IMAGES
of America

SUNBURY

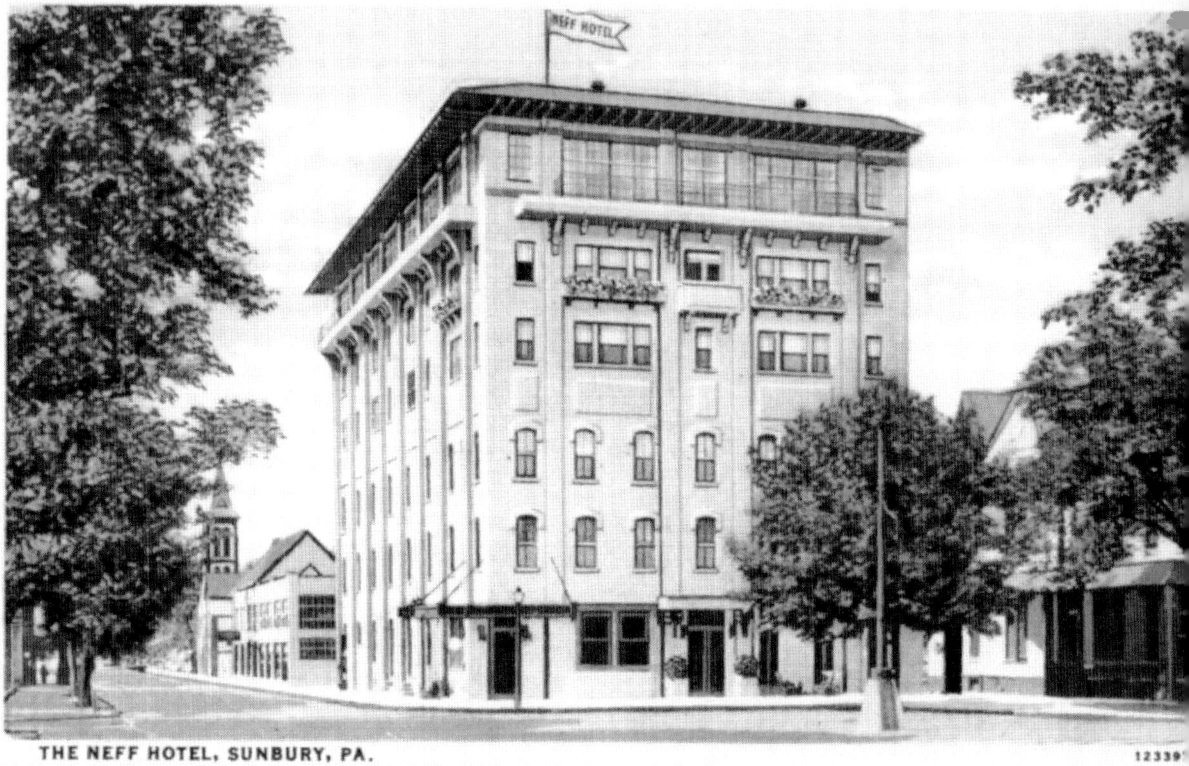

The Neff Hotel, a former distinguished edifice in town, was once a central meeting place for important residents of Sunbury. At one time, it was the only modern hotel in central Pennsylvania and stood at Second and Market Streets. The Neff Hotel was first called the Washington Hotel before Christian Neff, a prominent Sunbury resident, bought it. (Courtesy of Tim Auman.)

On the Cover: The Sunbury Beef Company was centrally located in the burgeoning market town of Sunbury in the early 1900s. (Courtesy of the Northumberland County Historical Society.)

IMAGES
of America

SUNBURY

Margaret Murray Thorell, PhD
Foreword by Mayor David Persing

ARCADIA
PUBLISHING

ISBN 978-1-4671-2071-5

Published by Arcadia Publishing
Charleston, South Carolina

Printed in the United States of America

Library of Congress Control Number: 2013945320

For all general information, please contact Arcadia Publishing:
Telephone 843-853-2070
Fax 843-853-0044
E-mail sales@arcadiapublishing.com
For customer service and orders:
Toll-Free 1-888-313-2665

Visit us on the Internet at www.arcadiapublishing.com

This book is dedicated to the Krippendorff, Maitin, and Moore families, owners of land in Sunbury where for many years the owners and their children, other family members, and friends enjoyed camping, hiking, swimming, and being together

Contents

FOREWORD

Sunbury has a unique history dating back to 1724 as the westernmost settlement in Pennsylvania. Fort Augusta, built in 1756, was the stronghold in the Susquehanna Valley providing protection for early settlers. Sunbury was founded in 1772, four years prior to our nation's independence. Magnificent historic buildings, dating back as far as the 18th century, still maintain their significant architectural facades. A family-oriented community, Sunbury has an outstanding community hospital, school district, new modern library, and 20 acres of recreational facilities that include a community pool, skate park, indoor ice-skating rink, lighted ball fields, neighborhood parks, and playgrounds. Lake Augusta is formed with the inflation in the spring of the Adam T. Bower Memorial Dam—the world's largest Fabridam—and provides for boating activities as well as sculling. The Edison Hotel, the first commercial building lit with a three-wire incandescent bulb by Thomas A. Edison, as part of the "Edison Experiment," is still in operation. A new water and sewer system supports municipal services and a 24/7 police force. Fire protection is made up of six volunteer fire companies. There are two outstanding universities 20 minutes away, as well as a business and trade school.

Sunbury is home to the corporate offices of a major supermarket chain, a large bakery, and a company that provides textiles internationally. Other well-established, stable industries and labor force meet additional employer needs. Local government helps to promote businesses and retain viable employers in the Susquehanna Valley. Sunbury is a great place to live, work, play, retire, and invest. Above all, it is a wonderful place to raise a family because of its low cost of living. It is a short distance to Philadelphia, New York, Baltimore, and Washington, DC.

—David Persing, mayor of Sunbury

Acknowledgments

I would like to thank the following people who helped make this book a reality: Tom Webb, Tim Auman, Michael Sherbon, Robin Simoneaux, Robert Dunkelberger, Jeanie Stout, Jason Nark, Howard Webb, Gail Broome, Elaine Borgese, Chris Zimmerman, Leonard DeGraaf, David Brown, Bonnie Wassmer, Ann Dzwonchyk, John Buxton, Bruce Marion, and, as always for their wonderful help, the staff of the Free Library of Philadelphia.

I would also like to thank David Persing, mayor of Sunbury, for his support and contributions to this book. His staff was also very helpful, especially Terry Specht and Cheryl E. Delsite. I am grateful to Meghan Beck, owner of the Edison Hotel.

I want to thank my proofreader, Dannette Bock, and my Arcadia acquisitions editor, Abby Henry, who pulled this all together. I would like to thank the Maitin, Moore, and Krippendoff families, and particularly, my husband, Klaus H. Krippendorff.

And this book would not have been possible without the support and help of the Northumberland County Historical Society (NCHS), especially Cindy Inkrote, who was gracious with her time and knowledgeable about the history of Sunbury.

Introduction

From earliest times, the valley of the Susquehanna River, a region in central Pennsylvania, was important because of its strategic location along the confluence of the north and west branches of the river. The area was first settled by a number of Indian tribes who used the Susquehanna River as a point of reference in their travels when seeking food and shelter. Soon, merchants and Indians developed paths along the river, which provided water for consumption, fresh fish, and a faster mode of transportation.

Several of the Indian tribes of the area formed a consortium of sorts, eventually led by Shikellamy, a famous Oneida chief and overseer for what became the Iroquois Confederacy. This collection of Indian nations became powerful in the region. Shikellamy, one of the first recognized leaders of this area, was highly respected, not only among the surrounding Indian tribes, but also by the white colonists whom he treated with kindness and respect. The region now known as Sunbury started out as a small Indian village called Shamokin. At the start of the French and Indian War (1757–1759), the Indians left the area, fearful of the military. Before departing, however, they set fire to their small encampment. Eventually, a fortress known as Fort Augusta (1756) was built by the English.

Fort Augusta, the largest of Pennsylvania's provincial forts, was constructed by the British and was used during the Revolutionary War as an American refuge for families fleeing the war, becoming an important stronghold. Its position at the confluence of the Susquehanna River contributed to its significance. After the Revolutionary War, it was used less and less and eventually became the dwelling of Col. Samuel Hunter. The current Hunter House was completed in 1852 after fire destroyed the commandant's quarters from the fort, where the family had lived. The Commonwealth of Pennsylvania purchased the building in 1930 as a historic edifice.

The name Sunbury came from an English village. Sunbury was one of seven proprietary towns in Pennsylvania and was originally governed by the British. The town was laid out as a city in 1772 when it was incorporated and took the name Sunbury. The town itself was surveyed and laid out by John Lukens, surveyor general, and his assistant William Maclay. Two main streets were constructed, and lots became available to anyone who was inclined to settle and build in the town, particularly tradesmen and others who would be encouraged to continuously improve the town.

Some of the businesspeople who created the mercantile town included William T. Grant, William M. Rockefeller, John Youngman, and others. Coal was one of the principal businesses of the town, providing employment for many—not so much in the mines, but on the wharves where barges ferried coal to the canals where it was then unloaded onto the canal boats and sent to Philadelphia, Baltimore, and other points along the system of canals. The coal business stimulated boatbuilding enterprises. Initially, it was the Pennsylvania Canal, a complex system of waterways, dams, locks, and aqueducts, which drove Sunbury's prominence. Private Pennsylvania companies built canals. Eventually, many waterways would be built, with a total length reaching

1,243 miles. Thus, transportation became one of the main reasons for the emergence of Sunbury as the most prominent frontier town in Pennsylvania.

By 1869, railroads would replace canals as the main transportation source. The first track of the Sunbury & Shamokin Railroad consisted of oak ties laid on the ground at intervals of several feet, fastened with wooden wedges, and covered with strips of iron. Horsepower was first used at this time—engines were too heavy, often resulting in trains going off the track. Using horsepower, the round-trip from Sunbury to the town of Shamokin took two days, using four and five horses hauling the train of cars filled with coal.

Eventually, Sunbury became a prosperous mercantile town, made famous because of Thomas Alva Edison, founder of the Edison Electrical Illuminating Company in 1883. He installed the first successful three-wire electric lighting system on July 4, 1883, in Sunbury. He switched on the current to a 100-candlepower light over the City Hotel entrance to cheers of residents and to marches, which were played by the local band. The City Hotel opened for business in January 1872. The hotel was renamed after Edison in 1922 during Sunbury's 150th anniversary. Still used today, the hotel is located on Fourth and Market Streets.

Sunbury was actually one of the first towns in the United States to have electric lights and was chosen by Edison because of its proximity to the anthracite coal region and the Susquehanna River. Edison was born in Milan, Ohio, and grew up in Michigan. He did not do well in school, and at the age of seven, his mother, an accomplished schoolteacher, began homeschooling him. He taught himself electronics, among other things. A bout of scarlet fever left him with hearing difficulties in both ears—he was virtually deaf as an adult. Nonetheless, Edison was a hard worker despite his many handicaps. The following was his favorite quote: "Opportunity is missed by most people because it is dressed in overalls and looks like work."

Sunbury is also important architecturally, with over 200 buildings depicting Federal or Georgian style in small inns and taverns from the canal days. Grander hotels and depots were built in Italianate, Romanesque, and Second Empire styles. Most notable were the Pennsylvania Railroad Passenger Depot, the Aldine Hotel, the Fairmount Hotel, the Central Hotel (originally the Sunbury Passenger & Ticket Office), and the Edison Hotel. Sunbury would eventually have a prominent minor-league baseball team.

Sunbury has contributed significantly in many areas to Pennsylvania and to the United States. While today it struggles, as many towns do, it is still contributing through its history, its splendid architecture, its verdant countryside, and the indomitable spirit of its citizens.

One

The Early History of Sunbury

Fort Augusta, named after the mother of King George III, was constructed by the British and was built on land that, at the time, was called Shamokin. That name would eventually be given to a premier coal-mining district several miles east of the current city of Sunbury.

Many important people came to or lived in the Sunbury area. But it was the Susquehanna River that contributed to the town's importance. The Susquehanna River is a beautiful waterway that drains 27,500 square miles, flowing through Pennsylvania, New York, and Maryland into the Atlantic Ocean. It is one of the oldest existing rivers in the world. The Iroquois Indians were the first recorded inhabitants of the west branch of the Susquehanna River valley. The British purchased large swathes of land in the valley from the Iroquois in 1768.

As important as the river was, the Indian pathways were also critical to the development of the city. Pennsylvania's temperate climate and relatively moderate rainfall contributed to the creation of more than 10 Indian paths, which kept the trails open and dry for foot traffic and, later on, for horses and wagons. The Great Shamokin Path is one of the most famous of the Indian trails because it connected two large Indian towns in the area, namely Shamokin and Kittanning.

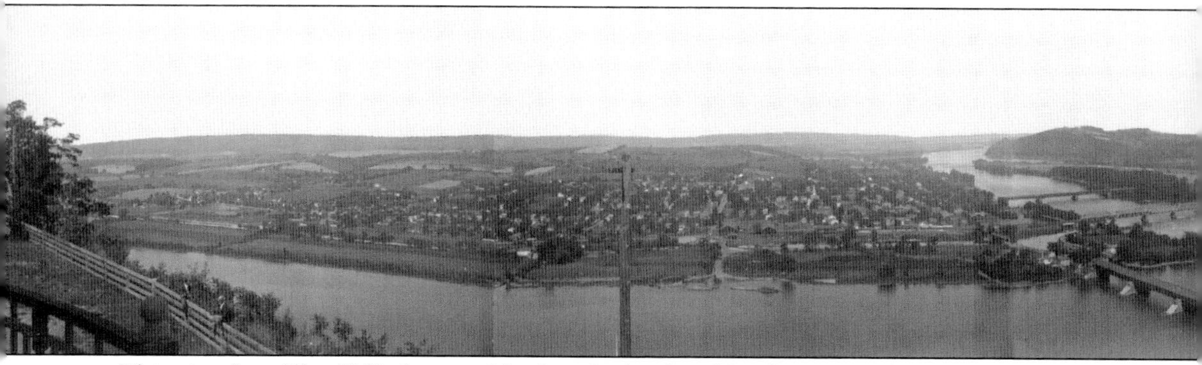

This view from Blue Hill, showing Northumberland and Sunbury, is at the junction of the north and west branches of the Susquehanna River. During the American Revolution, loyalists and Native Americans, who allied with the British, attacked Colonial settlements. From as far away as New York, these settlers were forced to find homes along the banks of the Susquehanna River in

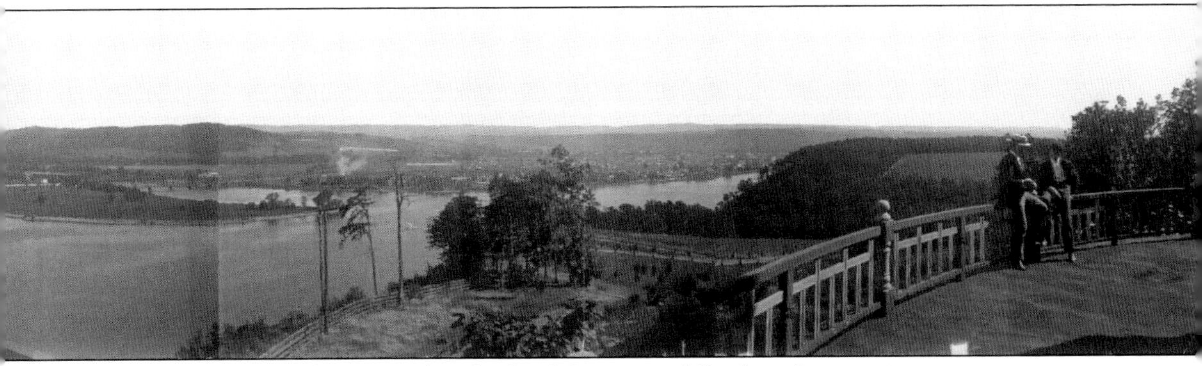

the area now called Sunbury. Northumberland County and Sunbury became important outposts and then marketing towns. The river became the primary mode of transportation during the early 19th century as a canoe route across the Allegheny Mountains and helped create the city of Sunbury. (Courtesy of the Library of Congress.)

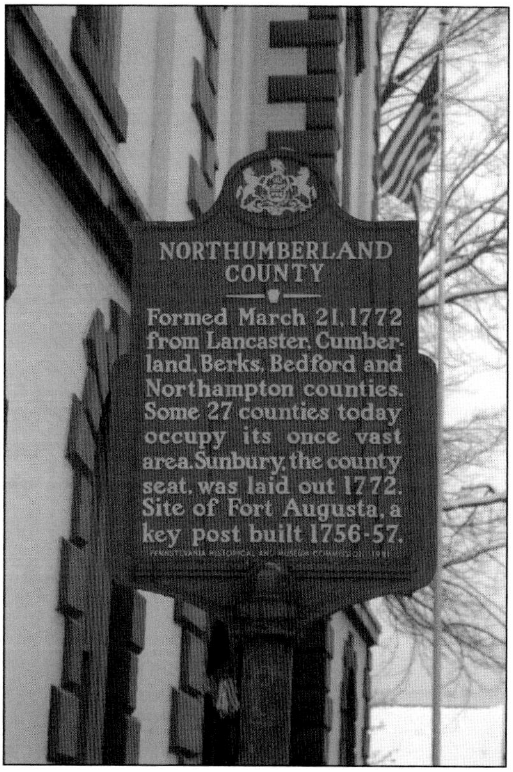

This historical marker celebrates the forming of Northumberland County on March 21, 1772, along the banks of the Susquehanna River. Today, some 27 counties occupy its once vast area. Today, Sunbury is the county seat. The county was originally formed from parts of what today are Lancaster, Berks, Bedford, Cumberland, and Northampton Counties and was almost half the size of Pennsylvania. It was first settled by Native Americans and explored by Europeans as early as 1615. Many famous people settled here, such as Joseph Priestley, the discoverer of oxygen. It is a rich architectural and historic area due to its location along the Susquehanna River, which is shown below in an early photograph. (Left, courtesy of Klaus Krippendorff; below, courtesy of the Library of Congress.)

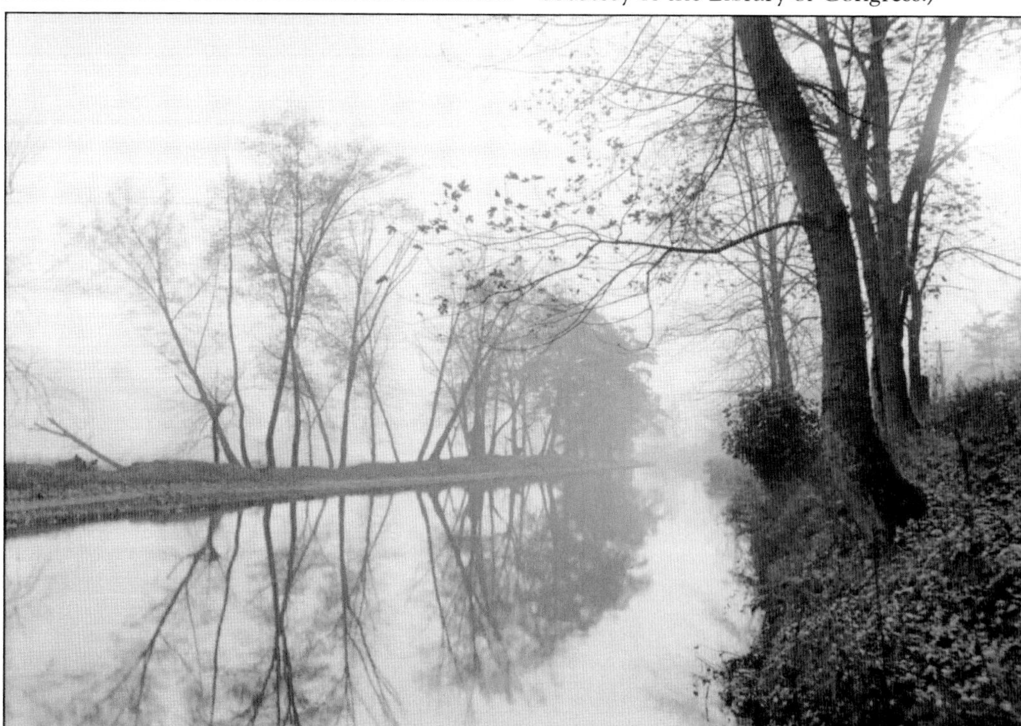

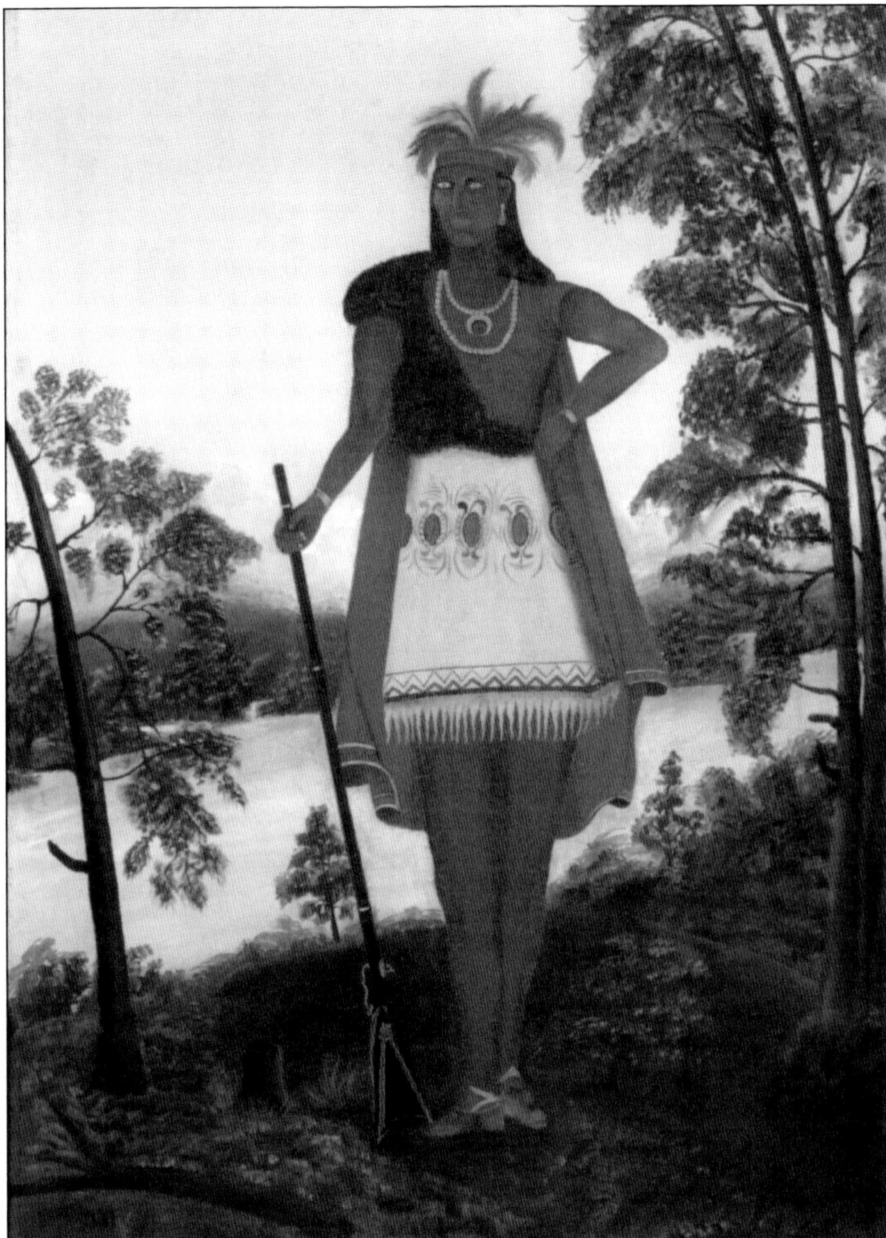

Shikellamy, a famous Oneida chief and overseer of the Iroquois confederacy, is depicted in this portrait. Shikellamy, one of the first recognized leaders of this area (unknown–1748), was highly respected, not only among the surrounding Indian tribes, but also by the white colonists, whom he treated with kindness and respect. This portrait of Shikellamy is from the collection of Edgar William and Bernice Chrysler Garbisch. It was made in the United States around 1820, and the artist is unidentified but thought to be an American. Shikellamy is depicted with strong features and an authoritative presence, dominating the foreground and standing before what is probably the Susquehanna River. The full-length pose shows him holding a matchlock, his left arm akimbo. He wears garments alluding to the fact that he is a leader—a decorative band of ovals on his apron, a large headdress, and a necklace. (Courtesy of the Philadelphia Museum of Art.)

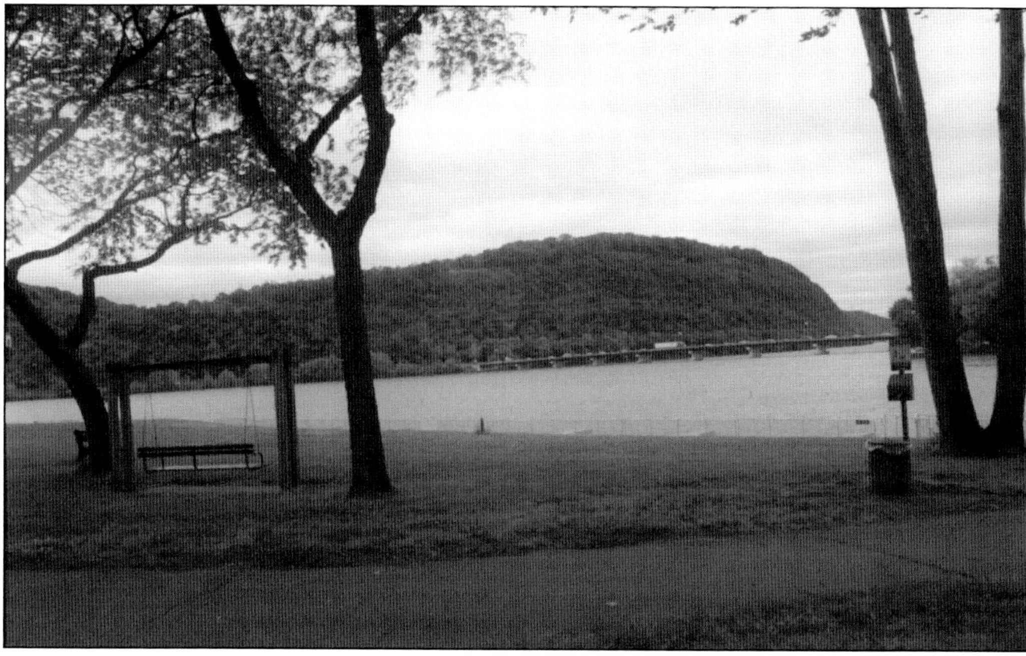

This image of Shikellamy State Park, from the marina side of the park, commemorates the great Indian leader. In 1728, Shikellamy was sent by the Great Federal Council of the Six Nations to watch over Delaware, Shawnee, and other Indian tribes in the Susquehanna River valley. In 1731, he was responsible for sending an ultimatum to the Pennsylvania government concerning liquor peddlers who were corrupting Indians. (Courtesy of Klaus Krippendorff.)

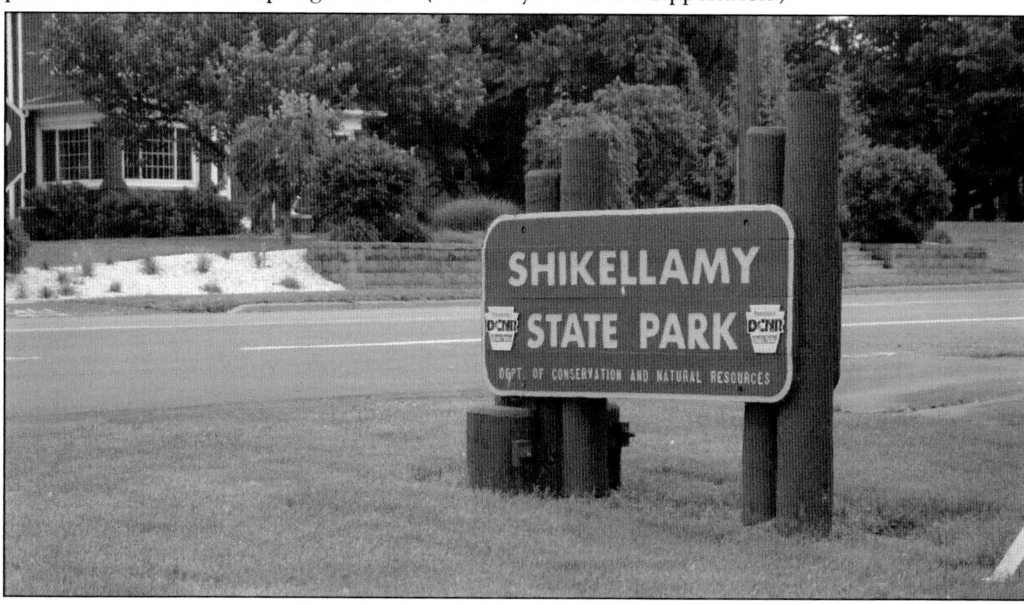

This sign welcomes visitors to Shikellamy State Park and celebrates the Oneida chief and overseer, or vice regent, of the Six Nations, who lived in the Shamokin Indian town Sunbury. He is said to have died in 1748. Many remembrances of him abound in the Sunbury area, such as several schools and the school district itself, located in the heart of the Susquehanna Valley. (Courtesy of Klaus Krippendorff.)

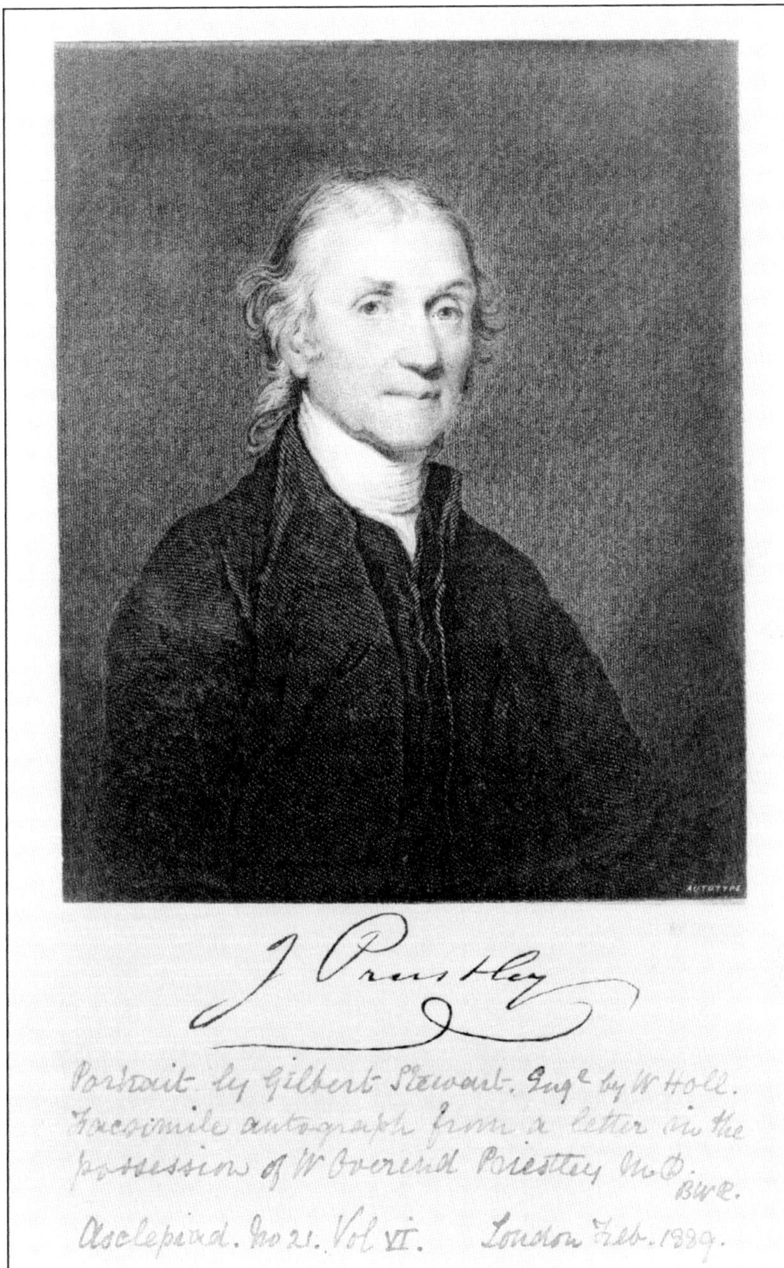

Joseph Priestly, discoverer of oxygen, noted theologian, political progressive, and author, lived most of his life in England, but when his controversial ideas forced him to leave the country of his birth, he came first to Philadelphia, where he was offered a position teaching at the University of Philadelphia, which he refused. He then came to Northumberland. It is here that he spent the last 10 years of his life. His home, located a few miles from the center of Sunbury, was designed by his wife, Mary Wilkinson, of Wrexham, England, whom he married on June 23, 1762. The home was of Georgian design with Federalist accents. The Priestleys lived there from 1798 until his death in 1804. The house has been carefully restored and is designated as a National Historic Landmark. (Courtesy of the Library of Congress.)

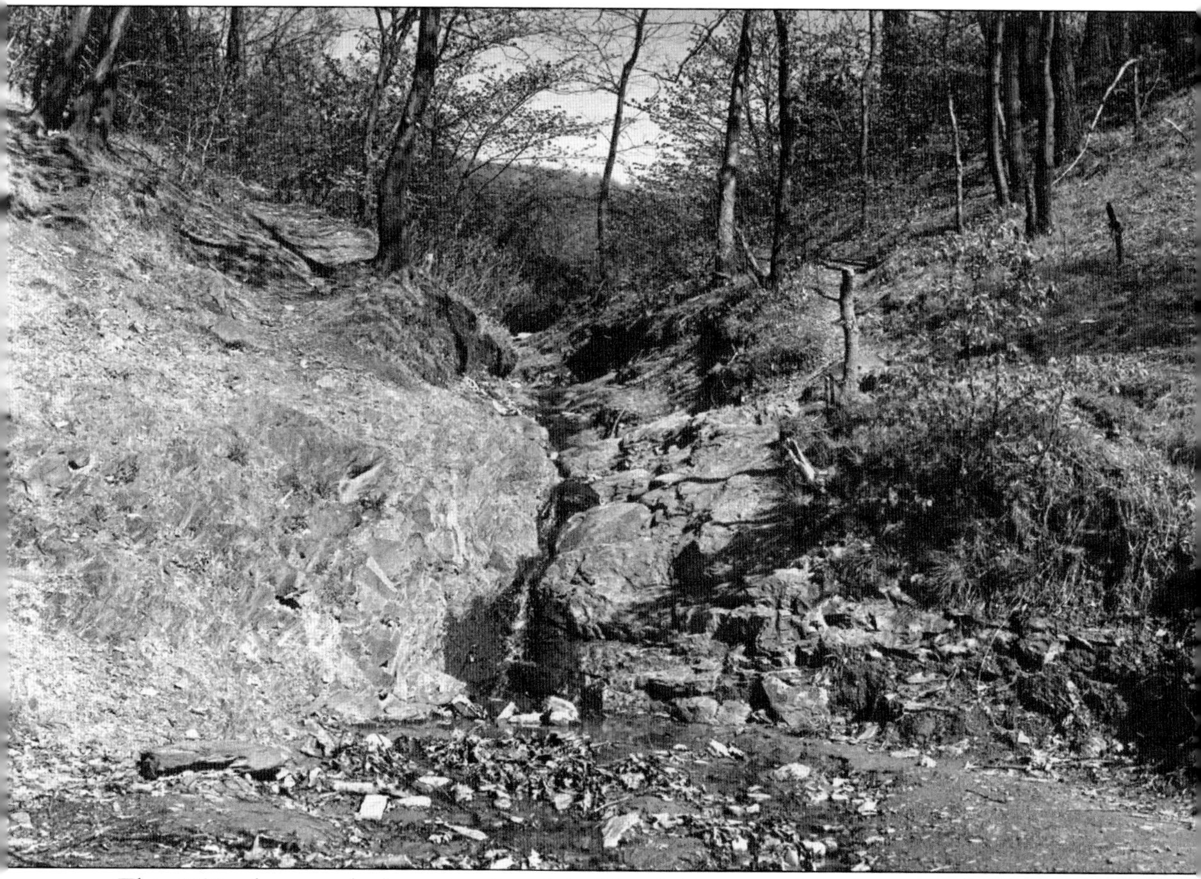

This 1930s photograph shows the site of the Bloody Spring and the location of a 1756 massacre during the French and Indian War. The spring was located about a half mile from Fort Augusta and is a historic spot of interest today. It was here that a Colonial soldier, John Pattin, a bullock guard who was tending cattle outside of Fort Augusta, left the security of the fort to find drinking water. He was fatally shot by Indians who feared that they might be discovered too near the fort. According to a marker, which stands there today, the scalped and shot soldier fell into the spring. It is said that his blood crimsoned the waters of the spring. Since that time, the spring has been called Bloody Spring. This incident is a reminder of the constant danger these early central Pennsylvania forts experienced. (Courtesy of NCHS.)

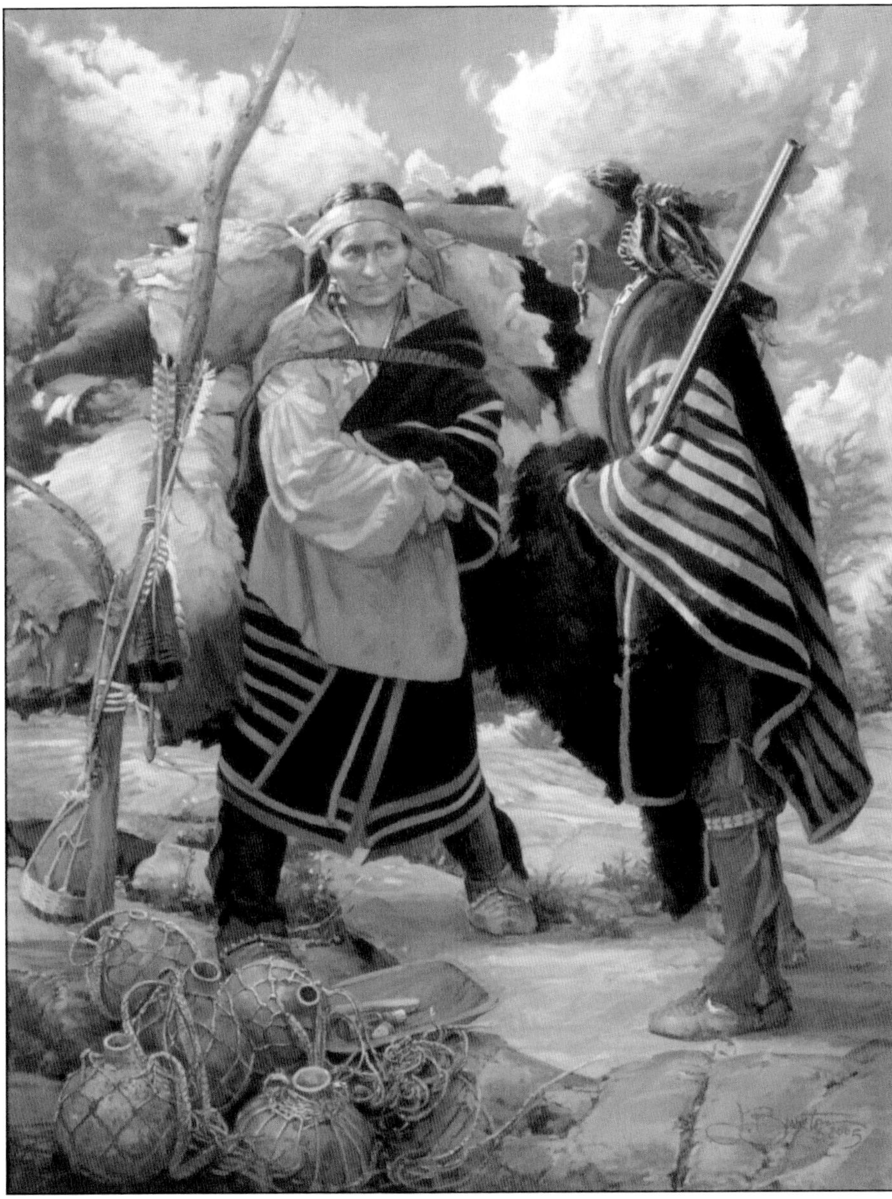

This painting of a woman (some say it is Madame Montour) was created by a Northumberland artist who called the painting *The Better Life*. John Buxton has said that he did not originally intend to recreate Madame Montour but wanted to show how greatly Native Americans' lives were changed by the arrival of the Europeans. Over the years, however, the painting has evolved into a portrait of the influential interpreter and diplomat. She came to Sunbury sometime around 1714, with her family first appearing in historic records in July 1727. She is recorded as the interpreter at a council in Philadelphia between the governor, Patrick Gordon, and an Iroquois group. Little but speculation is known about Montour's life, with many trying to sift through fact and fiction. It is known that she was important in the early days of life along the Susquehanna River near the area that is now called Sunbury. (Courtesy of John Buxton.)

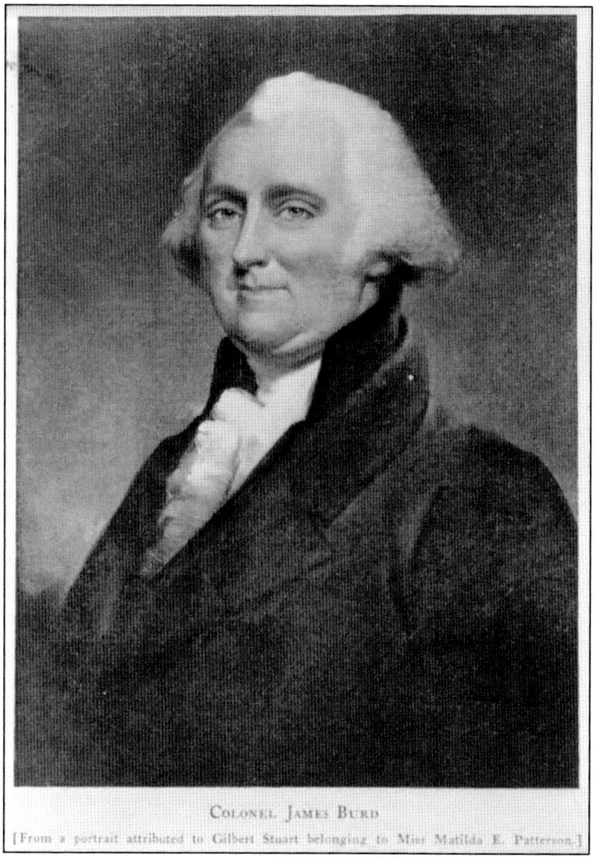

The historical marker below commemorates the establishment of Fort Augusta at the strategic junction of the Susquehanna River and its west branch. The marker indicates that the fort was built by Cols. James Burd and William Clapham. The governor sent Clapham with detailed instructions for building the fort. Burd, shown in this portrait, joined the Pennsylvania provincial military in 1756 at the outset of the French and Indian War when he was commissioned a major at Fort Augusta. On December 8, 1756, he took command after the resignation of Lieutenant Colonel Clapham. Burd resigned his commission following a dispute concerning rank and insubordination in his command. He returned in 1776 to his farm, named Tinian, where he died. (Left, courtesy of Klaus Krippendorff; below, courtesy of the Library of Congress.)

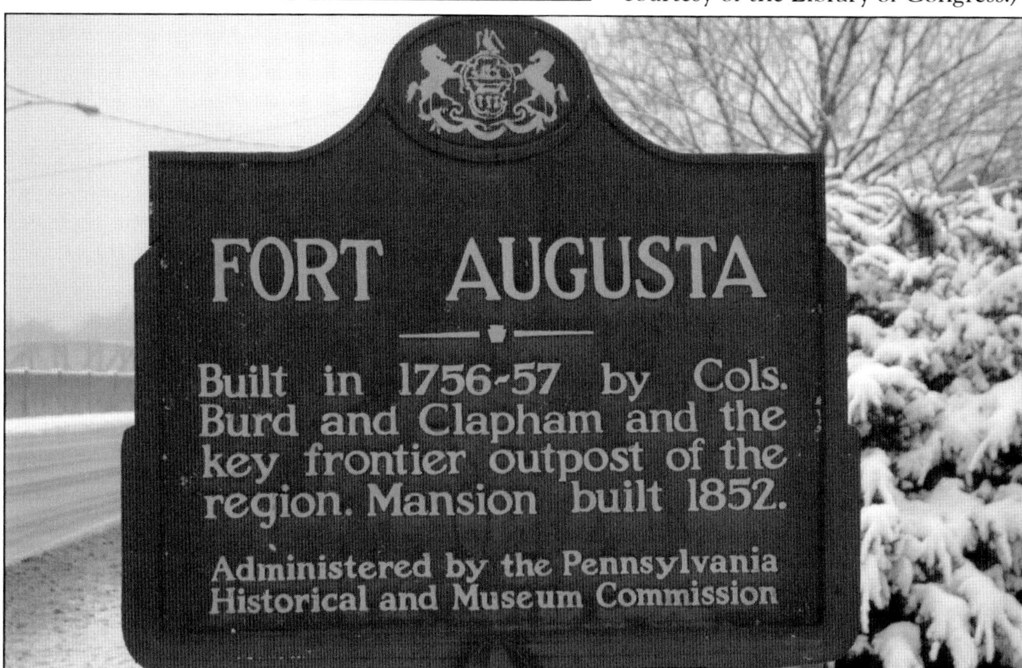

Johann Conrad Weiser Jr. was a Pennsylvania German and a pioneer, interpreter, and effective diplomat between the Pennsylvania colony and the Native Americans. He came to the New York colony via London. Shortly after his marriage to Anna Eve Feck, the couple followed the Susquehanna River south and settled in the area. His colonial service began in 1731 as an emissary to Chief Shikellamy. Weiser worked continuously for peace between the Native Americans and the settlers. He wrote this document. (Courtesy of the Library of Congress.)

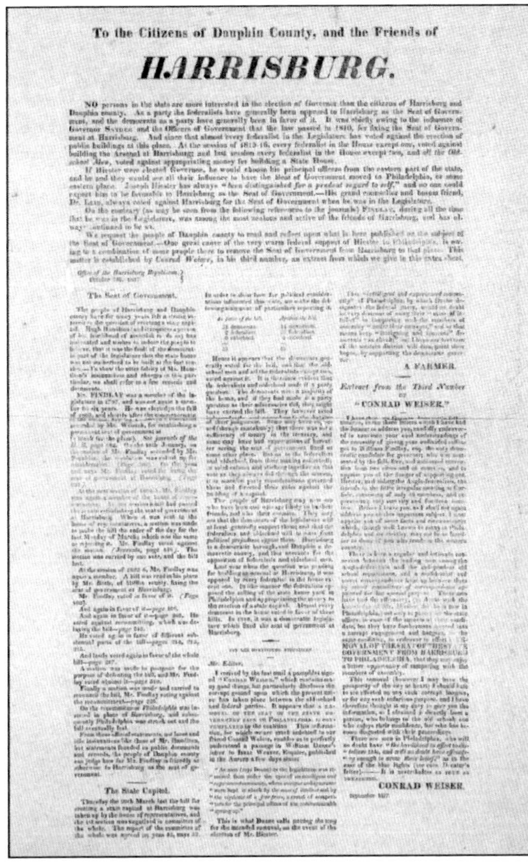

To the Citizens of Dauphin County, and the Friends of

HARRISBURG.

The Seat of Government.

A FARMER.

Extract from the Third Number of "CONRAD WEISER."

The State Capitol.

CONRAD WEISER.

This historical marker recognizes Col. William Thompson's Pennsylvania Rifle Battalion, part of the first battalion in the colonies authorized by Congress to be part of the army of the United Colonies, raised for the defense of American freedom. Capt. John Lowdon, a resident of Northumberland, organized it. (Courtesy of Klaus Krippendorff.)

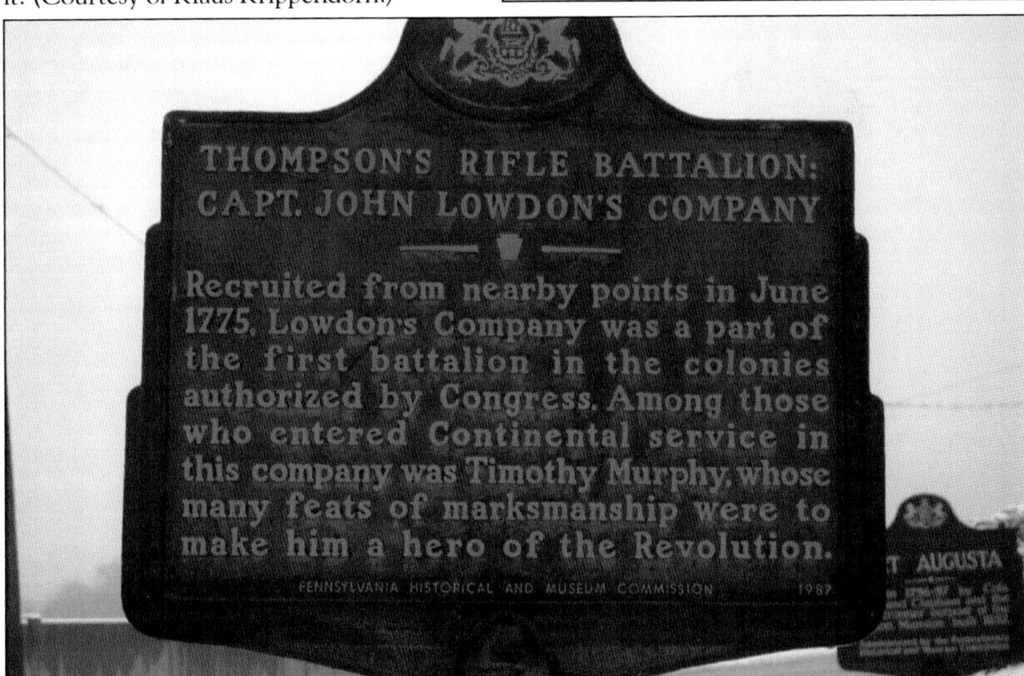

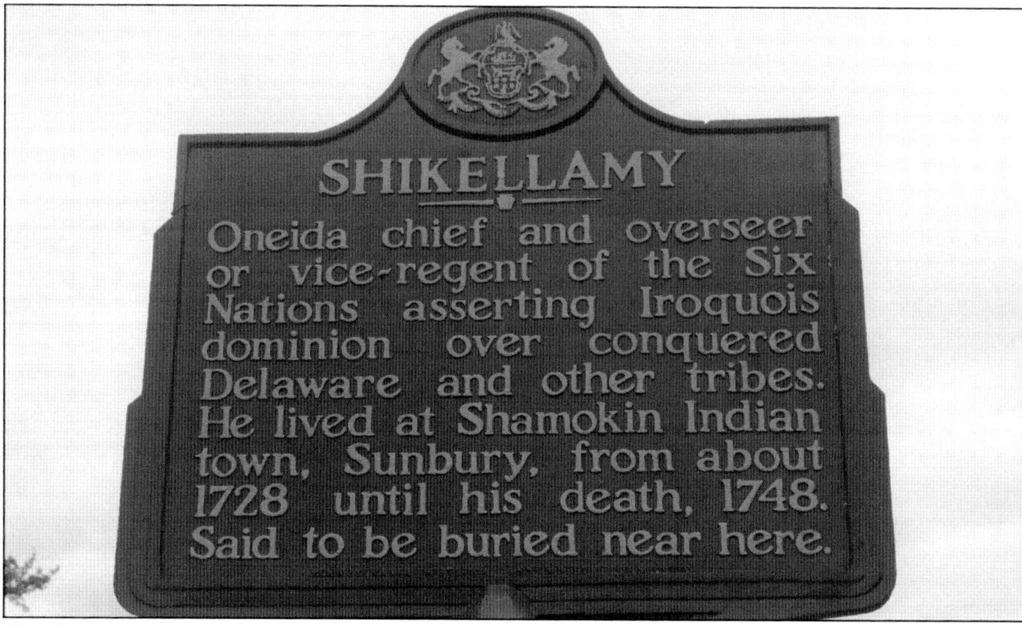

This historical marker in Sunbury celebrates the life of Shikellamy, who lived at the Shamokin Indian town from about 1728 until his death in 1748. Shamokin town would eventually become Sunbury. The marker is located at Front Street (Pennsylvania Route 147) between John and Julia Streets, at the Fort Augusta site, in Sunbury. (Courtesy of Klaus Krippendorff.)

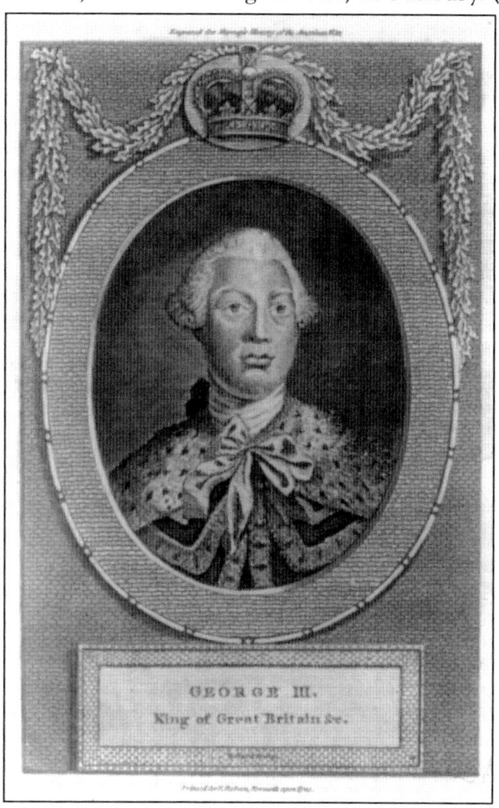

King George III became heir to the throne in 1751 upon the death of his father. He assumed the throne in 1760, upon the death of his grandfather George II. As king, he had to deal with unruly American colonists, a situation which came to a head with the passing of the Stamp Act (1765). Fort Augusta was established at the time of the French and Indian War and was operational until the close of the American Revolution. It was named for Princess Augusta of Saxe-Gotha-Altenburg, his mother, who was born in Gotha, a town in Thuringia, Germany. She married Frederick, Prince of Wales, at the age of 16, arriving in London without speaking a word of English. King George's strong defense of what he saw as the national interest and the prospect of long war made him, if anything, more popular than before. (Courtesy of the Library of Congress.)

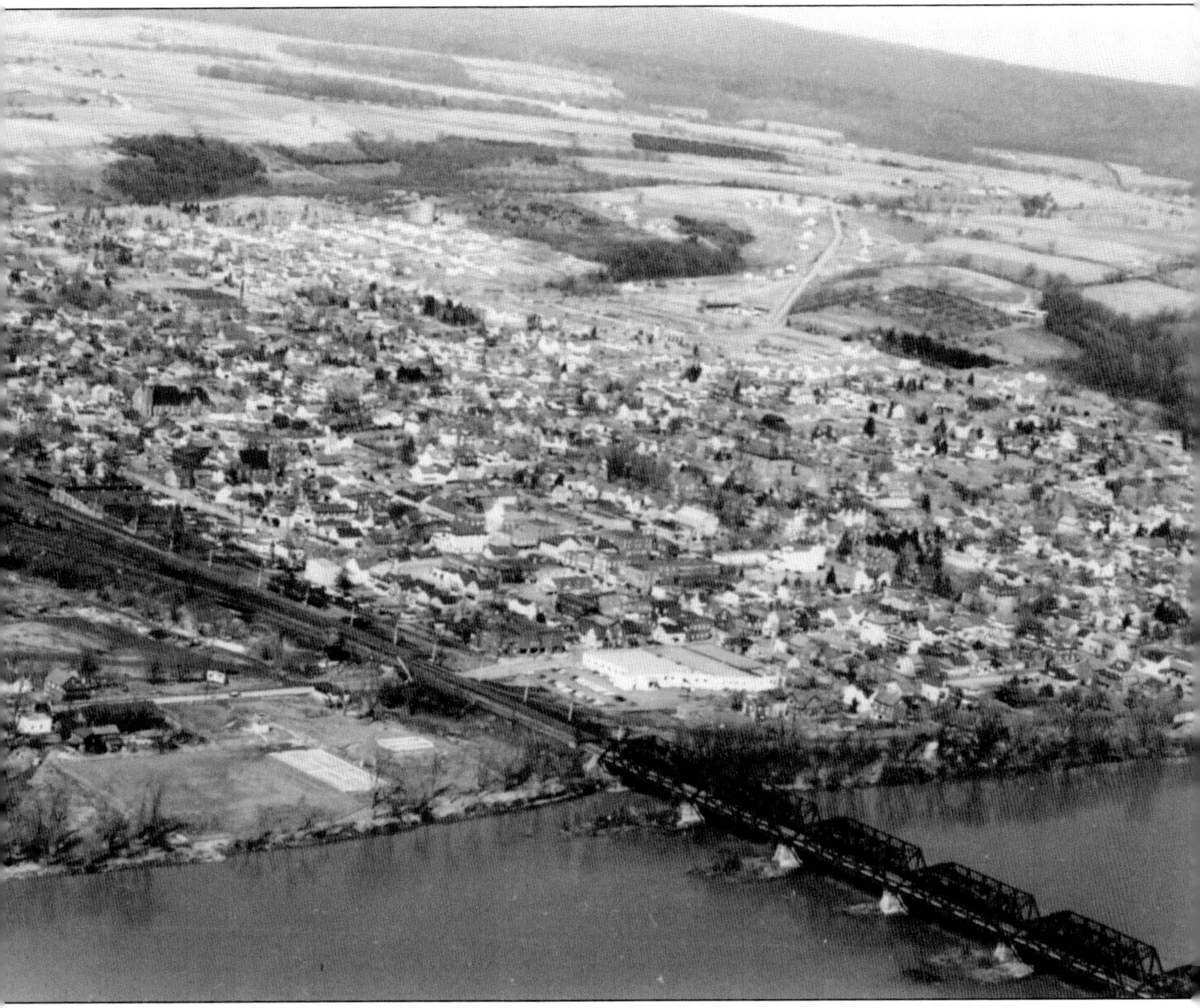

The world of Sunbury would change drastically following the Revolutionary War. Sunbury would become an important market town, and many of its residents became important Colonial leaders. Eventually, the town would become a center of transportation. The canals and the railroads would create great economic and social development in the area. This 1930s aerial view of Sunbury shows the old railroad bridge over the Susquehanna River and the growing city. The pillars of the old bridge are still visible today alongside the new bridge. (Courtesy of NCHS.)

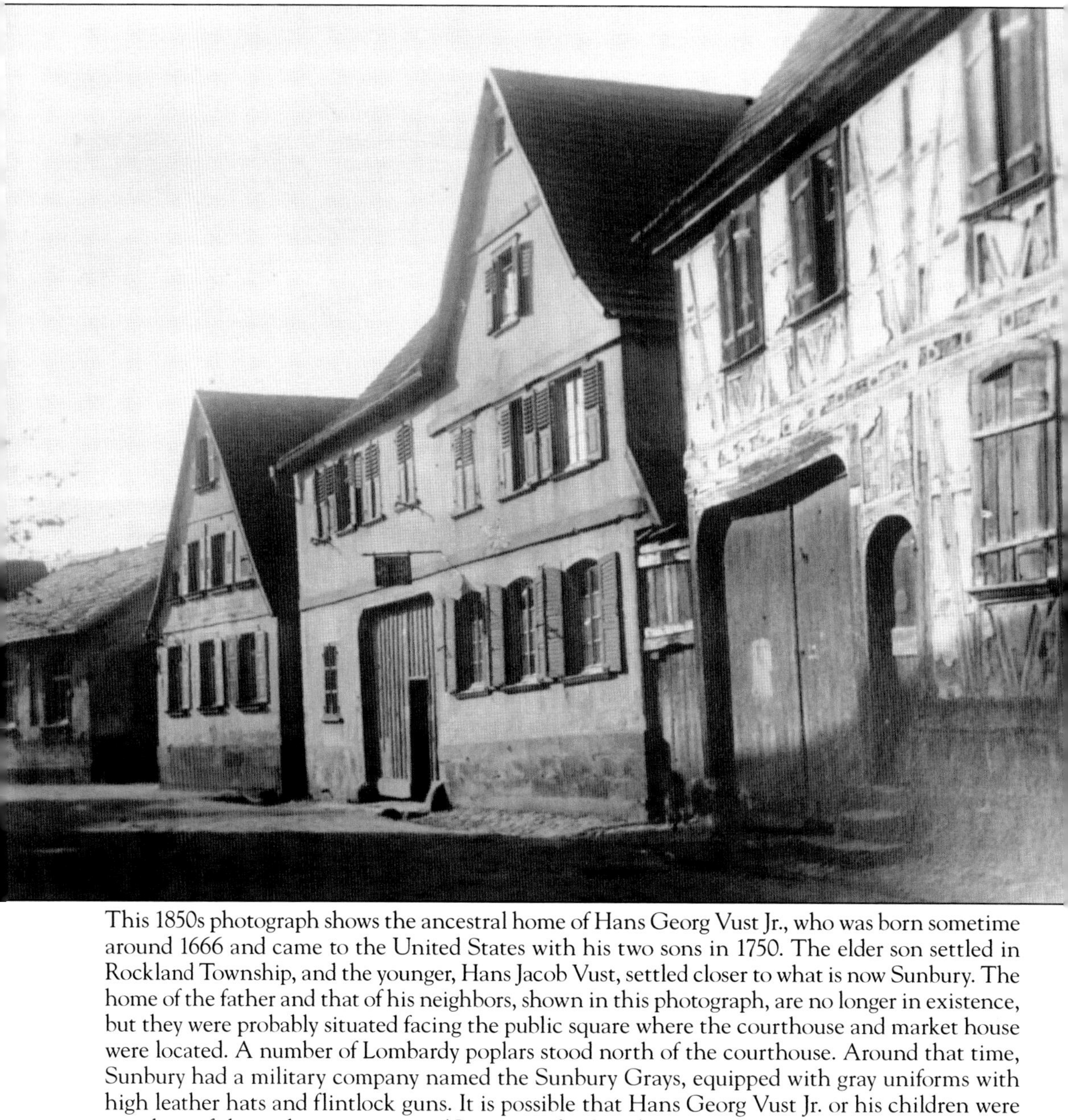

This 1850s photograph shows the ancestral home of Hans Georg Vust Jr., who was born sometime around 1666 and came to the United States with his two sons in 1750. The elder son settled in Rockland Township, and the younger, Hans Jacob Vust, settled closer to what is now Sunbury. The home of the father and that of his neighbors, shown in this photograph, are no longer in existence, but they were probably situated facing the public square where the courthouse and market house were located. A number of Lombardy poplars stood north of the courthouse. Around that time, Sunbury had a military company named the Sunbury Grays, equipped with gray uniforms with high leather hats and flintlock guns. It is possible that Hans Georg Vust Jr. or his children were members of this military company. (Courtesy of NCHS.)

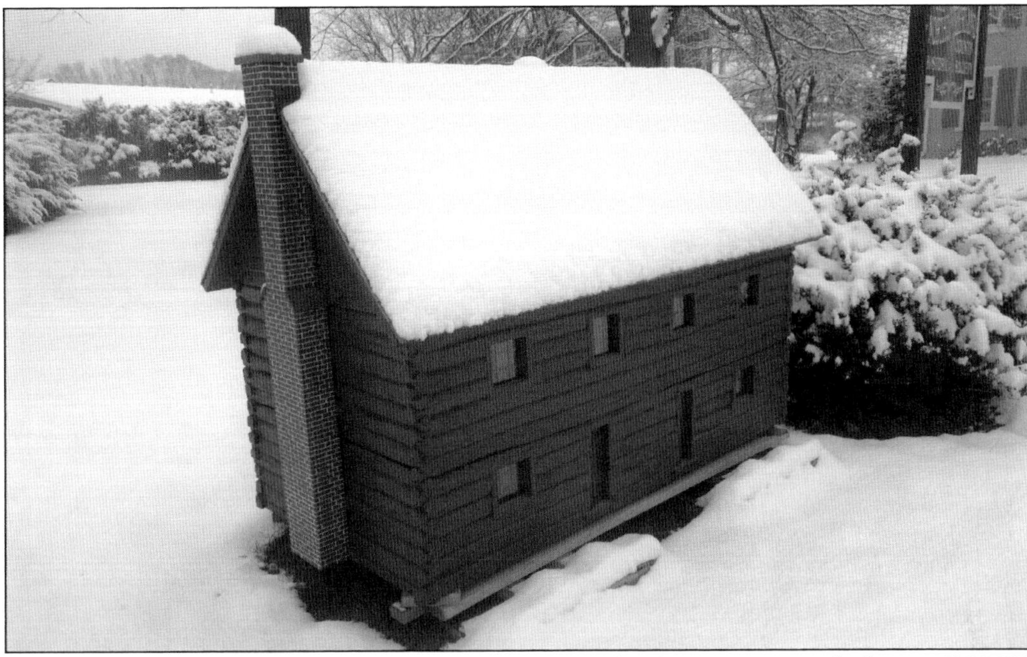

This replica of Fort Augusta is located today on the grounds of Hunter House, the home of NCHS. Fort Augusta was important in both the French and Indian War and the Revolutionary War. It was built following the destruction of the town of Shamokin by the Indians. That town would eventually become Sunbury. (Courtesy of Klaus Krippendorff.)

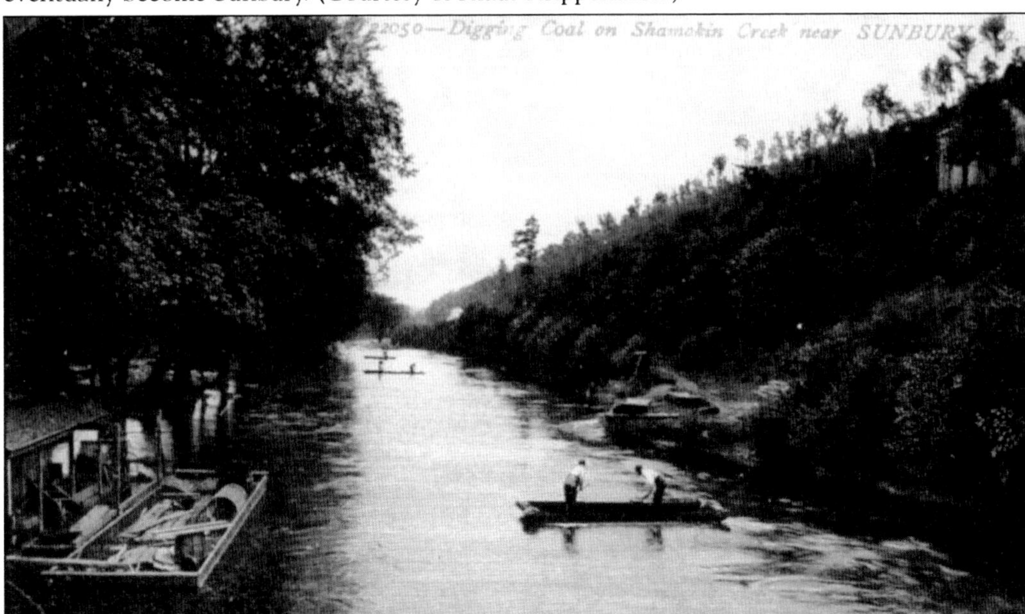

This bucolic scene on the Susquehanna River shows boaters digging for coal. Even in the early years of Sunbury and Northumberland County, the discovery of coal was an important one for the economic development of the area. Coal would eventually become important for Sunbury because it jump-started different business ventures, with many relating to the shipping industry. (Courtesy of Tim Auman.)

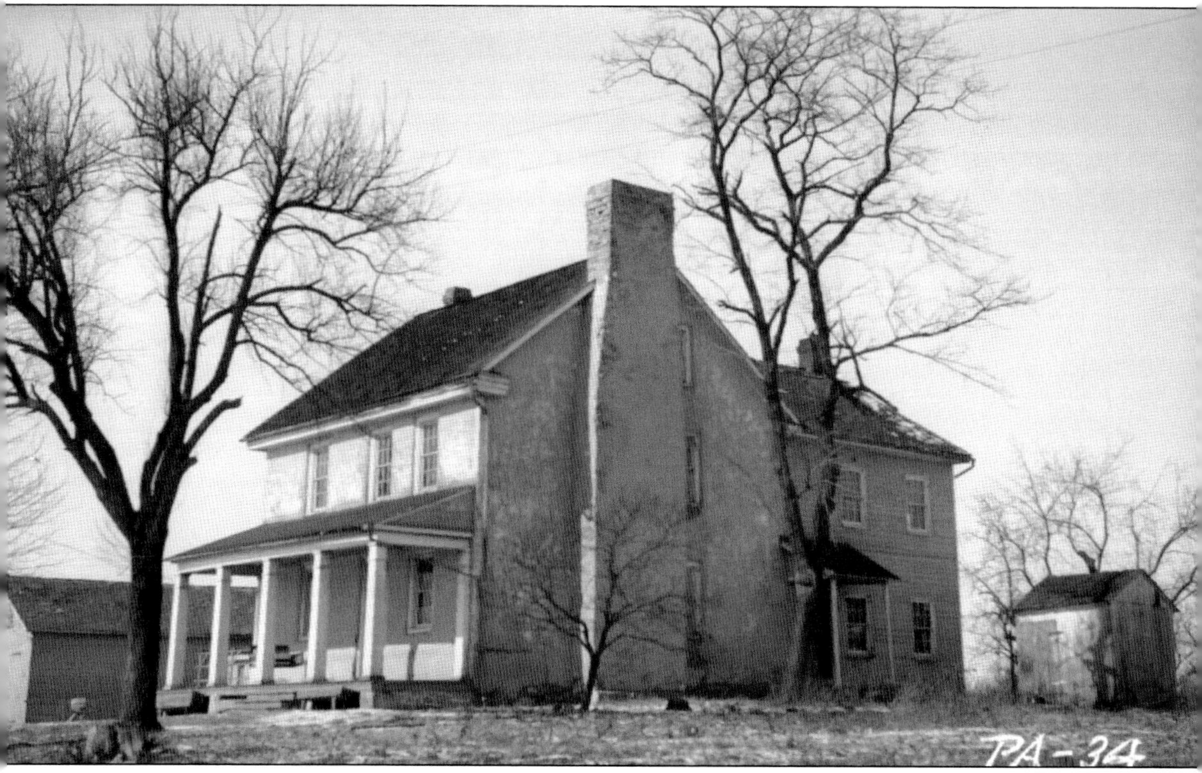

This 1935 photograph shows Tinian, the house of James Burd, the creator of Fort Augusta. The historic home is a short distance from Sunbury. It was built of limestone in 1767 and is mentioned in family correspondence as early as 1768. In 1766, Burd bought 500 acres of land along the Susquehanna River and built his residence, which would become the family estate. This was a typical agricultural estate, and, at one time, there were seven slaves. Burd served as justice of the peace, was active in the church, and at the time of his death in 1793, he was serving as one of the county judges for an area in Northumberland County that would eventually become Dauphin County. His wife, Sarah Shippen Burd, died in 1784. They are both are buried in the Middletown Cemetery. (Courtesy of the Library of Congress.)

Richard Penn Jr., a grandson of the founder of Pennsylvania, William Penn, gave the order to lay out the town of Sunbury, which was accomplished by William Maclay. Penn served as the lieutenant governor of the province of Pennsylvania from 1771 until 1773 and later returned to London, where he was a member of Parliament. (Courtesy of the Free Library of Philadelphia.)

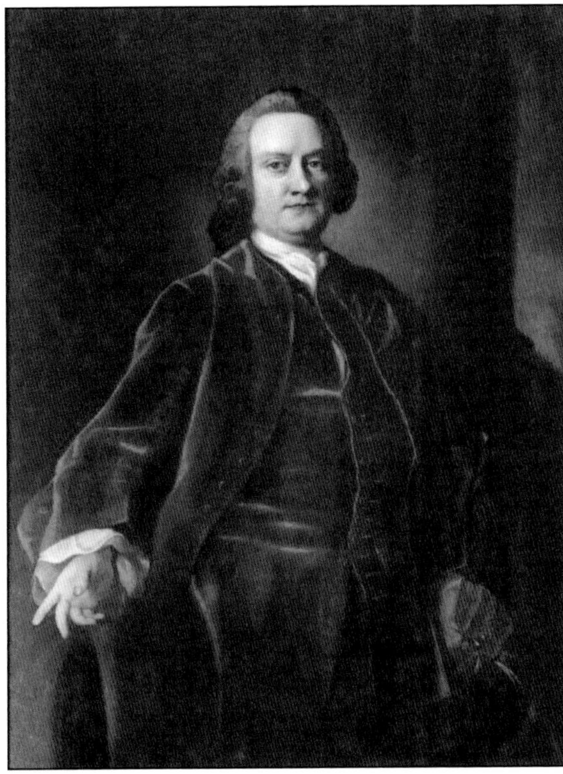

CONTENTS.

William Maclay was one of the first two senators from Pennsylvania. Within the first two months of the opening of the first session of Congress, he began to keep a diary, which he continued almost daily for the three sessions of the 1st Congress. The contents page of his diary is shown here. Senate sessions were closed to the public until 1795, so his diary is an important account of that time. (Courtesy of the Library of Congress.)

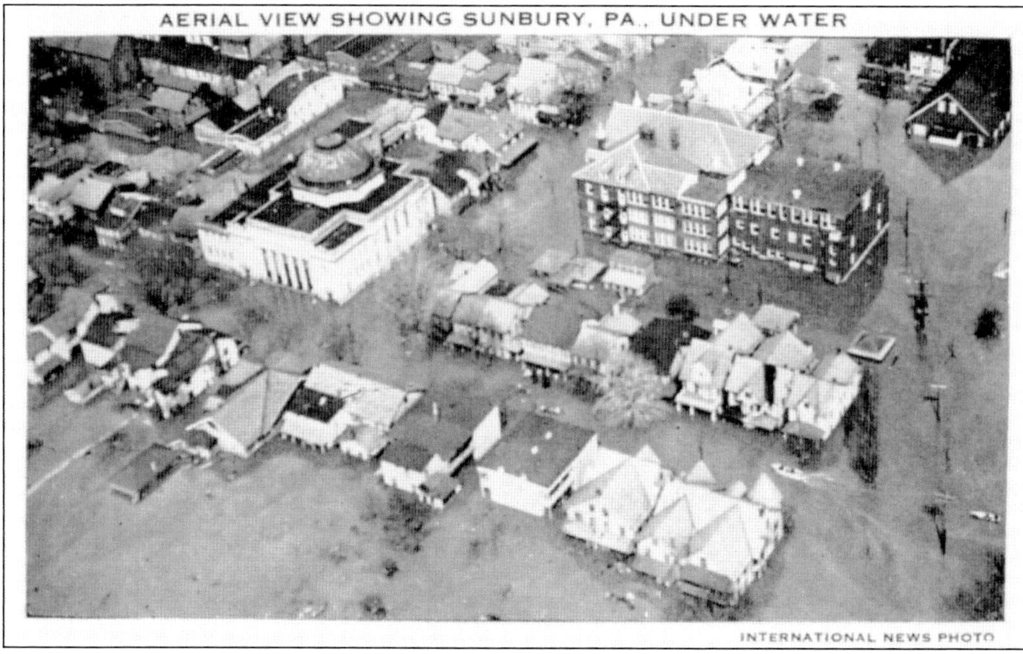

In the postcard above, the city is underwater from the ravaging overflow of the Susquehanna River. Floods were an unhappy part of the history of the town until a retaining wall was built. The image below shows the business section of Sunbury in 1935 when it was an important economic center. The business section, which was predominately located on Market Street, was a thriving center up until the 1980s, when recessions and economic downturns forced business owners to leave. The creation of malls across the river also helped create the loss of Sunbury as a mercantile center. (Both, courtesy of Tim Auman.)

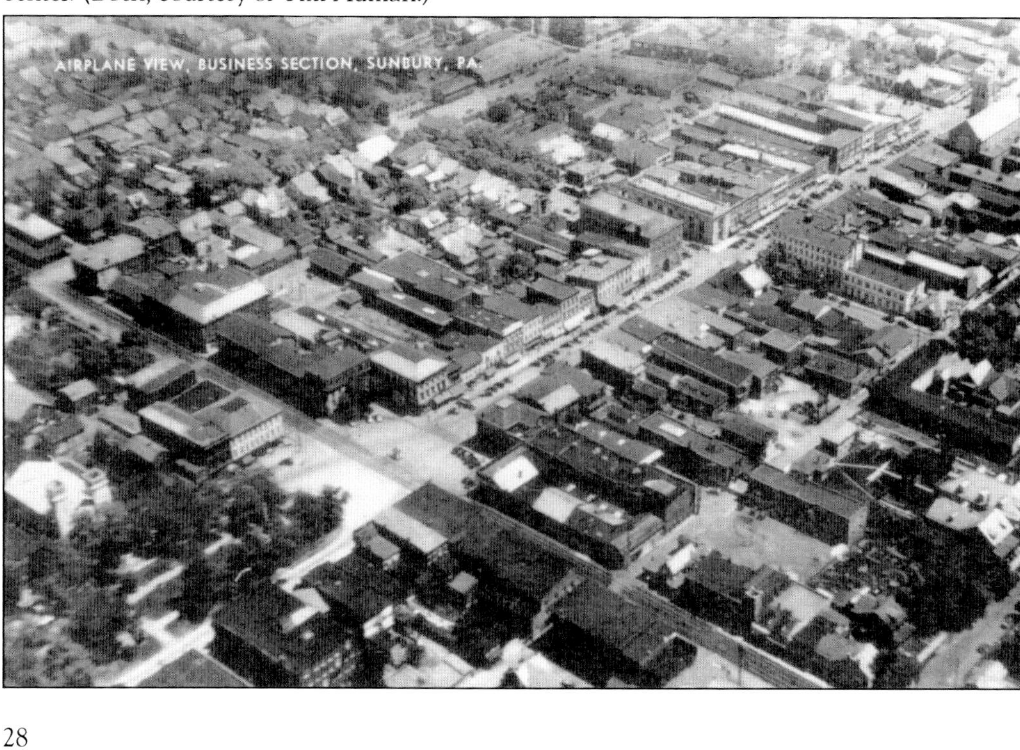

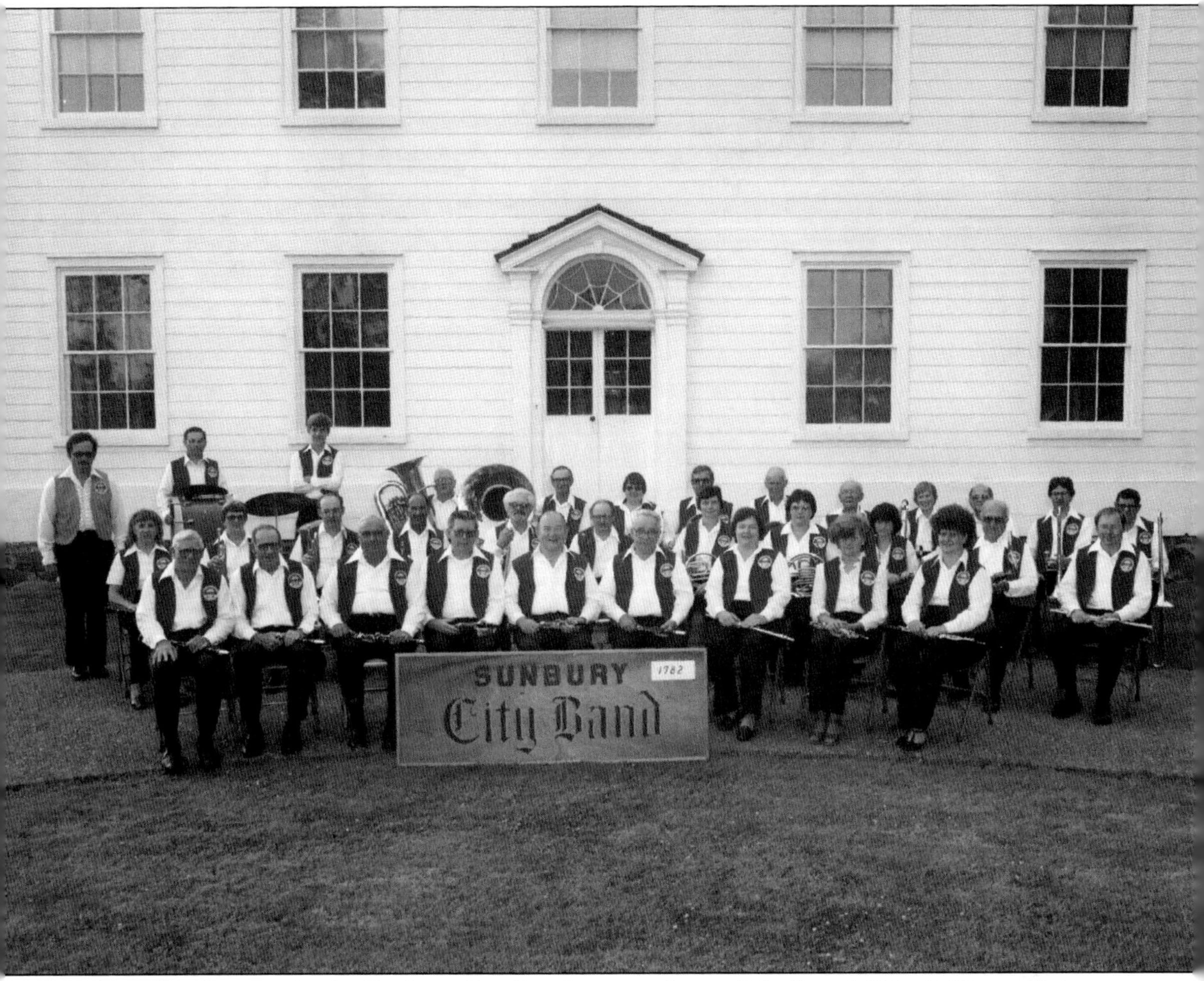

In this 1982 photograph, the Sunbury City Band poses in front of the Joseph Priestly House. Urias Wolf, who lived in East Sunbury along Catawissa Avenue, established the band in 1895. It was initially called the East Sunbury Band because five young men who lived near the Seven Points area of rural Sunbury enjoyed playing music together and decided to form the group. Soon, the band had more than 20 members and even bought uniforms. It has been in existence for more than 120 years now and changed its name to the Sunbury City Band in 1904. Today, the band is still a major form of entertainment in Sunbury and the surrounding area. It performs at multiple local venues each year, such as community centers, churches, senior living centers, and parks, and on special holidays in Sunbury, such as the annual Christmas Eve carol concert. (Courtesy of NCHS.)

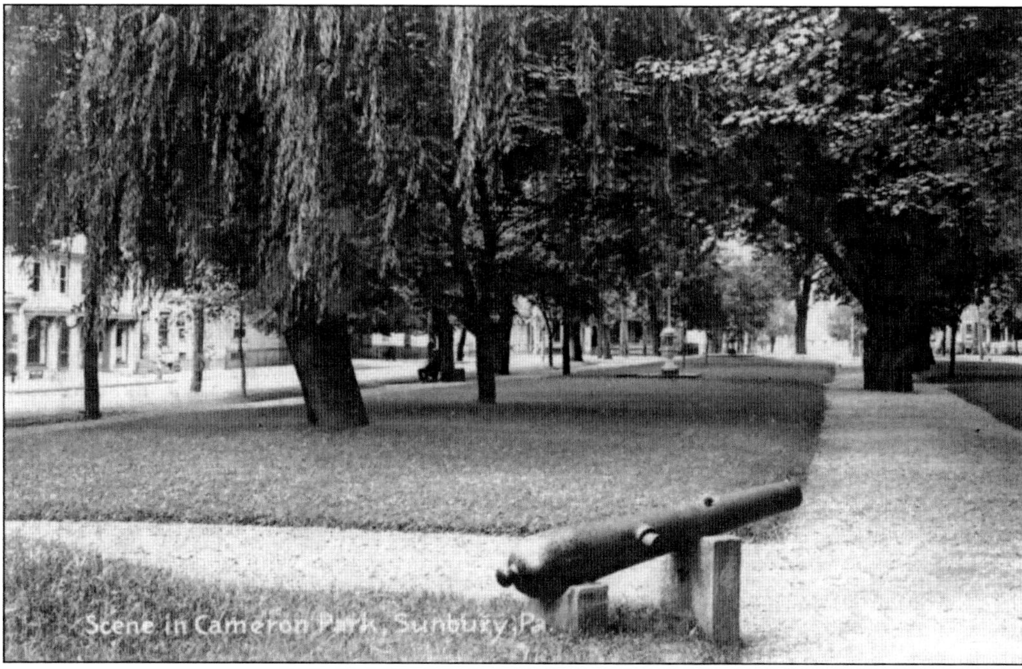

These two early postcards show Cameron Park, located in the center of Sunbury in the 200 block of Market Street. The park, named for Col. James Cameron, organizer of a regiment from the area during the American Civil War, is home to several memorials and has hosted many musical events over the years. Colonel Cameron was the first soldier of his rank from Northumberland County to lose his life in the Civil War. He died at the age of 60 as commander of the Cameronian Highlanders, the 79th New York Regiment at the Battle of Bull Run. (Both, courtesy of David Persing.)

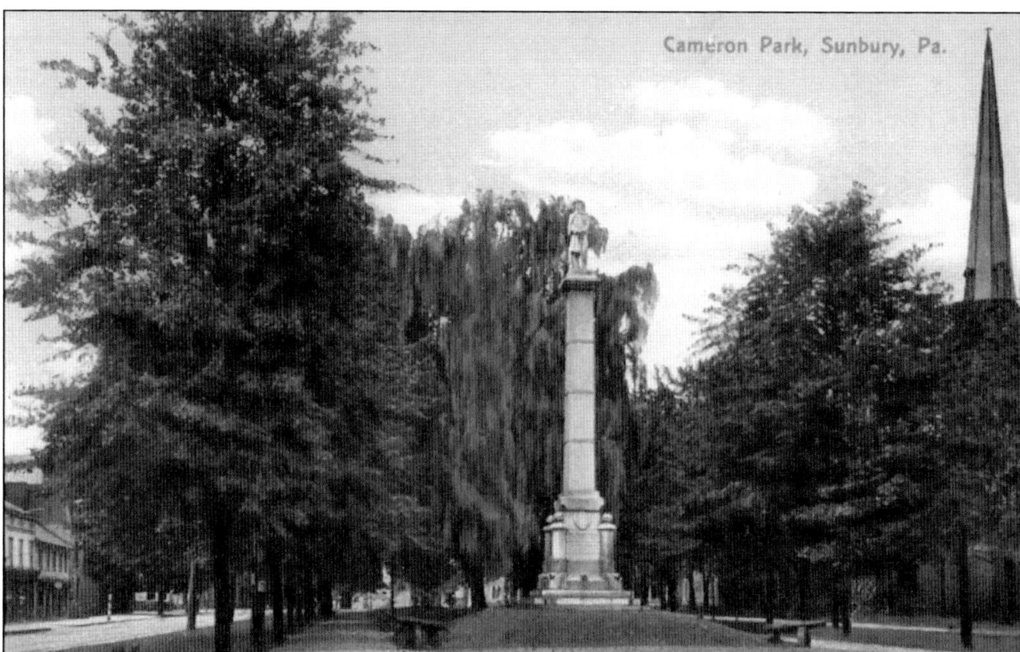

Two

Architecture and Monuments

Sunbury started its life as an Indian village with footpaths emanating from the area, like the spokes of a wheel. It then became an important trading center and the seat of Northumberland County. During the Colonial period, Sunbury was the most important town in north central Pennsylvania. Vestiges of this great era of Sunbury's history can still be seen today in its architecture and monuments. At the present time, there are approximately 238 buildings in the Federal, Colonial Revival, Italianate, and Queen Anne styles that represent the history of Sunbury.

This historic town was listed in the National Register of Historic Places in 1983. The historic district encompasses the land within the town's pre–Civil War limits and showcases the rich architectural heritage of the area. The Italianate courthouse, designed by Samuel Sloan (1815–1884), a Philadelphia-based architect and author, is a prime example of his style, which is seen in villas, country houses, churches, and institutional buildings around the United States. The great Sunbury Courthouse was built in 1865. The county jail (1876) is another example of Sunbury's historic architecture.

Both James Tilghman's house, the first house built after the survey, and Maclay-Wolverton's house are residences dating from the earliest days of Sunbury. Other buildings include Keithan's store (originally the Red Lion Inn Tavern), the Central Hotel (originally the Sunbury Passenger & Ticket Office), and the Edison Hotel (named after the famous inventor and formerly called the City Hotel). Other important buildings are the Masonic temple, a Romanesque edifice built in 1907; the Chestnut Street Opera House; and the Sunbury Market. All illustrate the town's history as an important trading post and market town.

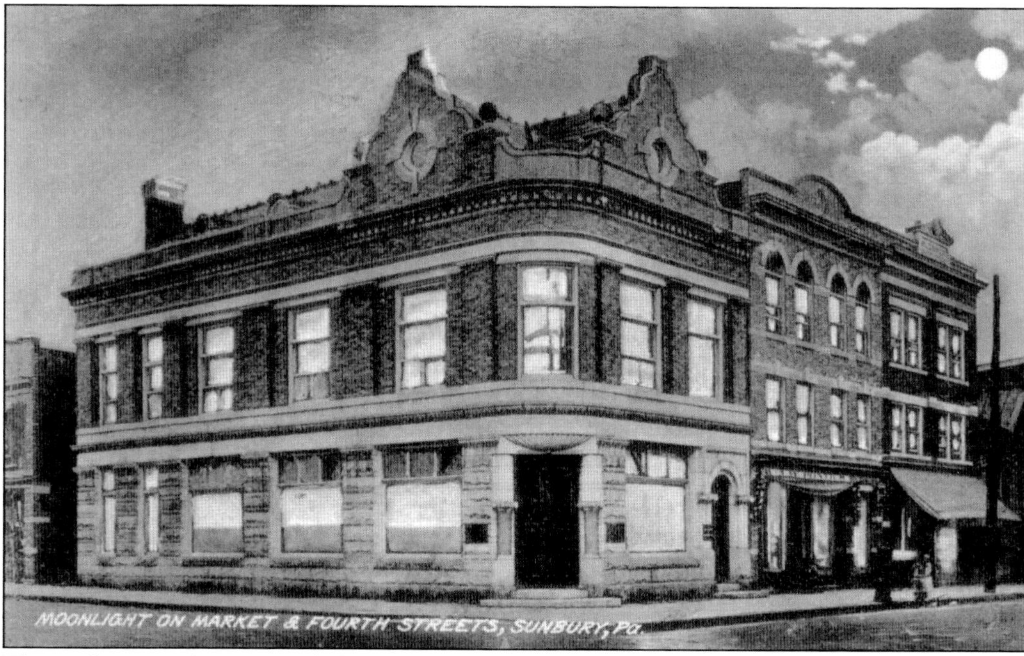

This night scene shows moonlight on Market and Fourth Streets. This is a view of the City Hotel, which is now the site of the Edison Hotel. E.J. Drumheller built the City Hotel in 1870. It caught fire on January 14, 1914, after which it was repaired and rebuilt. In the early years, there were nine hotels in Sunbury. Charles Weaver kept a hotel at the present site of this building, from which swung the sign of the Buck. (Courtesy of Tim Auman.)

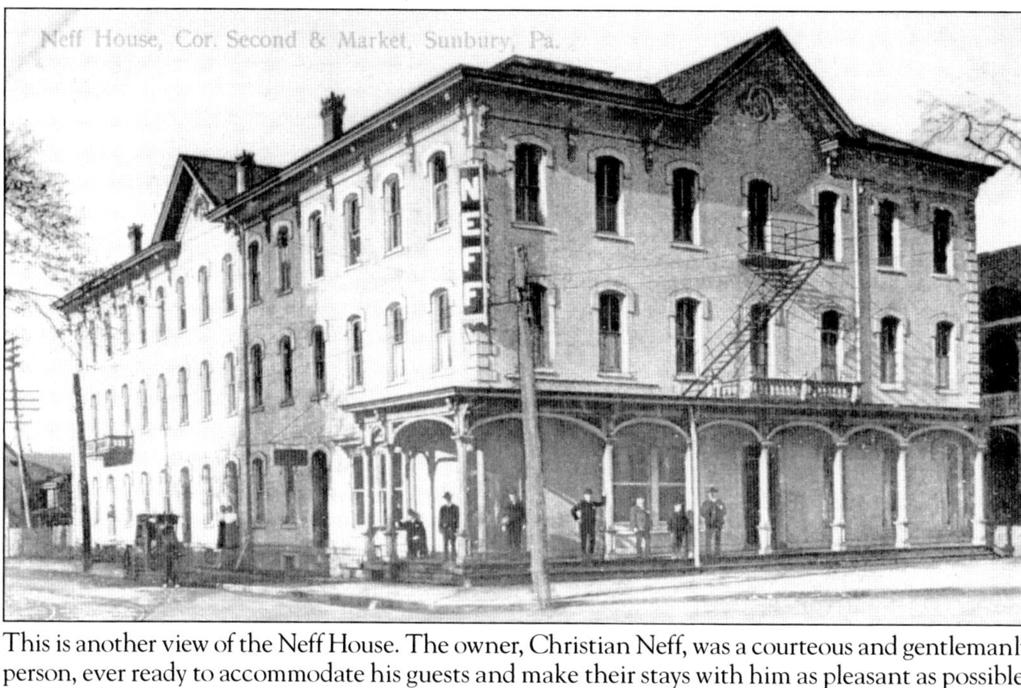

This is another view of the Neff House. The owner, Christian Neff, was a courteous and gentlemanly person, ever ready to accommodate his guests and make their stays with him as pleasant as possible. He thereby often merited a remark from travelers that he was one of the most open-hearted landlords they had ever met. (Courtesy of Tim Auman.)

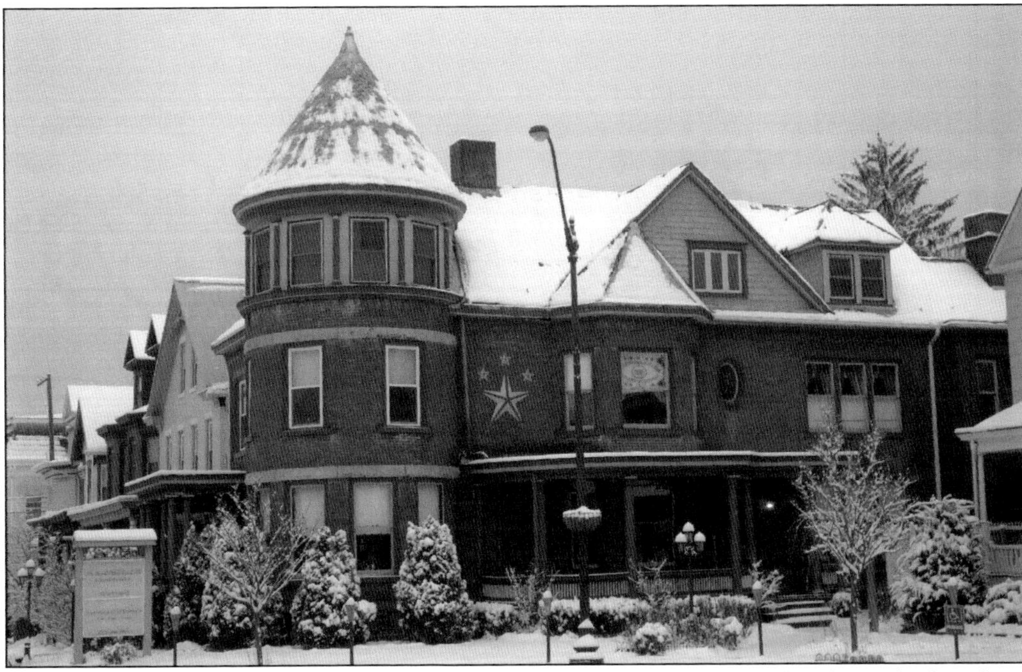

Ella Hutchinson was the original owner of this structure. She was the daughter of Edward and Mary Drumheller, who built the City Hotel, now called the Edison Hotel, in 1871. After her father Edward's death, her husband, Thomas, took over the running of the City Hotel and, with other family members, constructed additional buildings in the Sunbury area. (Courtesy of Klaus Krippendorff.)

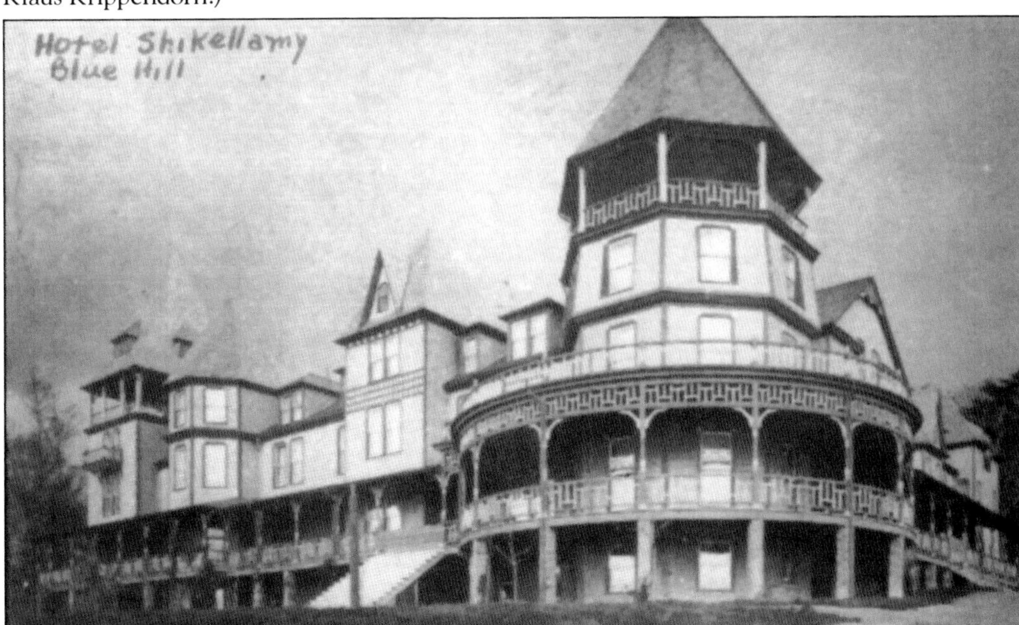

Edward Hutchinson also built the beautiful and infamous Hotel Shikellamy on top of Blue Hill, which only operated from 1890 until May 4, 1898, when it was destroyed by fire. Here, the hotel is shown in an early postcard. (Courtesy of David Persing.)

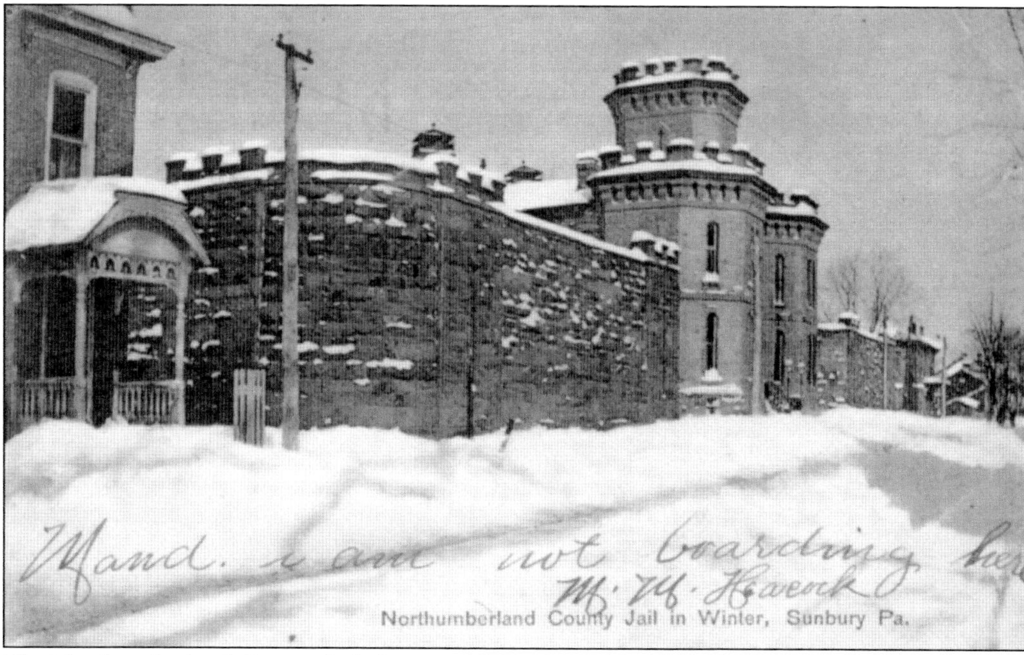

The Northumberland County Jail, shown in this postcard, is located on Second and Arch Streets and is the city's fifth jail. The jail was constructed in 1876 and was first used on August 7, 1877. The structure's dominant architectural style reflects Sunbury's preeminence during the Colonial period. The jail has been in continuous use ever since its beginning. (Courtesy of Tim Auman.)

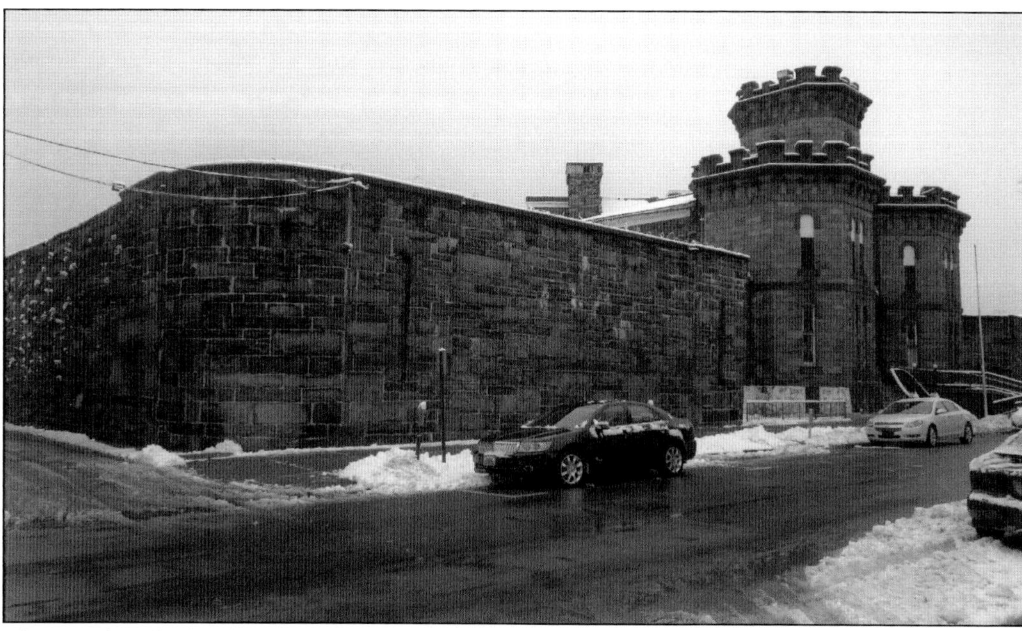

The Northumberland County Jail, shown here as it looks today, is still in operation in Sunbury. Located a few hundred feet from the Susquehanna River, it has been a part of Sunbury's history for many years. It is the fifth public county prison in Sunbury—the first having been located at Fort Augusta. (Courtesy of Klaus Krippendorff.)

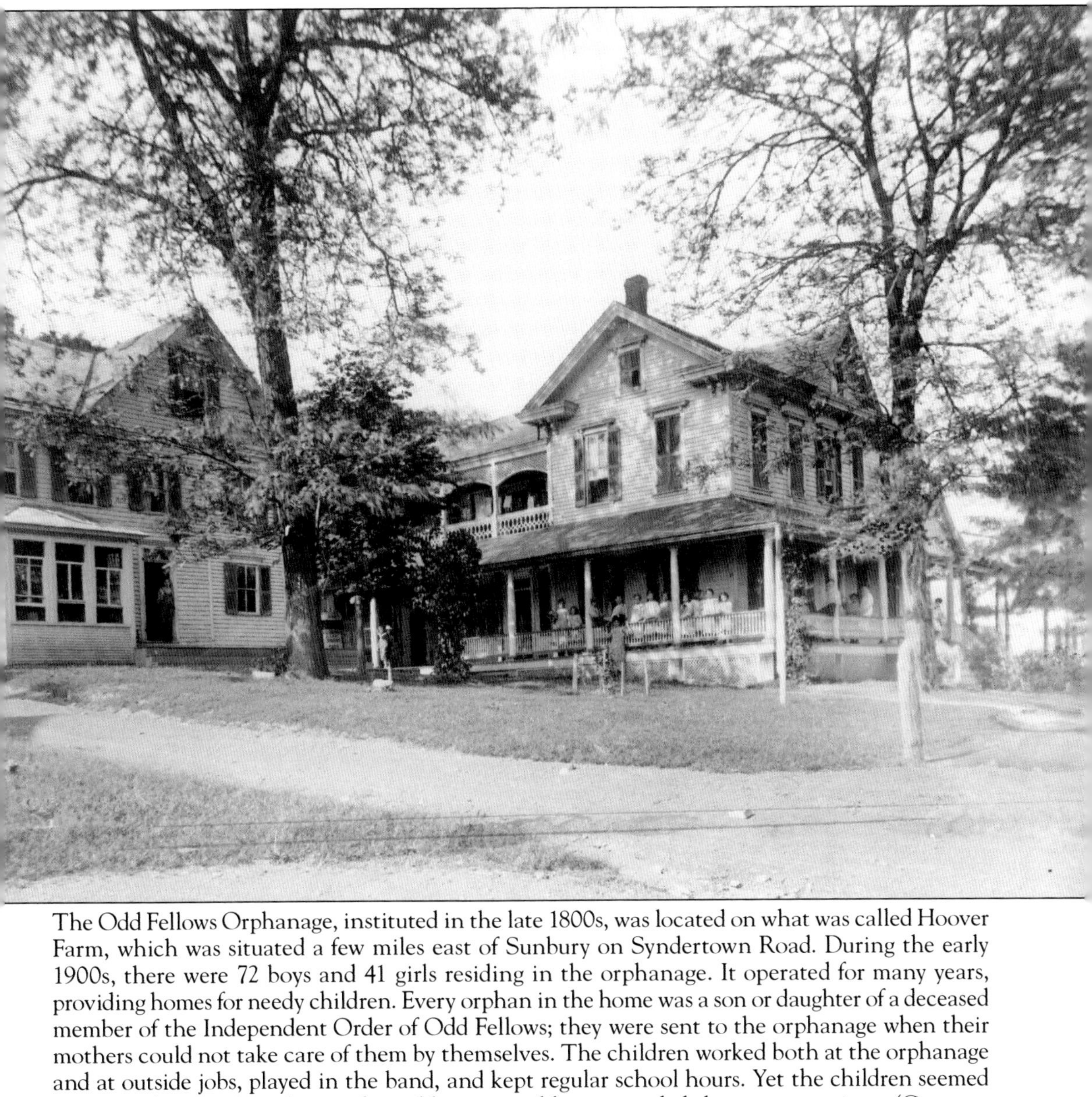

The Odd Fellows Orphanage, instituted in the late 1800s, was located on what was called Hoover Farm, which was situated a few miles east of Sunbury on Syndertown Road. During the early 1900s, there were 72 boys and 41 girls residing in the orphanage. It operated for many years, providing homes for needy children. Every orphan in the home was a son or daughter of a deceased member of the Independent Order of Odd Fellows; they were sent to the orphanage when their mothers could not take care of them by themselves. The children worked both at the orphanage and at outside jobs, played in the band, and kept regular school hours. Yet the children seemed to respond to the discipline in favorable ways and later attended the many reunions. (Courtesy of the Library of Congress.)

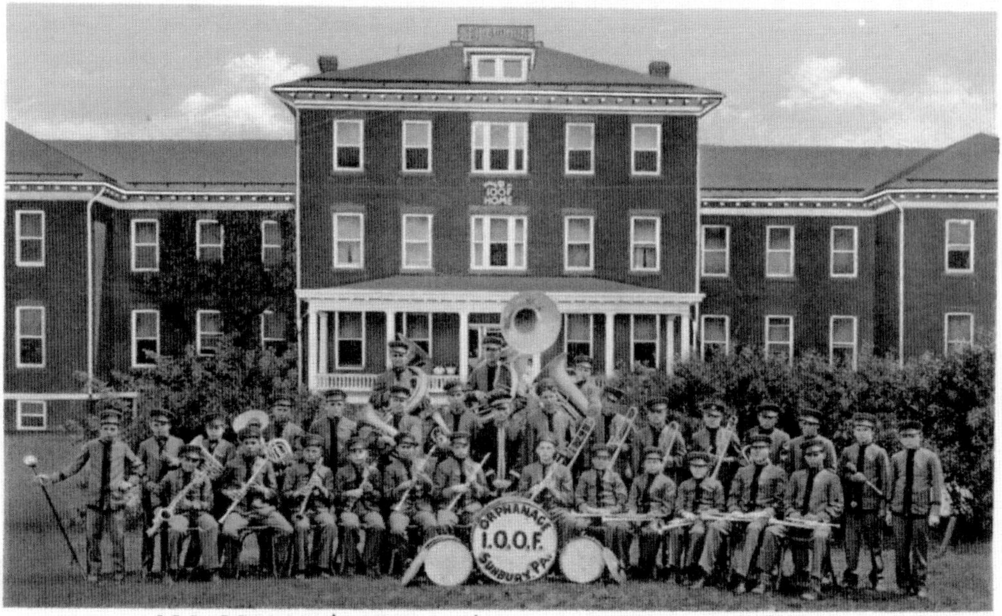
ODD FELLOWS' ORPHANS' HOME BAND — SUNBURY, PA. 2A1253

The Odd Fellows Orphans Home Band, shown above in a 1923 postcard, was very popular in the county. According to the October 3, 1923, edition of the *Reading Eagle*, the band played at the Rajah Theater in Reading, Pennsylvania and "made a great hit." The orphanage was designed and constructed by William Howard Lee, a county architect. The early postcard below depicts picnic grounds in a peaceful grove at the Odd Fellows Orphanage. The 1900 *Central Pennsylvania Odd Fellows' Orphans Home Report*, the third annual report of the home, includes a list of 33 children admitted to the home. (Both, courtesy of Tim Auman.)

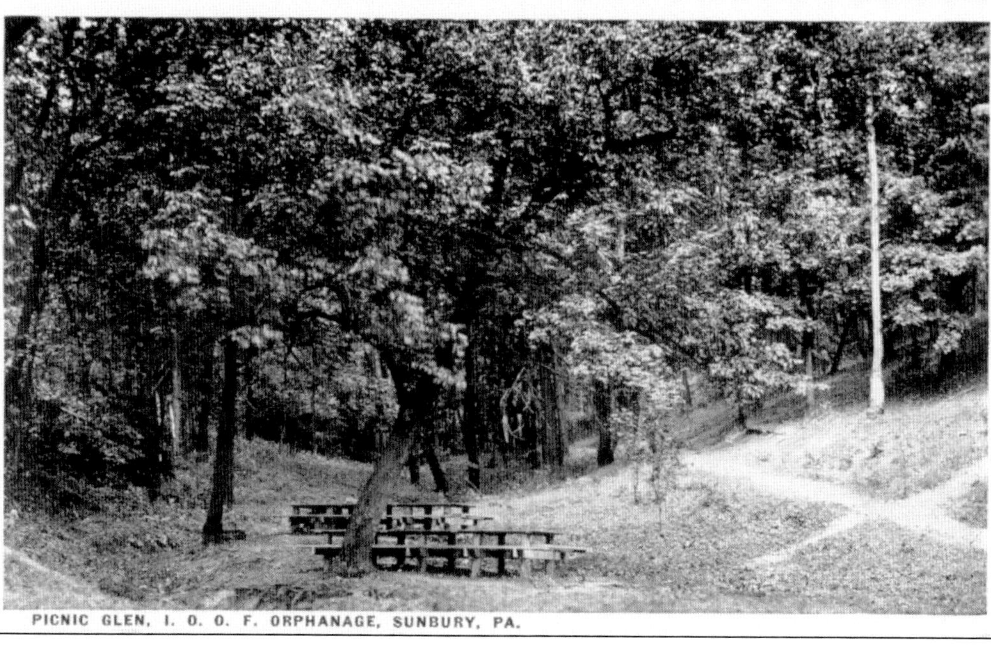
PICNIC GLEN, I. O. O. F. ORPHANAGE, SUNBURY, PA.

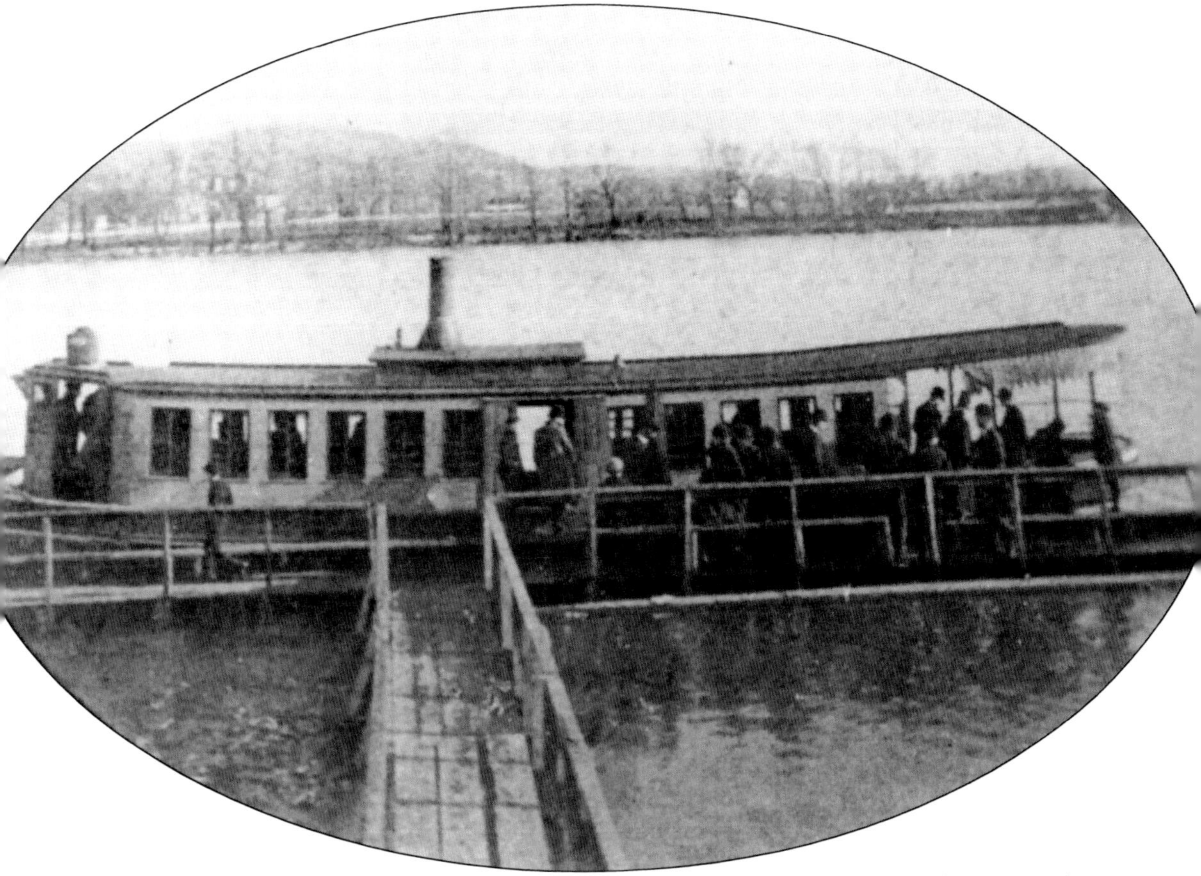

Sunbury became important because of its river access and its connection to Pennsylvania canals. Transportation on the river was critical, as it helped to create a thriving business district, as well as spawning many homes—both cottages and mansions. Before the ferries were created, flats with drivers using long poles took passengers across the river. With the advent of ferryboats, the borough of Sunbury sold the exclusive privilege of operating the ferry to the highest bidder. In 1854, one of those to whom the lease was given was Ira T. Clement, who used the wharf at the Market Street landing. This photograph shows his steamboat at the foot of Market Street waiting to take patrons across the river. Clement built several steamboats, one of which was named the *Sunbury*. It made hourly trips across the Susquehanna River to and from the Sunbury dock. (Courtesy of NCHS.)

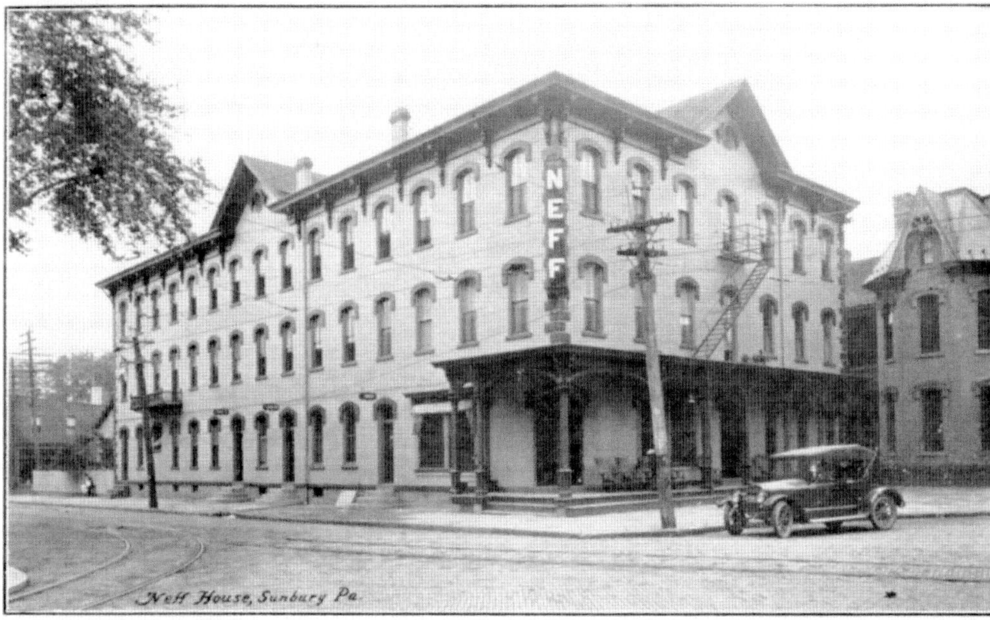

These 1920 postcards show the elegance of the Neff House, a hotel owned by C.D. Wharton and formerly called the Washington Hotel, which Wharton also kept. It was located at the corner of Second and Market Streets, across from the courthouse. Originally three floors, it was later expanded to six and was the only modern hotel between Harrisburg and Williamsport. The famous rooftop garden restaurant atop the six-story building overlooked the Susquehanna River and provided a panoramic view of central Pennsylvania. Lunch and dinner were served daily throughout the years. The hotel also had a soda fountain, grill, taproom, and dining room on the lobby floor. The Neff House was torn down in the mid-1970s. (Both, courtesy of Tim Auman.)

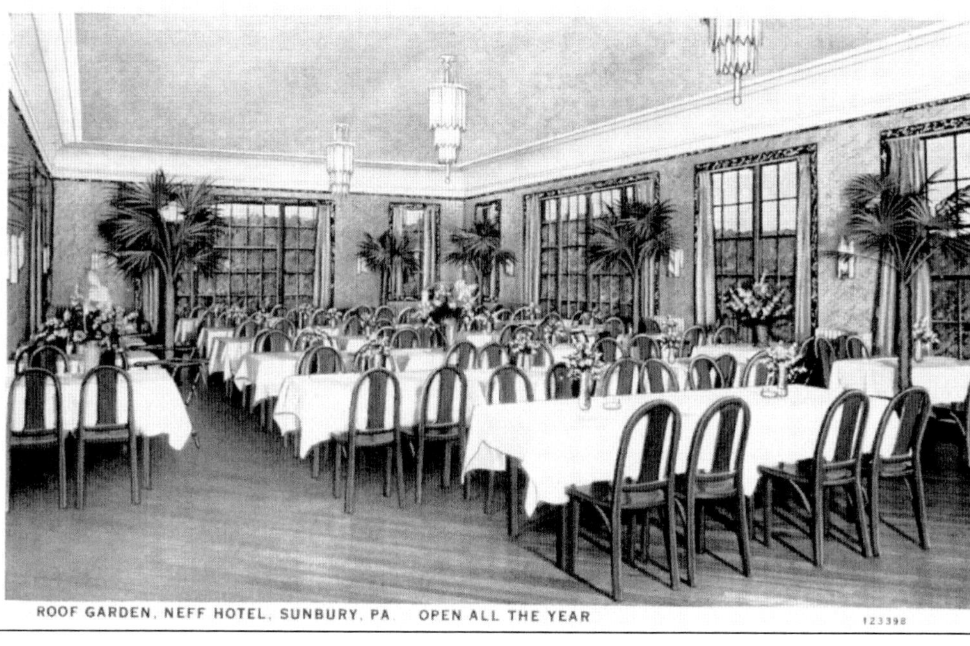

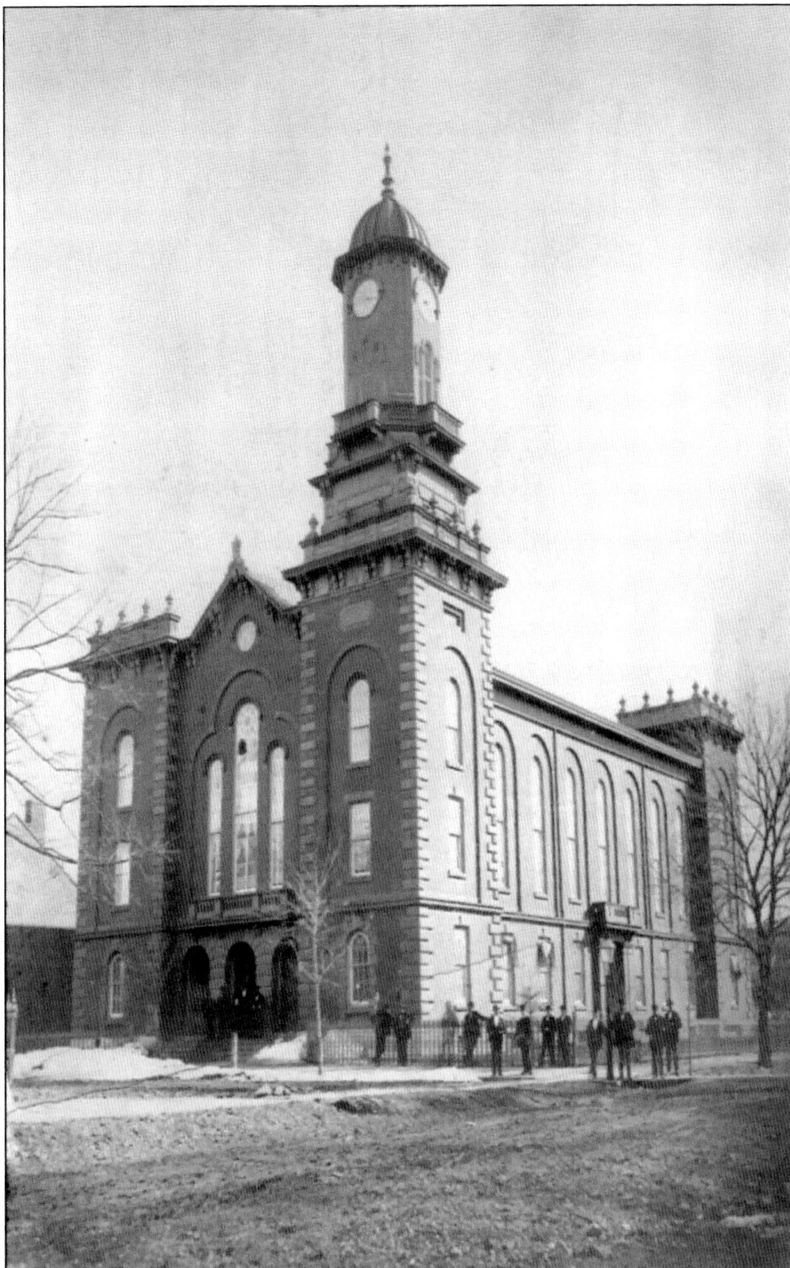

The present Northumberland County Courthouse was the fourth structure to be built in the county for the purpose of holding a court and was constructed in 1865 by Sunbury architect D.S. Russell. It was listed in the National Register of Historic Places. The two-story Italianate building features three arched doors on the front facade, brownstone quoins at the corners, and a clock tower with a copper dome. Simon Cameron donated the tower bell in 1878. The courthouse was also the site of the murder trial and conviction of the late Molly Maguire and Peter McManus (see page 109). The building was for some time the only public meeting place of any size in Sunbury and was used for various activities, including a Sunday school. Sunbury is the seat for Northumberland County. (Courtesy of NCHS.)

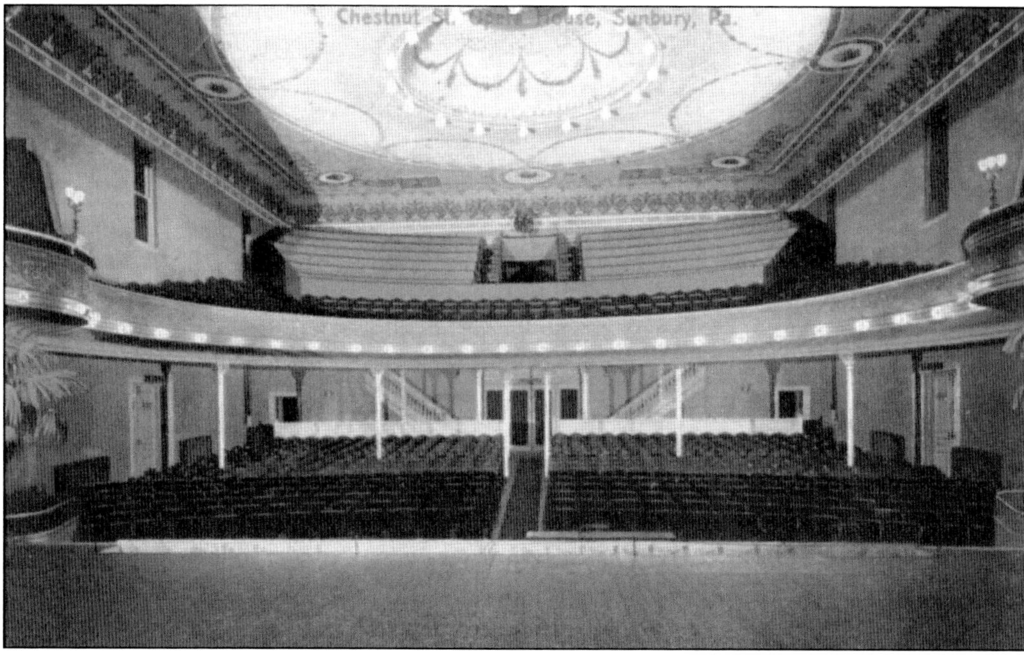

The Chestnut Street Opera House opened in Sunbury on September 12, 1901, and could seat up to 1,000 people. Records indicate that 571 road shows and 440 vaudeville acts performed there from 1915 to 1935. However, due to the flood of 1936 and the growing popularity of movies, the opera house was closed down. (Courtesy of Tim Auman.)

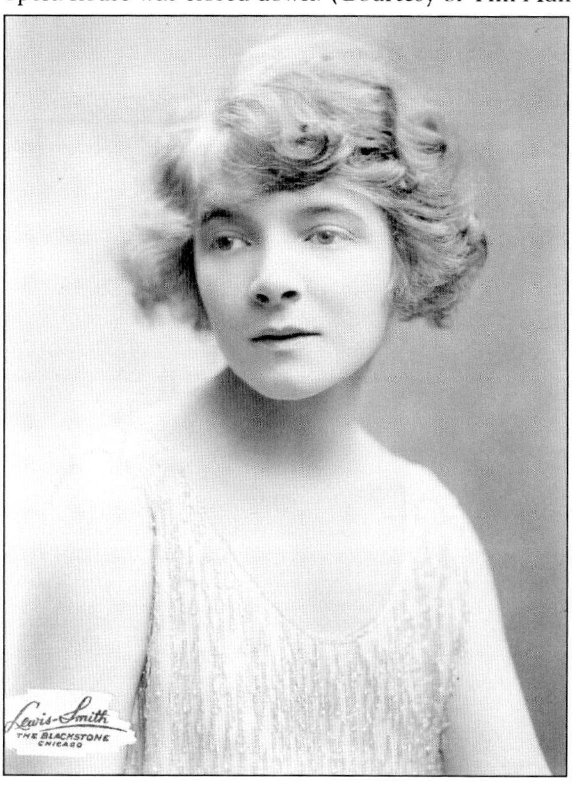

Helen Hayes was one of many famous entertainers who came to Sunbury. Considered the "First Lady of the American Theater," Hayes performed all over the world. She acted in everything from Shakespeare plays to Hollywood films. A Broadway theater is named for her. (Courtesy of the Library of Congress.)

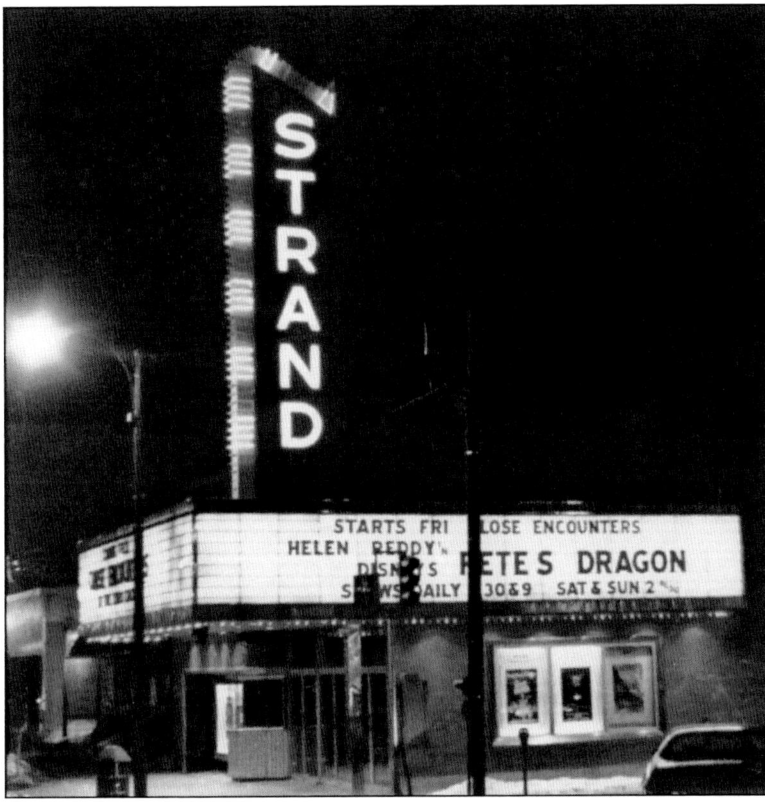

Strand Theatre, with the marquee advertising *Pete's Dragon*, starring Helen Reddy, was the larger of two theaters in Sunbury. Opened in 1910 as the People's Theater, it contained 1,104 seats and was located at 315 Market Street on the corner of Third Street. Its grand marquee featured moving lights, illuminating life on Market Street. In 1953, the theater possessed a large CinemaScope screen, which was installed for the movie *The Robe* in 1953. (Courtesy of NCHS.)

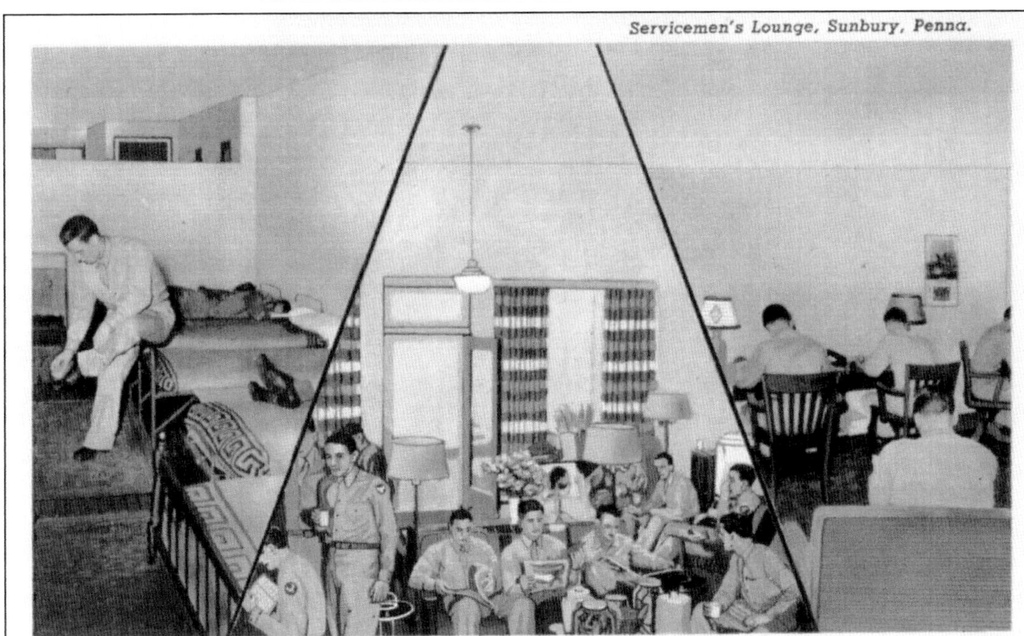

This 1945 postcard shows various scenes from the Servicemen's Lounge in Sunbury during World War II. This was a place where men could sleep, socialize, and have meals. There was also room for study and for writing letters home. (Courtesy of Tim Auman.)

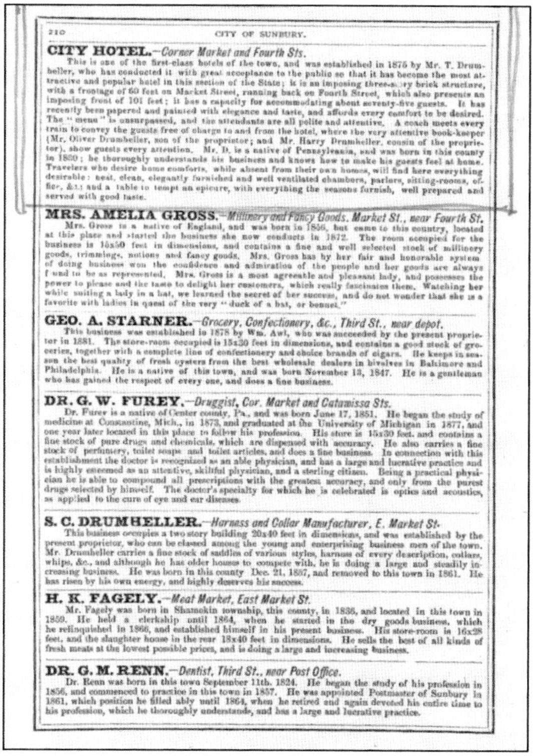

210 CITY OF SUNBURY.

CITY HOTEL.—*Corner Market and Fourth Sts.*

This is one of the first-class hotels of the town, and was established in 1875 by Mr. T. Drumheller, who has conducted it with great acceptance to the public so that it has become the most attractive and popular hotel in this section of the State; it is an imposing three-story brick structure, with a frontage of 60 feet on Market Street, running back on Fourth Street, which also presents an imposing front of 101 feet; it has a capacity for accommodating about seventy-five guests. It has recently been papered and painted with elegance and taste, and affords every comfort to be desired. The "menu" is unsurpassed, and the attendants are all polite and attentive. A coach meets every train to convey the guests free of charge to and from the hotel, where the very attentive book-keeper (Mr. Oliver Drumheller, son of the proprietor; and Mr. Harry Drumheller, cousin of the proprietor), show guests every attention. Mr. D. is a native of Pennsylvania, and was born in this county in 1830; he thoroughly understands his business and knows how to make his guests feel at home. Travelers who desire home comforts, while absent from their own homes, will find here everything desirable: neat, clean, elegantly furnished and well ventilated chambers, parlors, sitting-rooms, office, &c.; and a table to tempt an epicure, with everything the seasons furnish, well prepared and served with good taste.

MRS. AMELIA GROSS.—*Millinery and Fancy Goods, Market St., near Fourth St.*

Mrs. Gross is a native of England, and was born in 1856, but came to this country, located at this place and started the business she now conducts in 1872. The room occupied for the business is 15x50 feet in dimensions, and contains a fine and well selected stock of millinery goods, trimmings, notions and fancy goods. Mrs. Gross has by her fair and honorable system of doing business won the confidence and admiration of the people and her goods are always found to be as represented. Mrs. Gross is a most agreeable and pleasant lady, and possesses the power to please and the taste to delight her customers, which really fascinates them. Watching her while suiting a lady in a hat, we learned the secret of her success, and do not wonder that she is a favorite with ladies in quest of the very "duck of a hat, or bonnet."

GEO. A. STARNER.—*Grocery, Confectionery, &c., Third St., near depot.*

This business was established in 1878 by Wm. Awl, who was succeeded by the present proprietor in 1881. The store-room occupied is 15x30 feet in dimensions, and contains a good stock of groceries, together with a complete line of confectionery and choice brands of cigars. He keeps in season the best quality of fresh oysters from the best wholesale dealers in bivalves in Baltimore and Philadelphia. He is a native of this town, and was born November 13, 1847. He is a gentleman who has gained the respect of every one, and does a fine business.

DR. G. W. FUREY.—*Druggist, Cor. Market and Catawissa Sts.*

Dr. Furey is a native of Center county, Pa., and was born June 17, 1851. He began the study of medicine at Constantine, Mich., in 1873, and graduated at the University of Michigan in 1877, and one year later located in this place to follow his profession. His store is 15x30 feet, and contains a fine stock of pure drugs and chemicals, which are dispensed with accuracy. He also carries a fine stock of perfumery, toilet soaps and toilet articles, and does a fine business. In connection with this establishment the doctor is recognized as an able physician, and has a large and lucrative practice and is highly esteemed as an attentive, skillful physician, and a sterling citizen. Being a practical physician he is able to compound all prescriptions with the greatest accuracy, and only from the purest drugs selected by himself. The doctor's specialty for which he is celebrated is optics and acoustics, as applied to the cure of eye and ear diseases.

S. C. DRUMHELLER.—*Harness and Collar Manufacturer, E. Market St.*

This business occupies a two story building 20x40 feet in dimensions, and was established by the present proprietor, who can be classed among the young and enterprising business men of the town. Mr. Drumheller carries a fine stock of saddles of various styles, harness of every description, collars, whips, &c., and although he has older houses to compete with, he is doing a large and steadily increasing business. He was born in this county Dec. 21, 1857, and removed to this town in 1861. He has risen by his own energy, and highly deserves his success.

H. K. FAGELY.—*Meat Market, East Market St.*

Mr. Fagely was born in Shamokin township, this county, in 1836, and located in this town in 1859. He held a clerkship until 1864, when he started in the dry goods business, which he relinquished in 1866, and established himself in his present business. His store-room is 16x28 feet, and the slaughter house in the rear 18x40 feet in dimensions. He sells the best of all kinds of fresh meats at the lowest possible prices, and is doing a large and increasing business.

DR. G. M. RENN.—*Dentist, Third St., near Post Office.*

Dr. Renn was born in this town September 11th. 1824. He began the study of his profession in 1856, and commenced to practice in this town in 1857. He was appointed Postmaster of Sunbury in 1861, which position he filled ably until 1864, when he retired and again devoted his entire time to his profession, which he thoroughly understands, and has a large and lucrative practice.

This is a page from a travel book written in 1882 about Sunbury, which provides information about the City Hotel as well as other business owners, such as S.C. Drumheller. The City Hotel was considered a first-class lodging. The Drumhellers, who built the hotel, wanted to provide home comfort to those who stayed here. (Courtesy of Meghan Beck.)

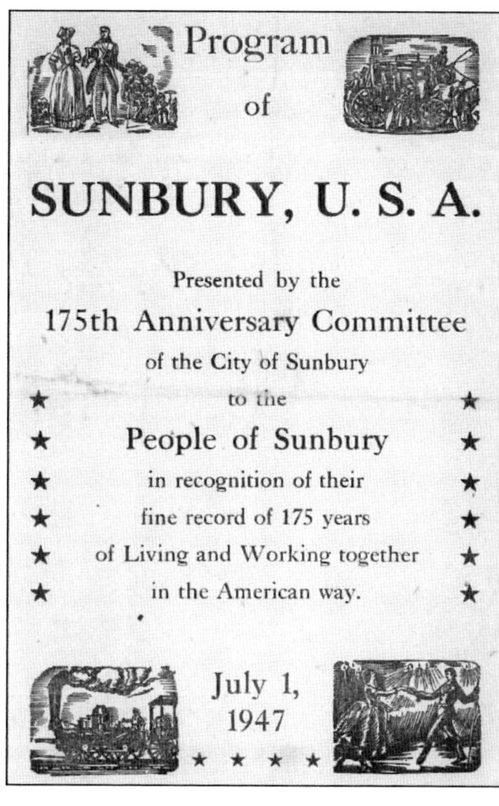

The Edison Hotel resides majestically at Fourth and Market Streets. Originally named the City Hotel, it was built by Edward T. Drumheller in 1871. It caught fire on January 14, 1914, after which it was repaired and rebuilt. It became the first building in the world to be lighted with incandescent electric lights, installed by Thomas A. Edison in 1883. On July 4, 1922, the anniversary of this event, it was renamed the Edison Hotel at a ceremony attended by Edison himself. There is a historic plaque to the right of the entrance door. This is the program for the 175th anniversary of the city of Sunbury, on July 1, 1947. Many events were conducted, and souvenirs were created to celebrate the anniversary, such as the 175th bronze medal and a 1947 wooden nickel flat bill. (Courtesy of Meghan Beck.)

This is a page from a tour book about hotels along Route 41 from Harrisburg to Williamsport. It shows the City Hotel, now the Edison Hotel, as one of the leading hostelries in the area when it was still under the ownership of the builder, Edward T. Drumheller. (Courtesy of Meghan Beck.)

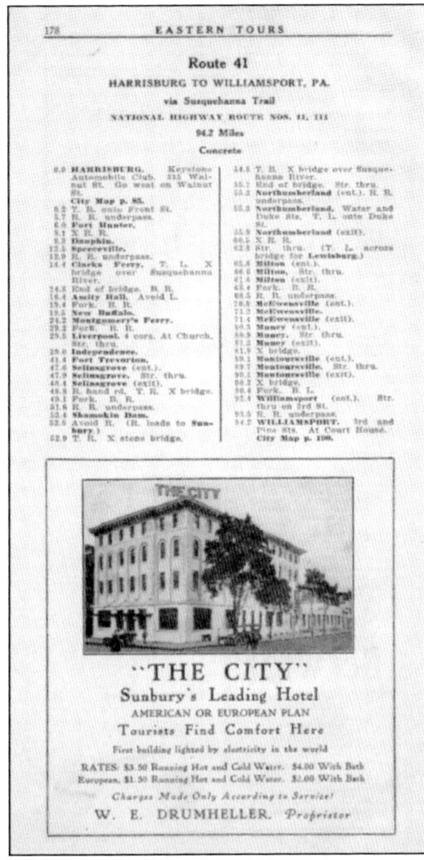

178 EASTERN TOURS

Route 41

HARRISBURG TO WILLIAMSPORT, PA.

via Susquehanna Trail

NATIONAL HIGHWAY ROUTE NOS. 11, 111

94.2 Miles

Concrete

0.0 **HARRISBURG.** Keystone Automobile Club, 115 Walnut St. Go west on Walnut St.
City Map p. 85.
2.2 T. R. onto Front St.
3.7 R. R. underpass.
6.0 **Fort Hunter.**
8.1 X R. R.
9.3 **Dauphin.**
12.5 **Speeceville.**
12.9 R. R. underpass.
14.4 **Clarks Ferry.** T. L. X bridge over Susquehanna River.
14.8 End of bridge. R. R.
16.4 **Amity Hall.** Avoid L.
19.4 Fork. B. R.
19.5 **New Buffalo.**
24.2 **Montgomery's Ferry.**
29.2 Fork. B. R.
29.5 **Liverpool.** 4 cors. At Church. Str. thru.
39.0 **Independence.**
41.4 **Fort Trevorton.**
47.6 **Selinsgrove** (ent.).
47.9 **Selinsgrove.** Str. thru.
48.4 **Selinsgrove** (exit).
48.8 R. hand rd. T. R. X bridge.
49.1 Fork. B. R.
51.8 R. R. underpass.
52.4 **Shamokin Dam.**
52.8 Avoid R. (R. leads to **Sunbury.**)
52.9 T. R. X stone bridge.
54.5 T. R. X bridge over Susquehanna River.
55.1 End of bridge. Str. thru.
55.2 **Northumberland** (ent.). R. R. underpass.
55.5 **Northumberland.** Water and Duke Sts. T. L. onto Duke St.
55.9 **Northumberland** (exit).
60.5 X R. R.
62.8 Str. thru. (T. L. across bridge for **Lewisburg.**)
65.8 **Milton** (ent.).
66.6 **Milton.** Str. thru.
67.6 **Milton** (exit).
68.4 Fork. B. R.
68.5 R. R. underpass.
70.8 **McEwensville** (ent.).
71.2 **McEwensville.**
71.4 **McEwensville** (exit).
80.3 **Muncy** (ent.).
80.5 **Muncy.** Str. thru.
81.2 **Muncy** (exit).
81.9 X bridge.
89.1 **Montoursville** (ent.).
89.7 **Montoursville.** Str. thru.
90.1 **Montoursville** (exit).
90.2 X bridge.
90.4 Fork. B. L.
92.4 **Williamsport** (ent.). Str. thru on 3rd St.
93.5 R. R. underpass.
94.2 **WILLIAMSPORT.** 3rd and Pine Sts. At Court House.
City Map p. 190.

THE CITY

"THE CITY"

Sunbury's Leading Hotel

AMERICAN OR EUROPEAN PLAN

Tourists Find Comfort Here

First building lighted by electricity in the world

RATES: $3.50 Running Hot and Cold Water. $4.00 With Bath
European, $1.50 Running Hot and Cold Water. $2.00 With Bath

Charges Made Only According to Service!

W. E. DRUMHELLER, *Proprietor*

The Edison Hotel is a cornerstone of the downtown area. Early innovations at the hotel included a hand-operated elevator. Part of the hotel burned down on January 14, 1914, but was renovated with a new facade and the addition of the fourth floor. The hotel is reputed to be haunted by a spirit named Ramona. (Courtesy of Klaus Krippendorff.)

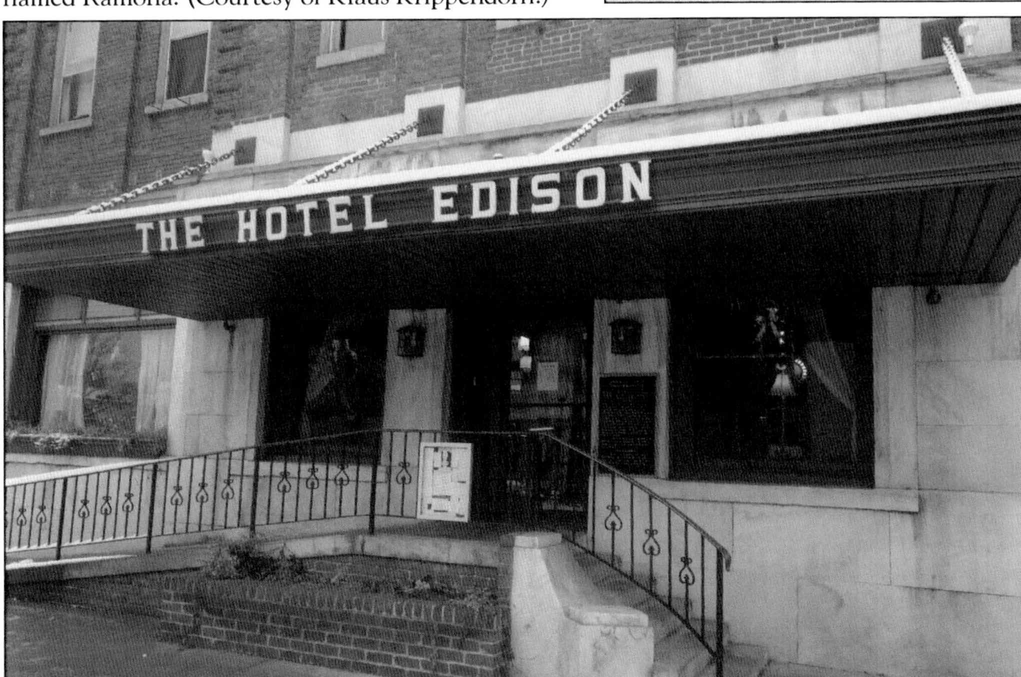

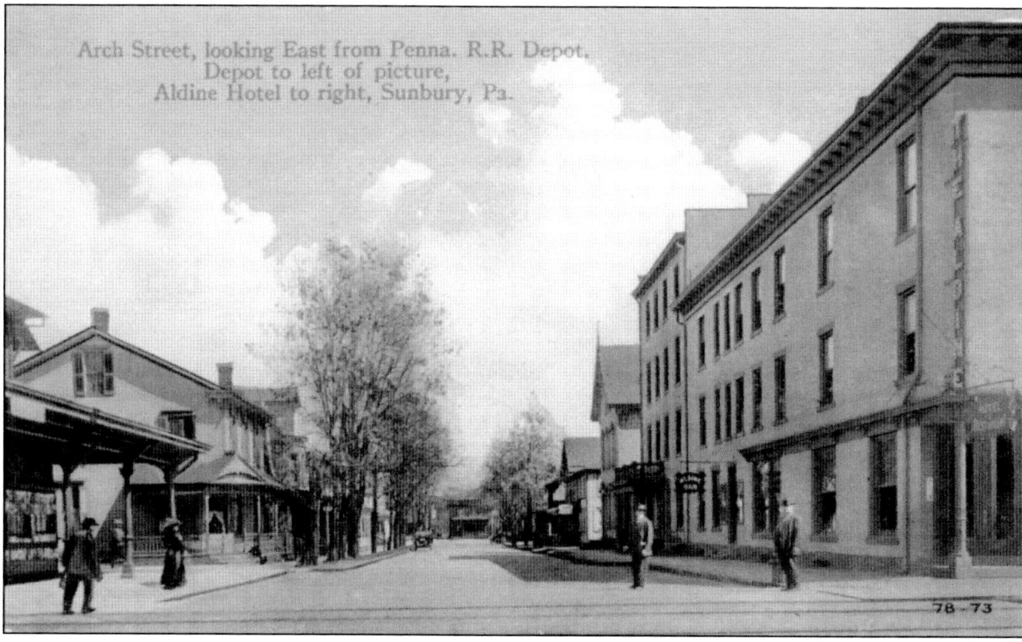

The view of the city seen in this vintage postcard is of Arch Street, looking east from the Pennsylvania Railroad depot on the left of the picture and the old Aldine Hotel on the right. Both the depot and the hotel are examples of the Second Empire styles from the railroad era. (Courtesy of Tim Auman.)

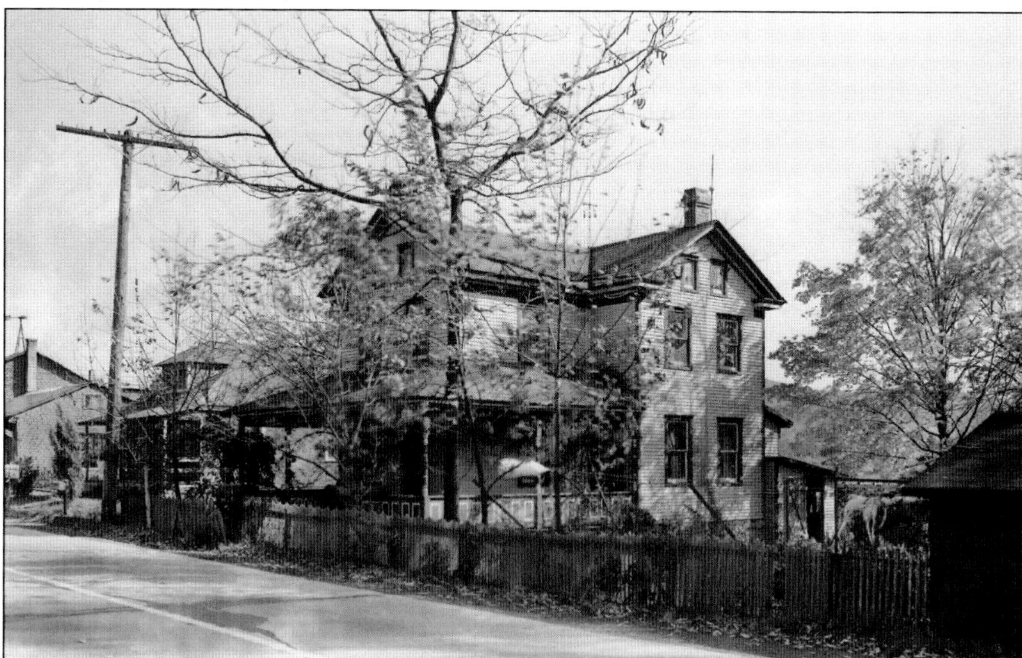

This lovely old house, which was once owned by Pansy L. family, was located on the south side of State Highway Route 61 on the outskirts of Sunbury in Stonington. It stood near the site of land owned by the author's family and two other families and is near the present-day Northumberland County Memorial Park, one of the largest cemeteries in the county. (Courtesy of NCHS.)

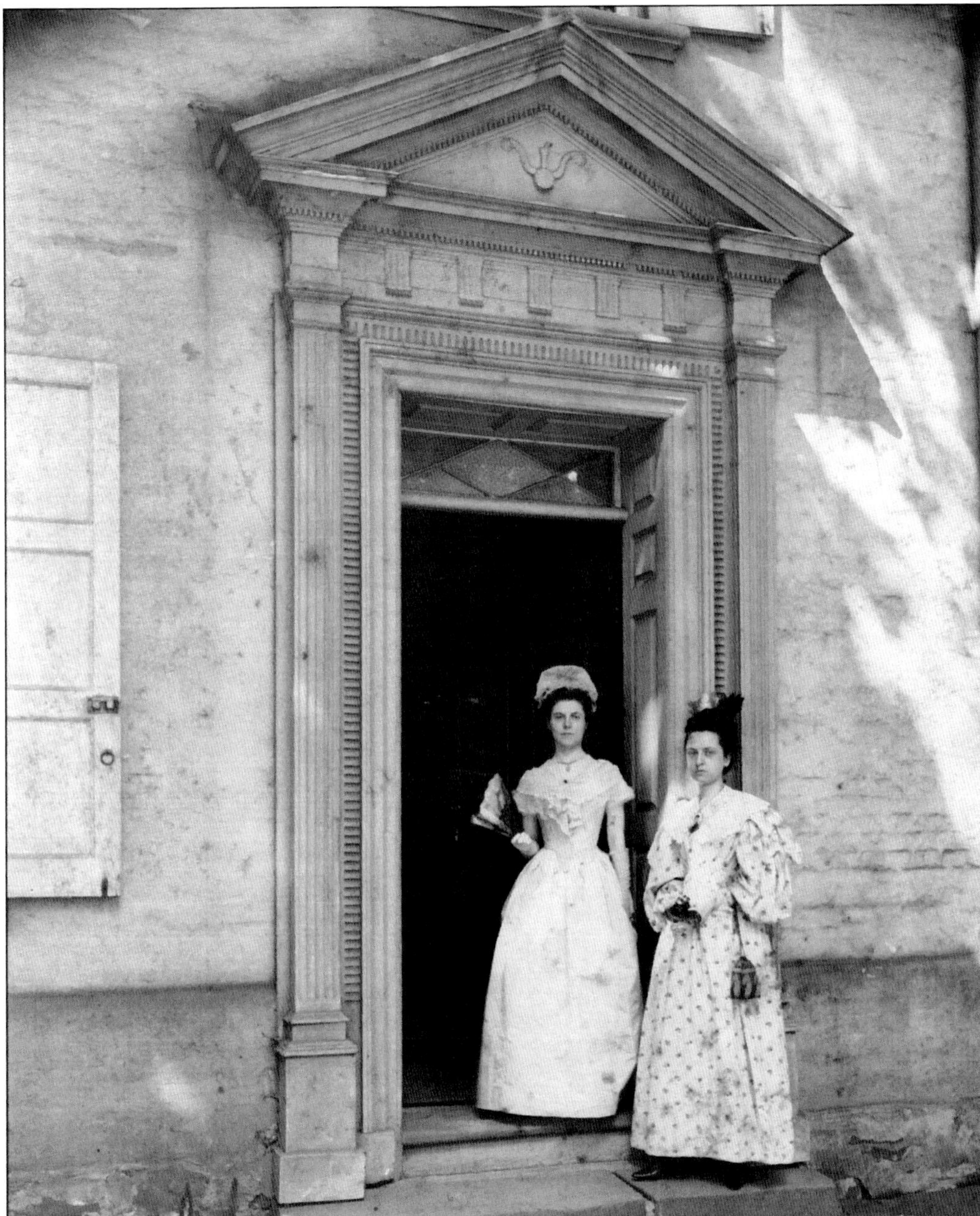

Here are two girls in period dress at the Donnel House on the north side of Market Street at Second Street in about 1910. Formerly a hotel, the house is still standing and is between the Masonic temple and the offices of the *Daily Item* (the Sunbury newspaper), opposite Cameron Park. The girls are Emile Clay (left) and Lucy Gibson, granddaughters of Judge Charles Gobin Donnel. Judge Donnel paid $1,000 for the house, which is believed to be oldest brick structure in Sunbury. The building was constructed in sections, the oldest of which dates back to 1779 by Jacob Preisinger. The prothonotary, register, and recorder rented apartments in the house until the new courthouse was completed. At least two duels were fought here, and the second duel involved Gen. Hugh Brady and Capt. Daniel Levy in 1812. (Courtesy of NCHS.)

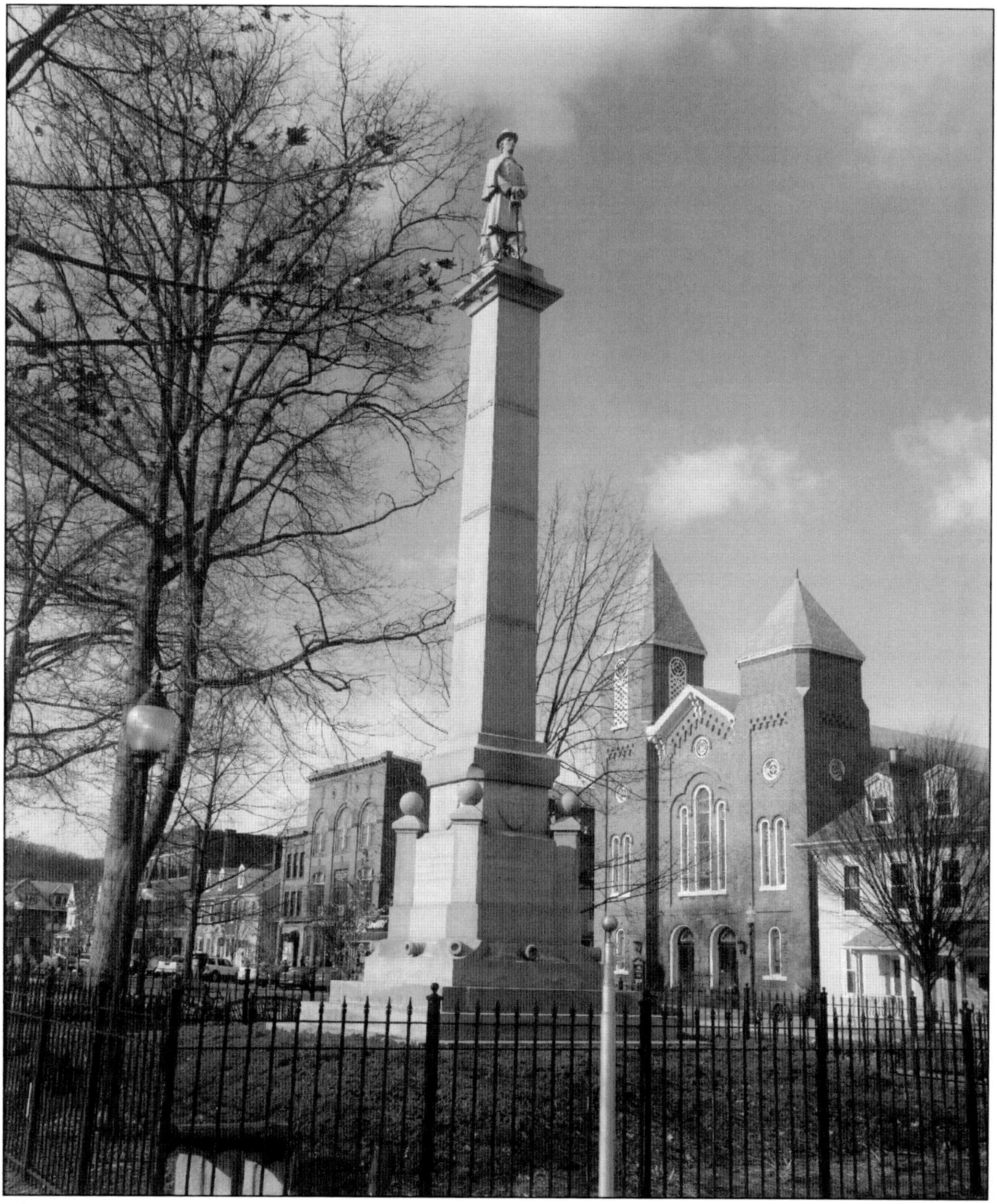

This contemporary photograph shows the city behind the Northumberland County Soldiers' Monument, located in Cameron Park. Behind the monument is Market Street. Situated next to the First Presbyterian Church, shown behind the monument, is the Paul Baldy House, built in 1820 by Paul Baldy, a blacksmith and a veteran of the Revolutionary War. Baldy had maintained his smithy on the site of the Presbyterian church. After his death in 1823, Samuel J. Packer purchased the property. Packer was a young attorney, publisher of the *Public Inquirer*, and postmaster of Sunbury from 1822 to 1824. In 1997, the monument was restored and the iron fence surrounding it was added. It was rededicated during Sunbury's 225th anniversary celebration that year. At one time, a whipping post stood in the center of the park. A second war memorial is at the western end of the park. (Courtesy of Klaus Krippendorff.)

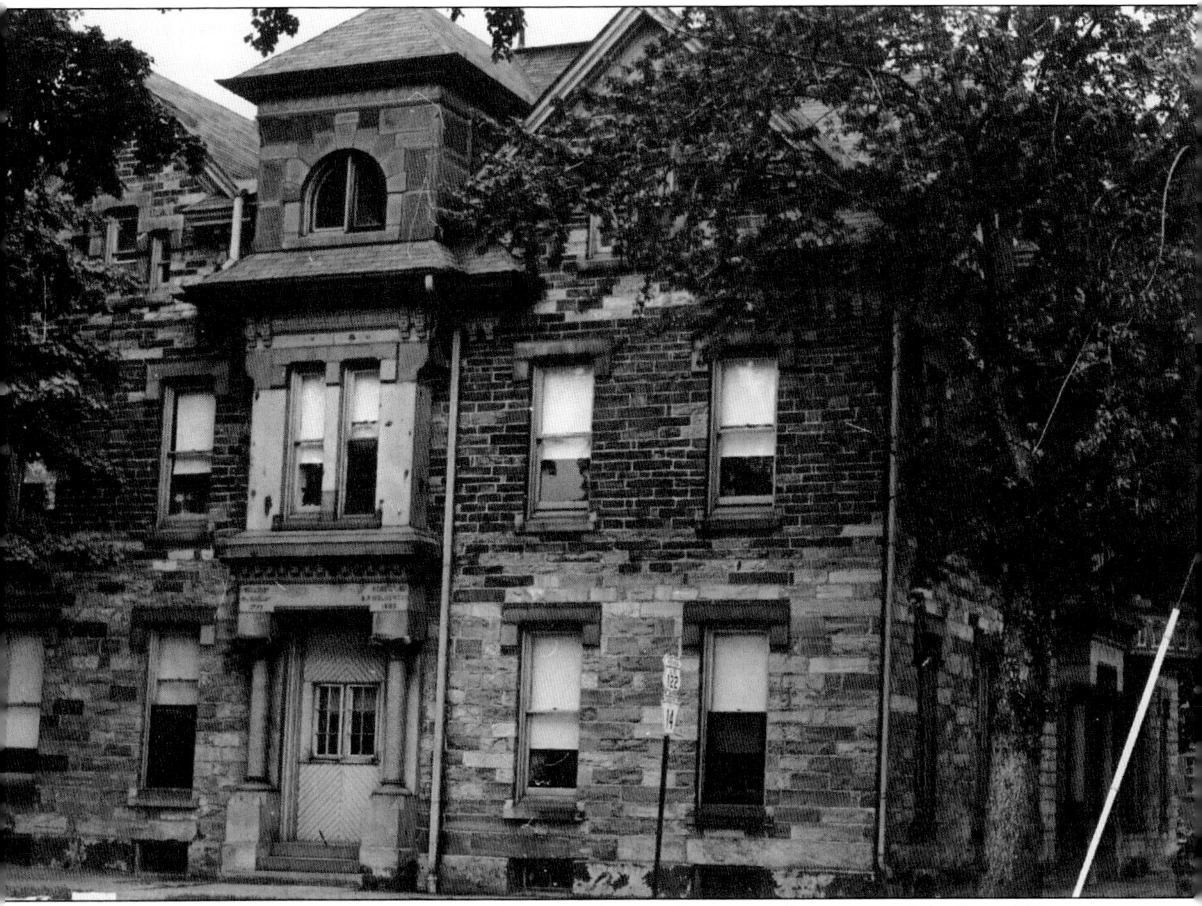

William Maclay built this house facing the Susquehanna River on the corner of Arch and Front Streets, the Maclay-Wolverton House, in 1773. It was the second house constructed in Sunbury. The residence was constructed of dressed limestone quarried on the farm that Maclay owned, near Sunbury. It was built in a rectangular shape, with two stories and an attic. The first floor had a large center hall, with two rooms on each side, with huge fireplaces. From 1786 to 1788, Maclay served as a member of the Supreme Executive Council of Pennsylvania, and from 1789 to 1791, he represented Pennsylvania as one of its first two US senators. The house was leased to a doctor for a brief time and served as hotel and taproom; it was willed to Jane, Maclay's daughter, in 1804. (Courtesy of NCHS.)

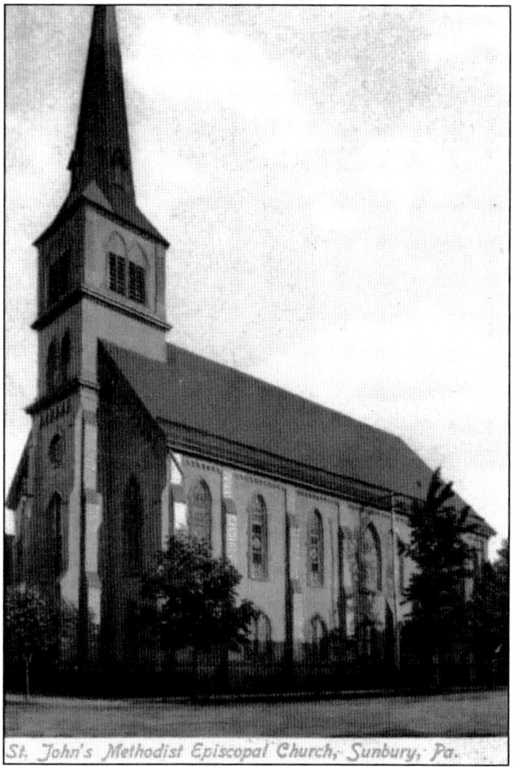

St. John's Methodist Episcopal Church was located on the southeast corner of Arch and North Second Streets. The first mention of preaching by Methodists in Sunbury was in 1793 when Bishop Francis Asbury traveled here to preach an afternoon sermon. Since many of the inhabitants of Sunbury were German Lutherans, the Methodist preachers rarely secured many listeners. (Courtesy of Tim Auman.)

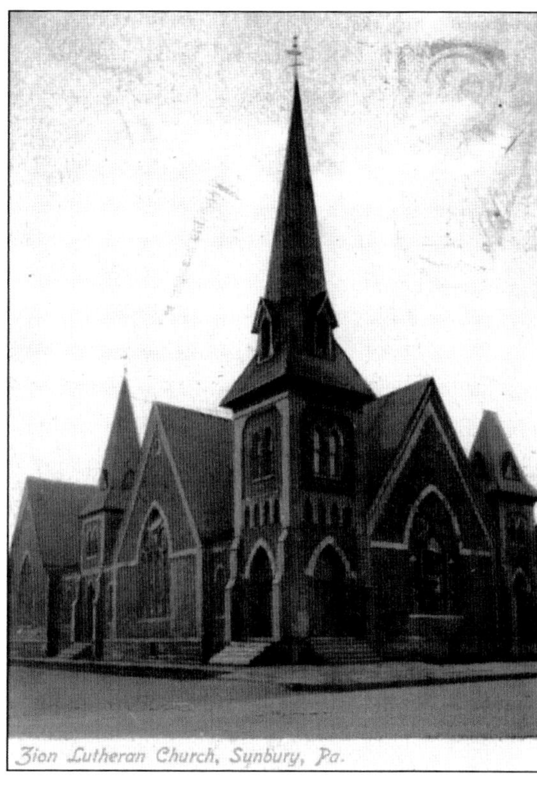

The Zion Lutheran Church is located on the southwest corner of Market and Fifth Streets. It had another location, but the noise and vibrations from passing trains were too distracting. Consequently, the church was relocated to its present site. This building was completed in 1888. (Courtesy of Tim Auman.)

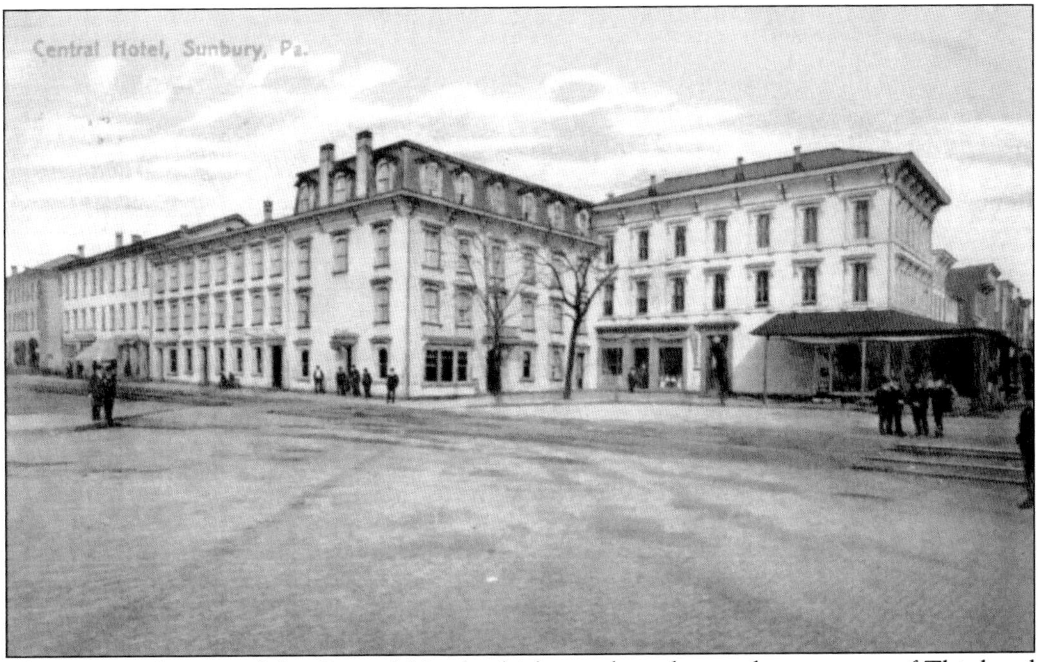

This is an early view of the Central Hotel, which stood on the northeast corner of Third and Market Streets. It was torn down in 1996. The original building was the residence of John B. Packer. In 1859, he sold it to James Van Dyke, the county sheriff at the time. Van Dyke remodeled it, adding the third floor, and opened it as the Central Hotel. (Courtesy of Tim Auman.)

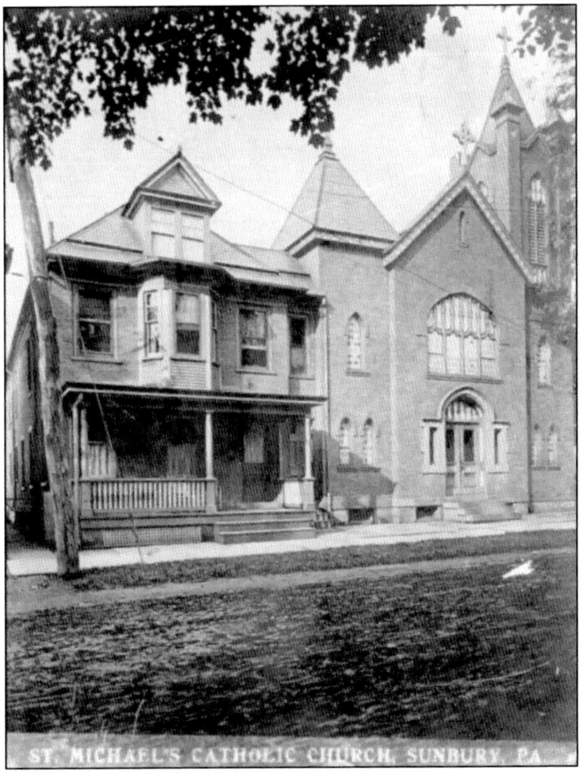

St. Michael the Archangel Catholic Church was built in 1910. In the fall of 1863, Fr. John Joseph Koch organized the mission of St. Michael in Sunbury. Mass was celebrated once a month at a home on Third and Chestnut Streets and, later, at a home on Fourth Street prior to the construction of the church. In 1995, the name of the church was changed to St. Monica. (Courtesy of Tim Auman.)

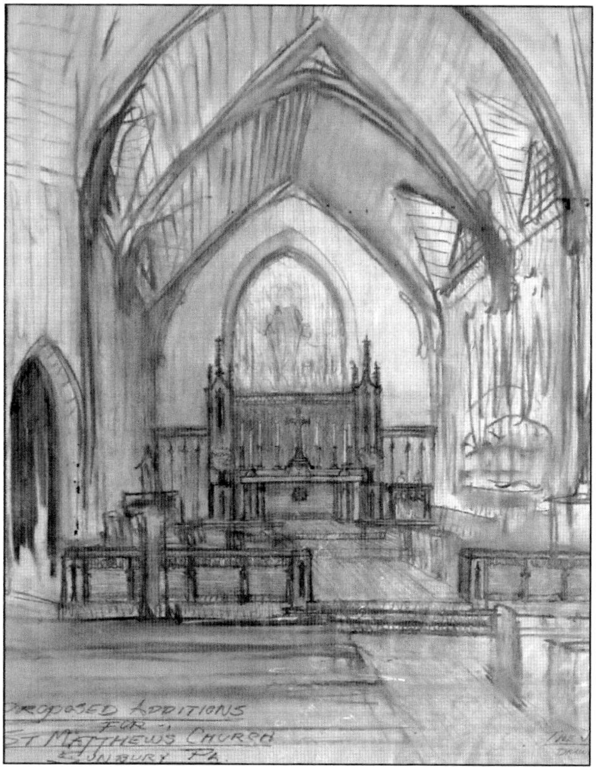

This is a design drawing for architectural elements for proposed additions to St. Matthew's Episcopal Church in Sunbury, Pennsylvania. J&R Lamb Studios created the design around 1857. The drawing was created using a graphite colored pencil. (Courtesy of the Library of Congress.)

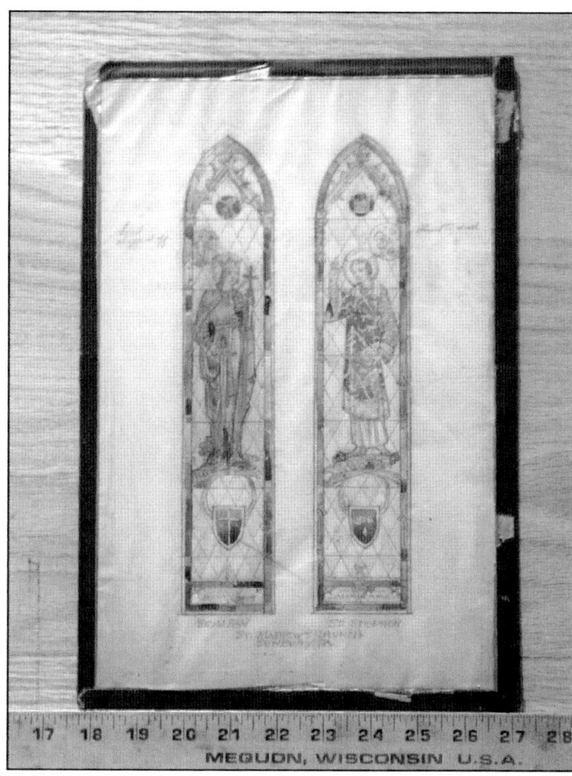

This image shows the proposed stained-glass windows for St. Matthew's Church, which was created by J&R Lamb Studios sometime around 1857. The stained-glass windows, which would face one another, show St. Alban and St. Stephen. The design was done in watercolor. (Courtesy of the Library of Congress.)

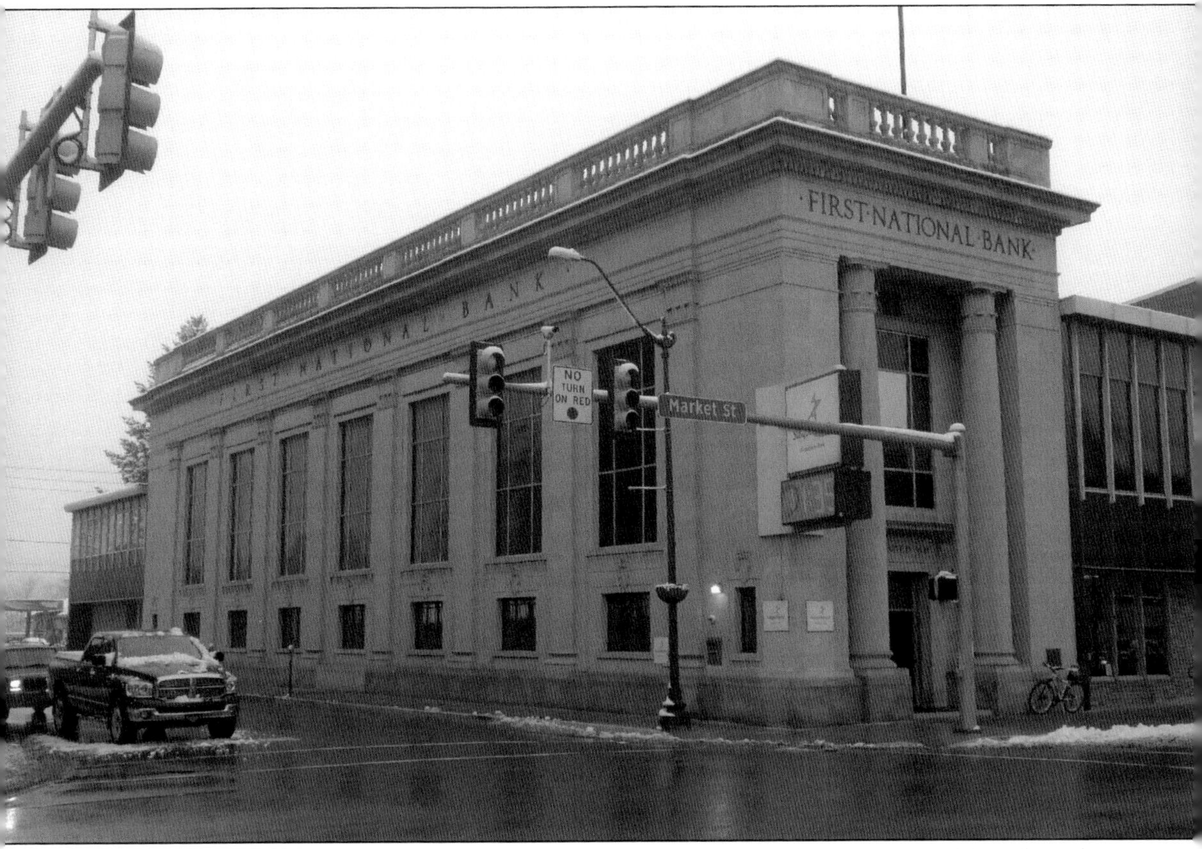

The First National Trust Bank currently occupies a site on the northeast corner of Fourth and Market Streets. Formerly the Bank of Northumberland, it moved to Sunbury in 1864, due in large part to the shift of business activity from the canals to railroads, manufacturing plants, and lumber mills. Initially, the building was located on the north side of Market Square, between Second and Third Streets. On August 23, 1905, the bank relocated to the structure at the southeast corner of Market and Center Streets, known then as the Harrison Building but later as the old YMCA building. In 1923, the First National Bank purchased the assets of the Sunbury National Bank. The old structure at Fourth and Market Streets was then torn down, and the present building was erected on that site. On June 4, 1932, the old Sunbury Trust and Safe Deposit Company became a part of the First National Trust Bank of Sunbury. (Courtesy of Klaus Krippendorff.)

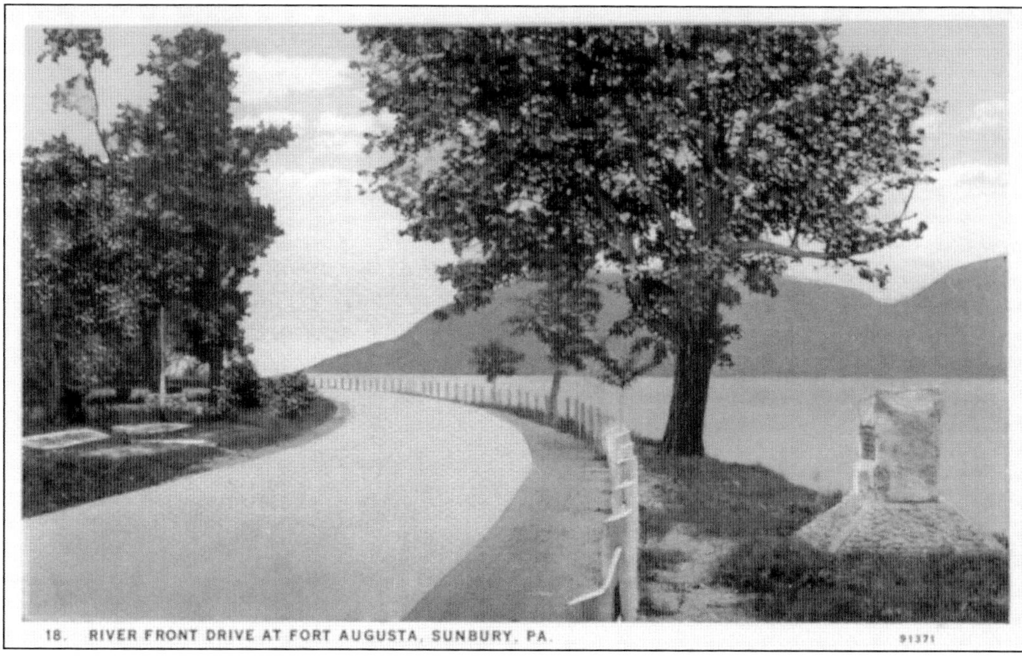

This vintage postcard shows the lovely river drive in front of Fort Augusta. The area was, for many years, open to the overflowing river, but today a flood wall has been built that keeps the waters of the Susquehanna River from flooding the town and causing the destruction that blighted the area for many years. Also shown is the Masonic temple, located between Center and Second Streets. The Masonic lodge is as old as the town itself and is the oldest Masonic lodge in northern Pennsylvania. The lodge was first established when nine officers of General Sullivan's army met at Fort Augusta. (Both, courtesy of David Persing.)

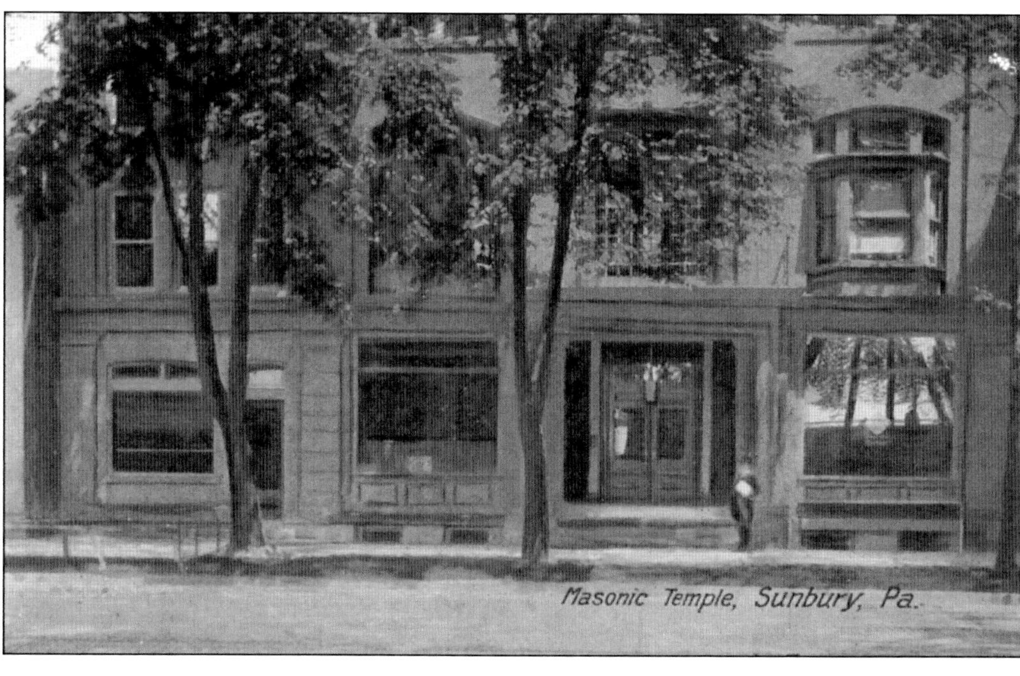

Three

The People of Sunbury

Although Sunbury can be said to be far from the corridors of power—the East and West Coasts—it has nevertheless influenced the culture, politics, and industry of the United States through the important people who have lived there, worked there, or traveled though Sunbury and Northumberland County.

A famous visitor to Sunbury was Thomas Edison, called "the Wizard of Menlo Park," who, in 1883, lit the City Hotel using his three-wire system, which is a system of distribution of electric current for multiple arc or constant service. Three main wires start from the central station and send electric current to a district or building to be lighted. Edison founded the Edison Electronic Illuminating Company in 1883, making Sunbury one of the first towns in central Pennsylvania to have electricity.

Many other prominent citizens have contributed to the history of Sunbury, such as James Tilghman, secretary of the land office. On the corner of Front and Market Streets, his house was possibly the first house built after the 1772 survey of Sunbury. Then there is J.O. Mertz, founder of the Sunbury Motor Company, who established his business in 1914 selling Ford Model Ts. William Maclay's survey laid out the town square of Harrisburg, which was modeled on his previous survey of Sunbury's town square. Maclay was not only a surveyor but also a judge and US senator, as well as an officer in the Continental army. Edward T. Drumheller, entrepreneur, was the builder of the Edison Hotel, which was erected in 1871 and opened as the City Hotel in January 1872.

On March 5, 1895, a group of prominent citizens met in the Central Hotel to discuss securing a general hospital for the area. The Mary M. Packer Hospital was thus born in 1895. At that time, a committee consisting of James C. Packer and others was appointed to procure a charter for a hospital. Mary M. Packer, sister of James, made the offer at this meeting of $6,000 toward starting the charity, with the sole proviso that it forever remain nonsectarian in character and free to all. There were six private patient rooms and a ward for 24 others. The Victorian building that housed the hospital was once the residence of T.H. Purdy, Esq.

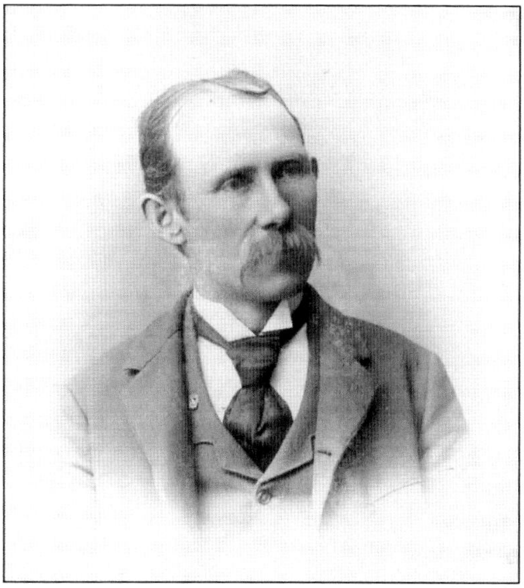

This early-1918 photograph is of William Reddick, who worked in Sunbury while his family lived back home in Virginia. He came to Sunbury to find work on railroads. The 14th US Census, dated February 3, 1920, indicates that he lived in a boardinghouse in Sunbury. (Courtesy of Robin Simoneaux.)

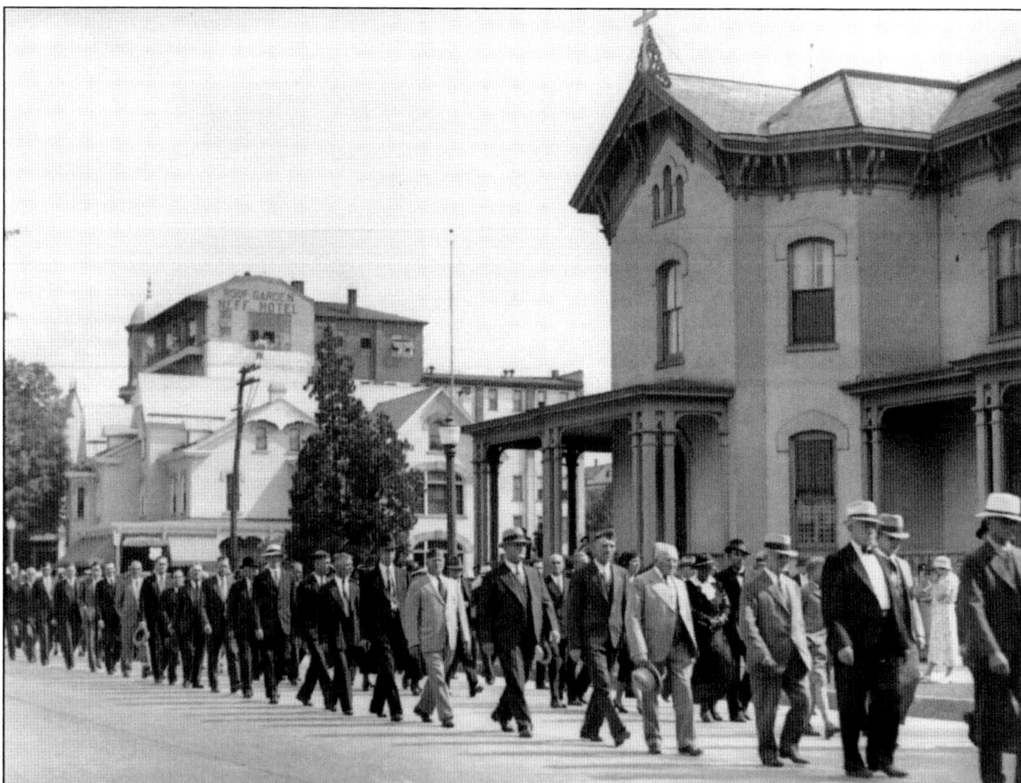

The funeral procession of Maj. Gen. Charles Maxwell Clement, who was born in Sunbury and served his country during the Spanish-American War, was the largest ever seen in the city. Here, mourners walk through Sunbury to honor him. On July 17, 1917, he became the first commander of the 28th Infantry Division (Keystone) unit of the Army National Guard during World War I. This particular unit is the oldest division-sized unit in the armed forces of the United States. (Courtesy of NCHS.)

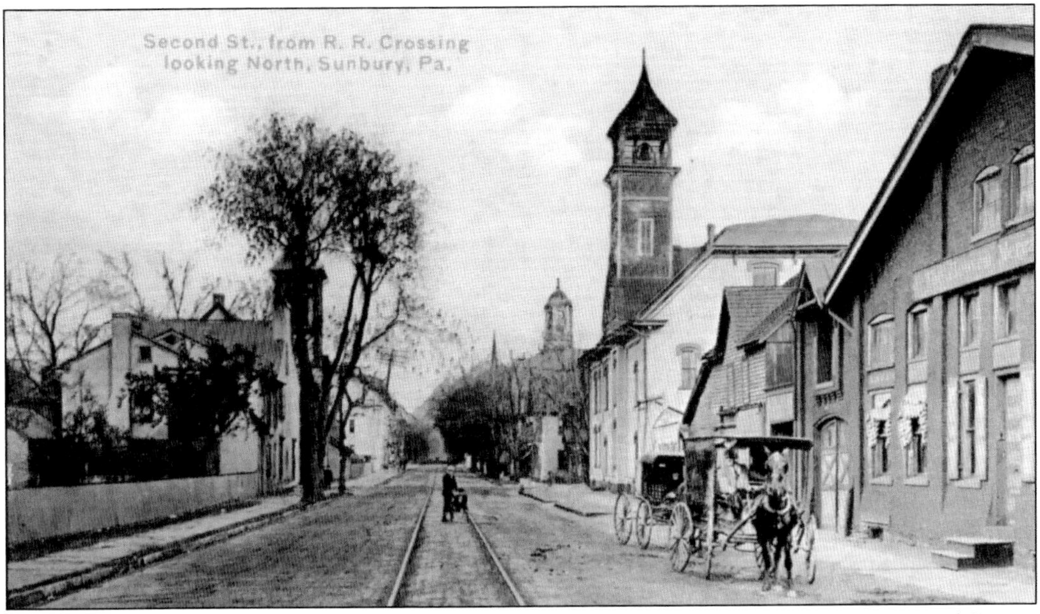

Looking northward, the view in this vintage postcard shows the railroad crossing at Second Street, with tracks running through the town. On the right side is the Hoover Mercantile Company, a store owned by a family well known in Northumberland County. The original Hoover family came from Germany, where their name was Hubers. (Courtesy of Tim Auman.)

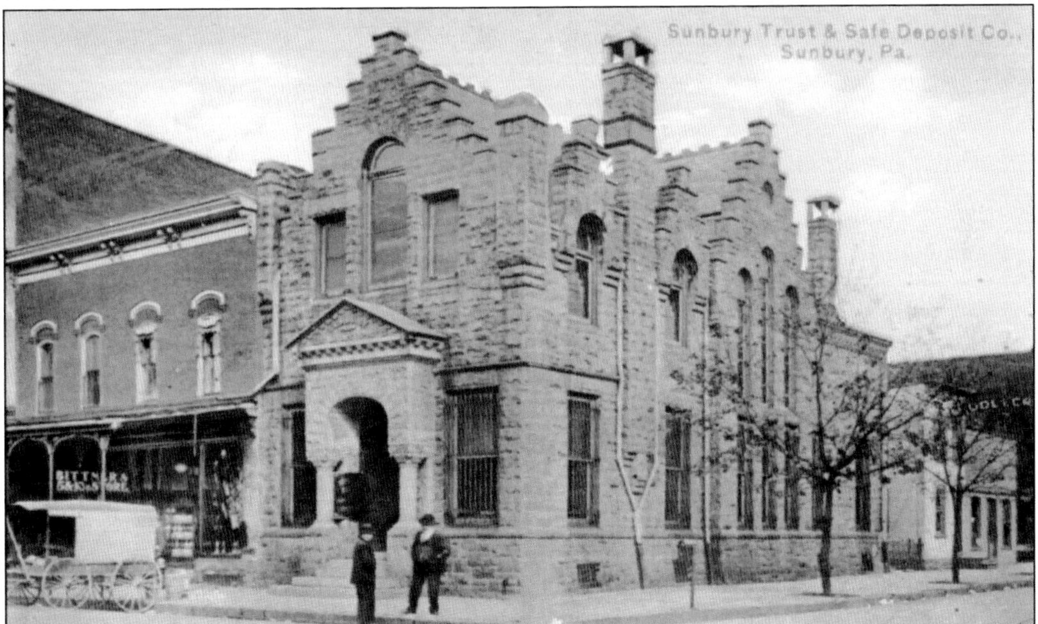

The Sunbury Trust and Safe Deposit Company was formed on July 15, 1890, and was situated on the corner of Fourth and Market Streets. Several leaders of Sunbury organized it. Charles W. Nickerson served as president, with Hiram Long as vice president. The authorized capital was $250,000. A.L. Bastress became secretary and treasurer on March 1, 1891. On June 4, 1932, the First National Trust Bank of Sunbury absorbed the old Sunbury Trust and Safe Deposit Company. (Courtesy of Tim Auman.)

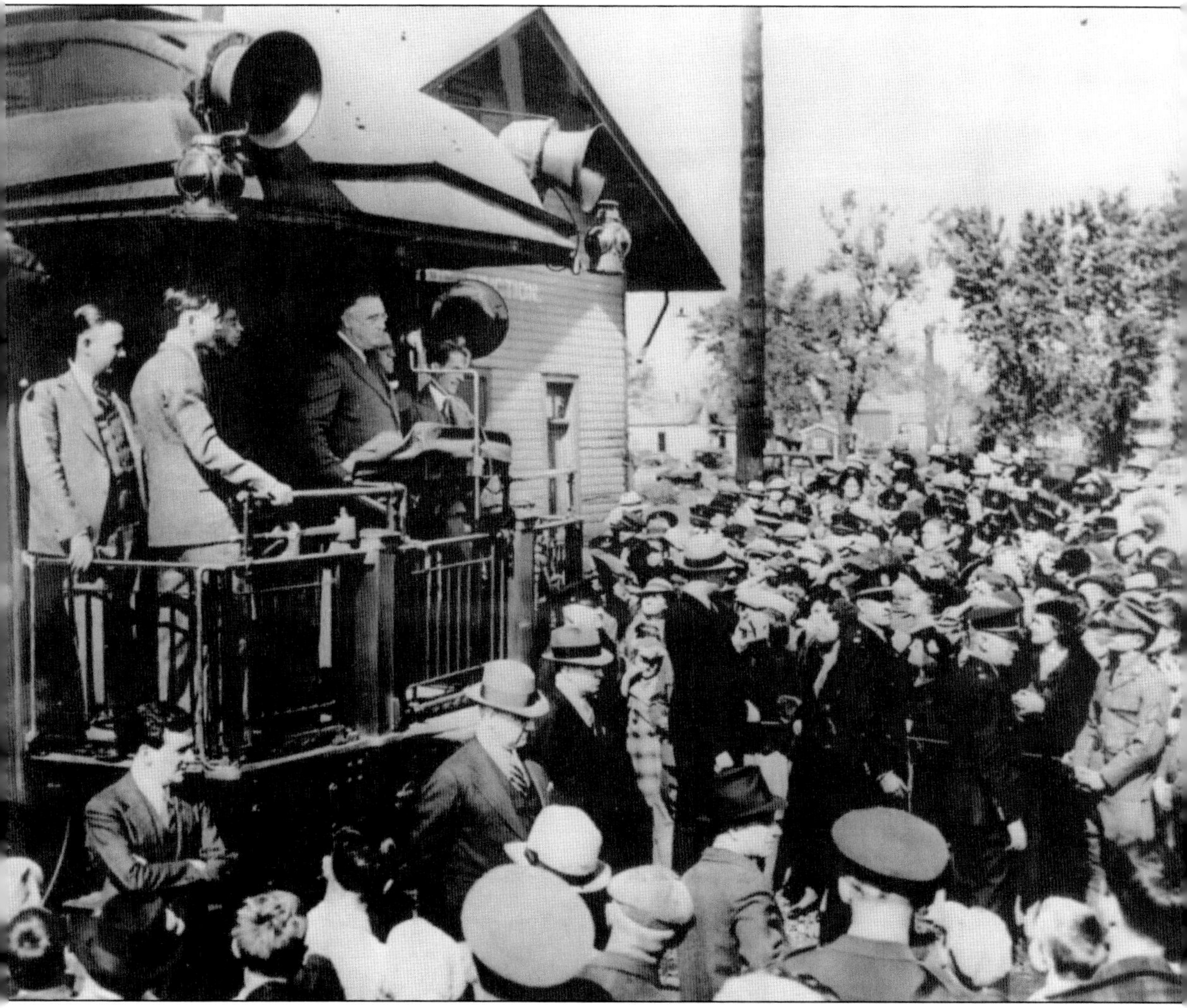

Franklin Delano Roosevelt, also known as FDR, was the 32nd president of the United States. He is shown here during his 1936 whistle-stop campaign for reelection to a second term as president. He is speaking from the platform of his private railroad car, the *Pioneer*, which stopped in Sunbury. When he visited Sunbury, thousands of people came to Market Street to hear him. Roosevelt was elected as president four times, and he was the only person to ever do so. He died of a cerebral hemorrhage in Warm Springs, Georgia, before completing his fourth term of office. (Courtesy of the Franklin D. Roosevelt Presidential Library.)

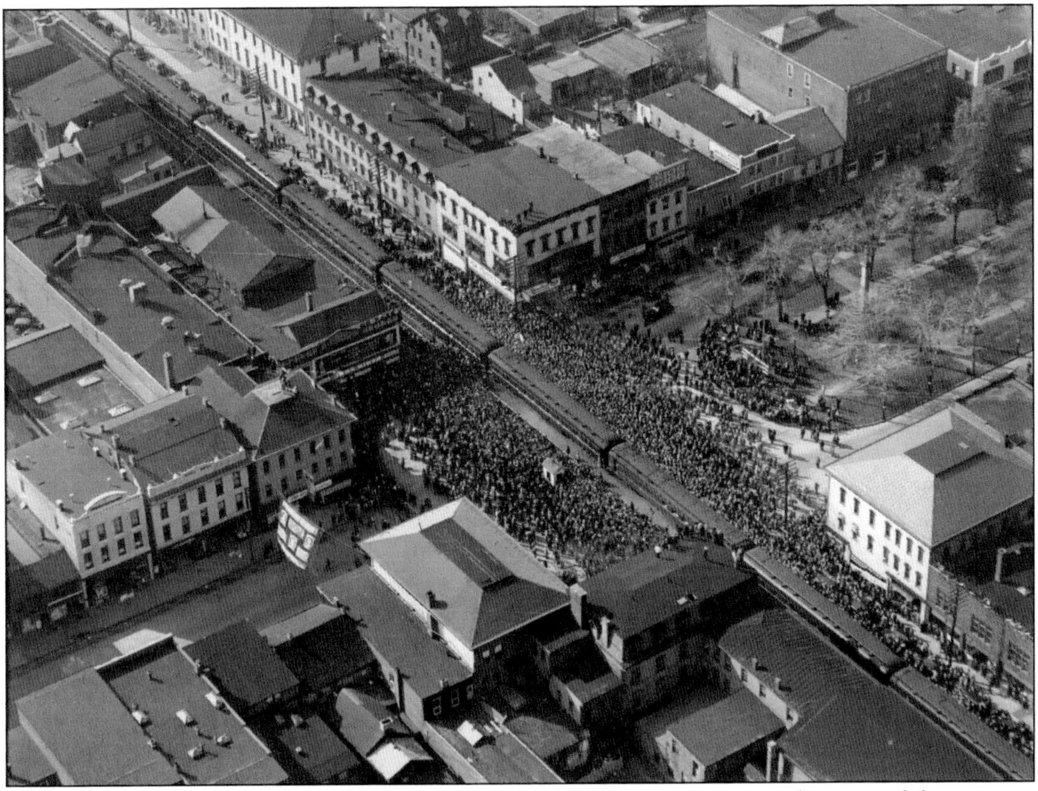

This aerial view of Franklin D. Roosevelt's visit to Sunbury gives some indication of the massive numbers of people who came to see the president along Market Street. Roosevelt was a dominating international figure. He ushered in many domestic programs and carried the United States through World War II. He is considered by many to be one of the greatest US presidents. (Courtesy of the Pennsylvania Archives.)

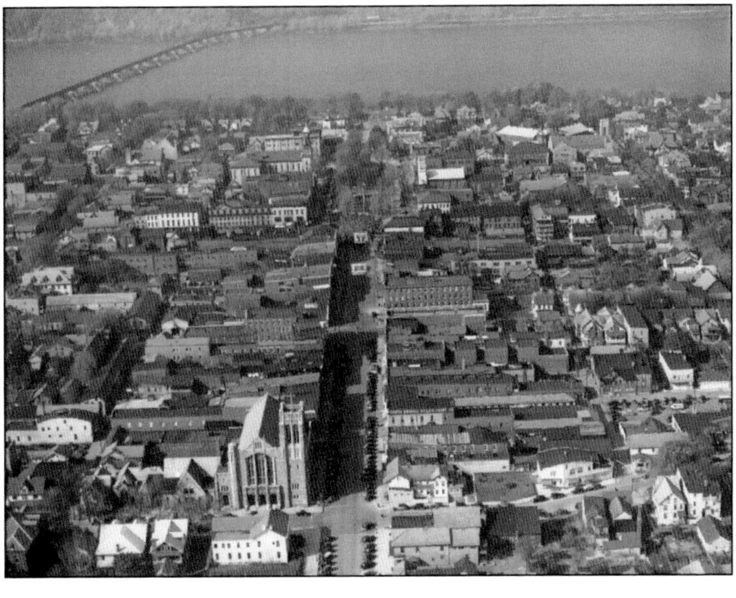

This 1936 photograph of Franklin D. Roosevelt's campaign stop in Sunbury, with a view facing the Susquehanna River, provides a panoramic look at the city as well as an aerial view of the crowds lining Market Street to see the president, who would go on to win election to a second term. (Courtesy of the Pennsylvania Archives.)

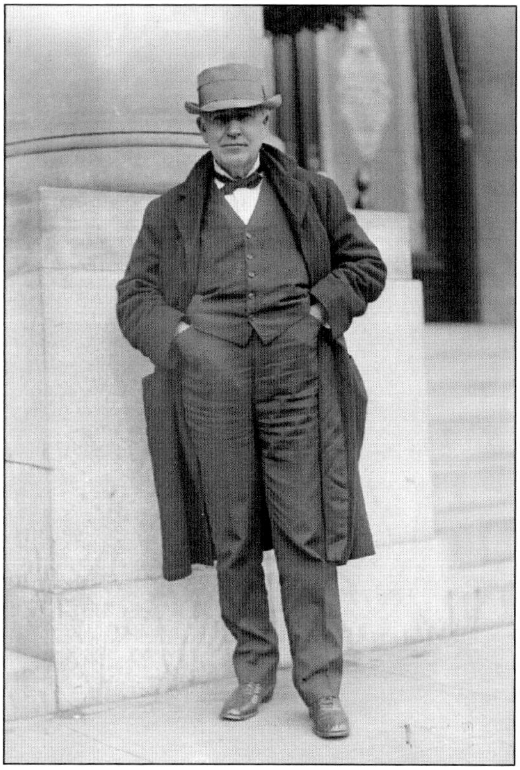

Thomas Alva Edison was born in Ohio and grew up in Michigan. He was not very attentive in school and was considered to be addled by one of his teachers. He was eventually educated at home by his mother. Edison has said that she was the making of him. Eventually, he grew up to be one of America's greatest inventors. In 1883, he came to Sunbury, and using Sunbury's City Hotel as a base, he built a coal-fired power plant. This is a photograph of Edison in later years. (Courtesy of the Library of Congress.)

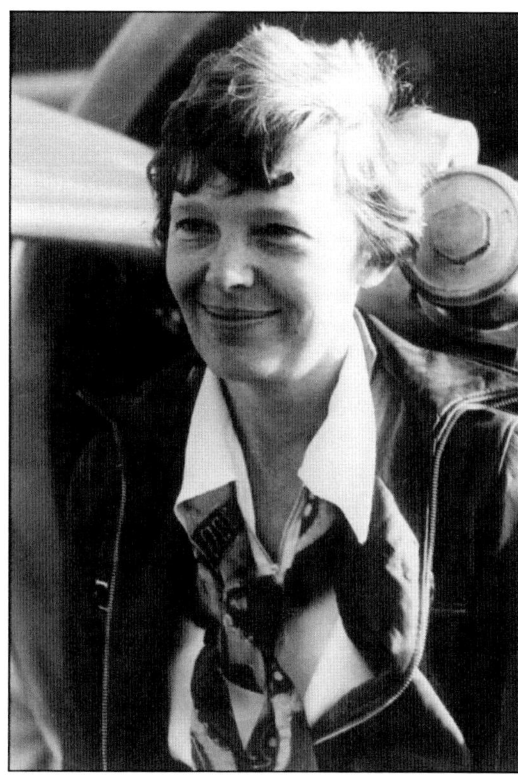

Shown in a c. 1935 photograph, Amelia Earhart was born on July 24, 1897, and disappeared on July 2, 1937. An American aviation pioneer, she flew into Sunbury's Island Park Airport in 1929. (Courtesy of the Free Library of Philadelphia.)

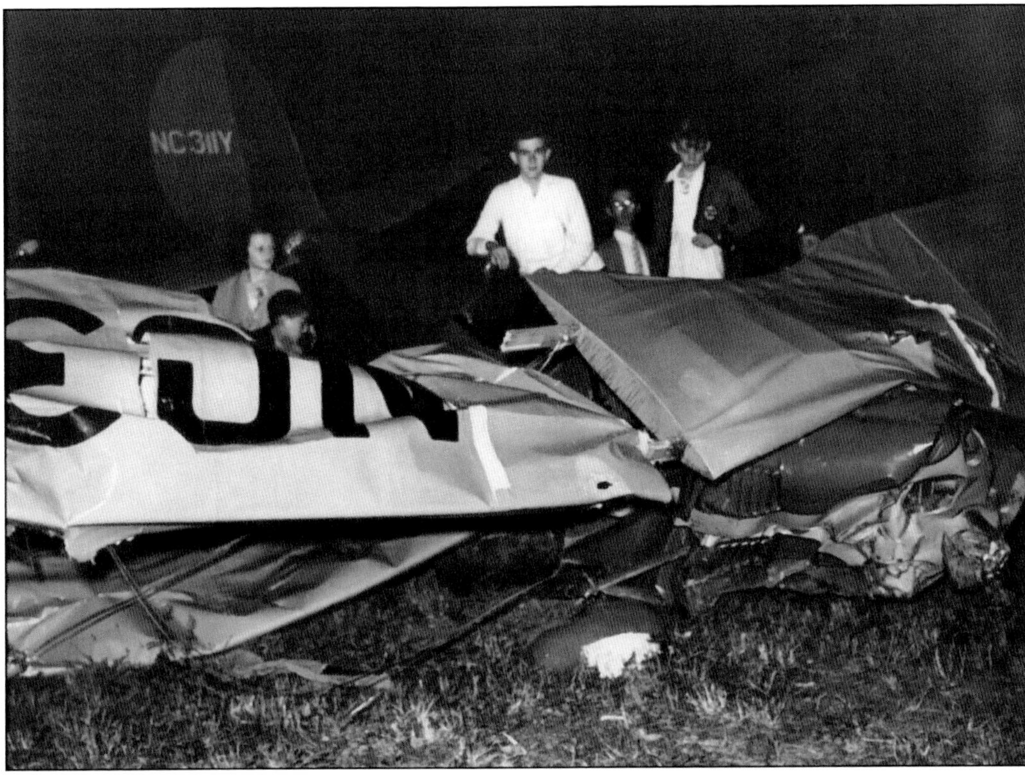

This plane crash at the Sunbury airport happened in 1936. The student pilot was not hurt. At the time of the crash, the weather conditions of low clouds and fog also forced airmail pilot E.M. Allison to land in a farmer's field. Created in 1920, the airport was known as Island Park Airport and located between Sunbury and Northumberland. The US Department of Commerce designated the spot on the farm a charted airfield. (Courtesy of the Pennsylvania Archives.)

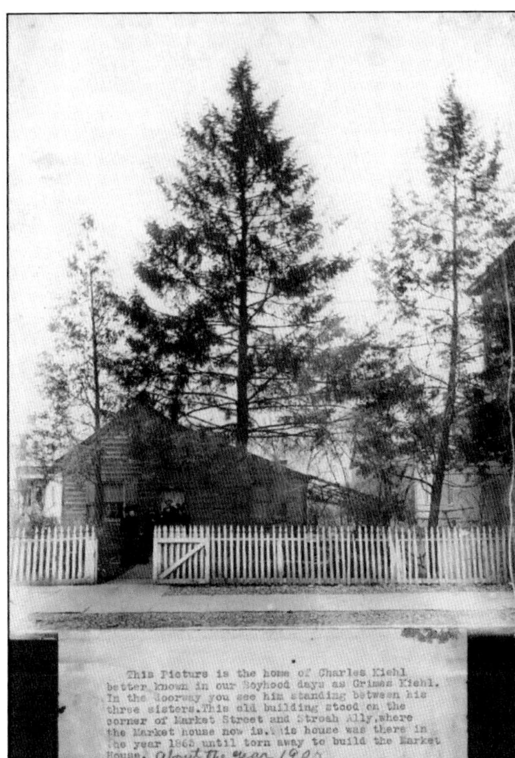

The home of Charles Kiehl is shown in this 1906 photograph. He stands in the doorway between his three sisters. The building stood on the corner of Market Street and Stroah Alley (today called Stroh Alley) and was torn down in order to build the Sunbury Market House. The Kiehl family is an old Sunbury family, with many mentions of their name in various historic records. (Courtesy of NCHS.)

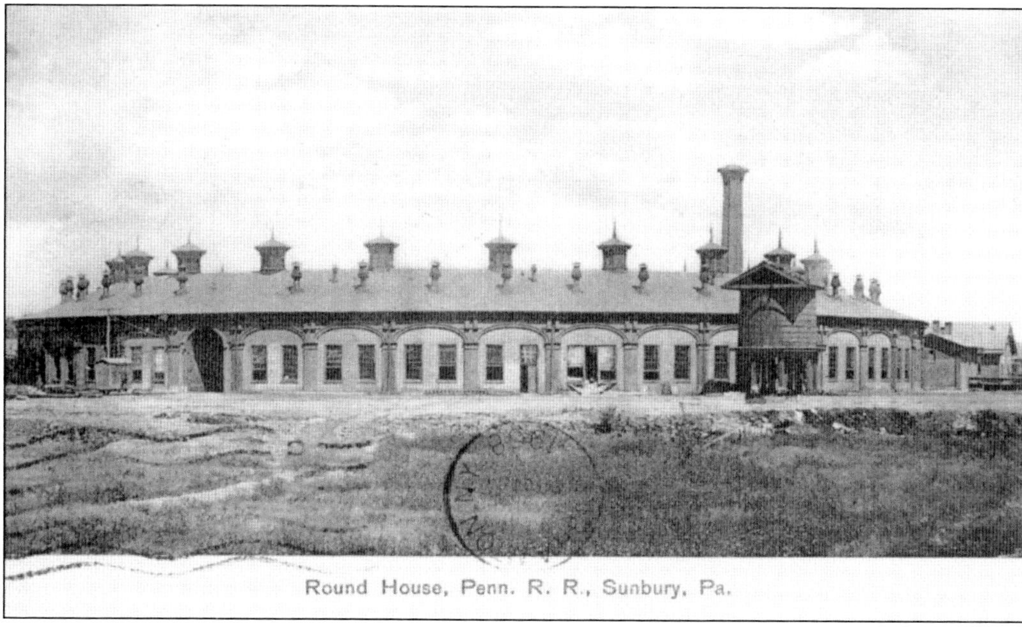

This postcard, mailed from New York, shows the roundhouse of the Pennsylvania Railroad. Completed on August 6, 1911, the Northumberland Classification Yard contained an area of 700 acres and 70 miles of track, roundhouse, and shops. During the 1950s, over 1,500 railroad cars passed through the yard each day for receiving, dispatching, or reclassifying. (Courtesy of Tim Auman.)

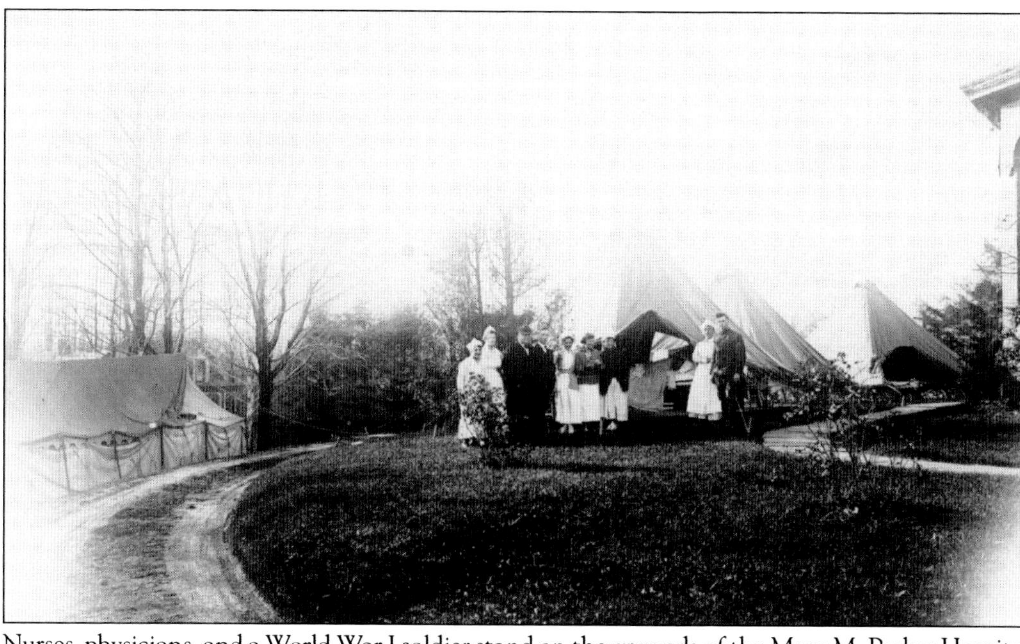

Nurses, physicians, and a World War I soldier stand on the grounds of the Mary M. Parker Hospital in front of tents, which Dr. William L. Shindel helped to set up. The tents were used to care for patients during the influenza pandemic of 1918. Very few paid attention to the account of an unusual sickness first reported by a Spanish wire service. Before the year was out, a total of 75,000 people from Pennsylvania would die. (Courtesy of NCHS.)

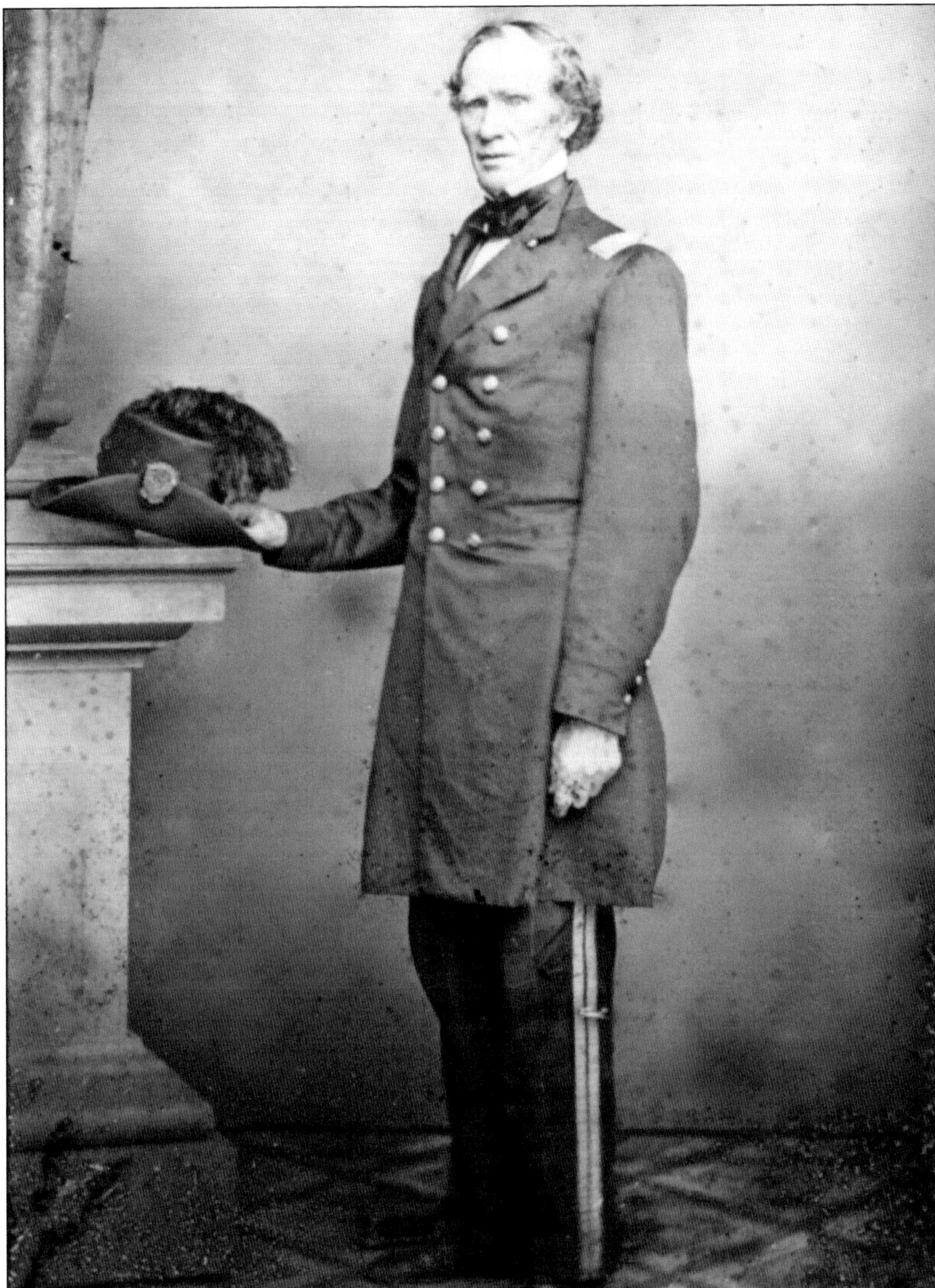

This 1870s photograph shows Col. James Cameron, who organized a regiment from Northumberland County and fought in the American Civil War. A native of Sunbury, he fell during the Battle of Bull Run in 1861. Cameron Park in the center of Sunbury is named after him. (Courtesy of the Library of Congress.)

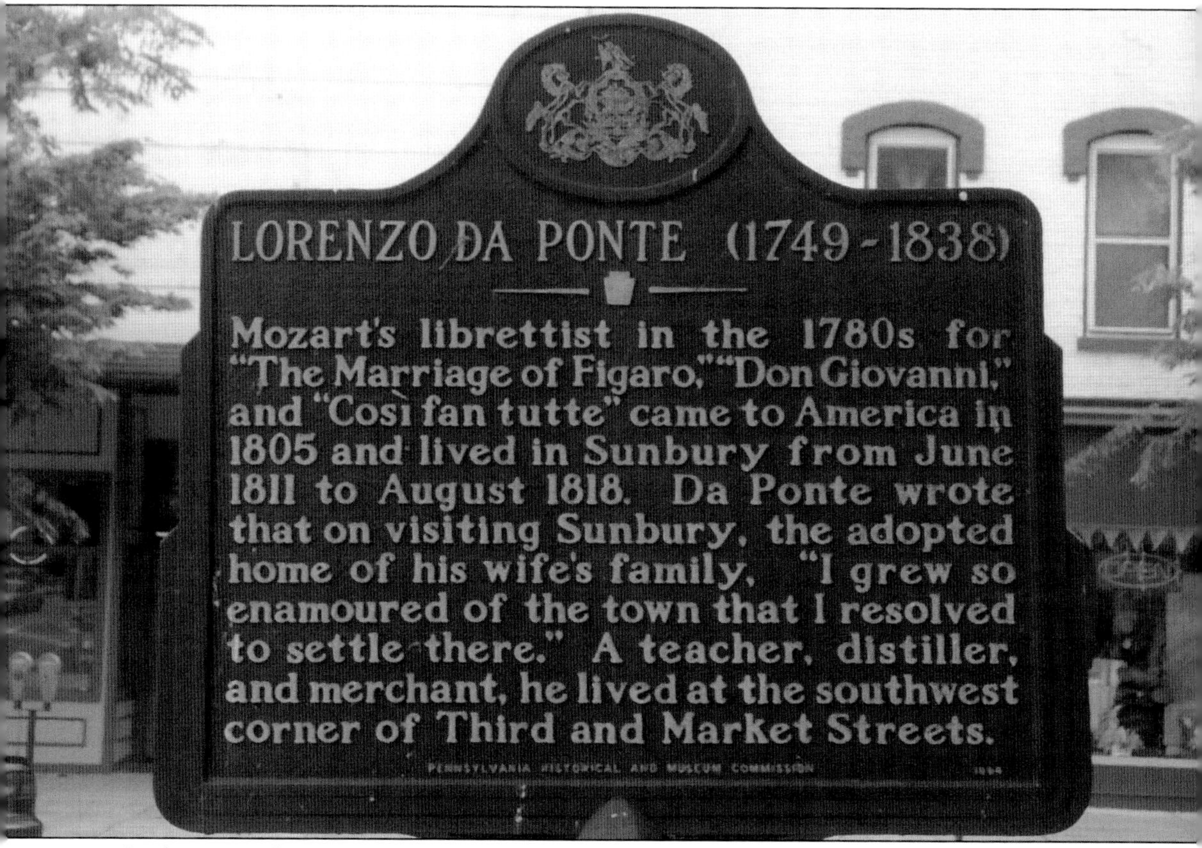

As the sign indicates, Lorenzo Da Ponte was an opera librettist and poet. He is most well known for writing the librettos for three of Mozart's greatest operas—*Don Giovanni*, *The Marriage of Figaro*, and *Così fan tutte*. (Author's collection.)

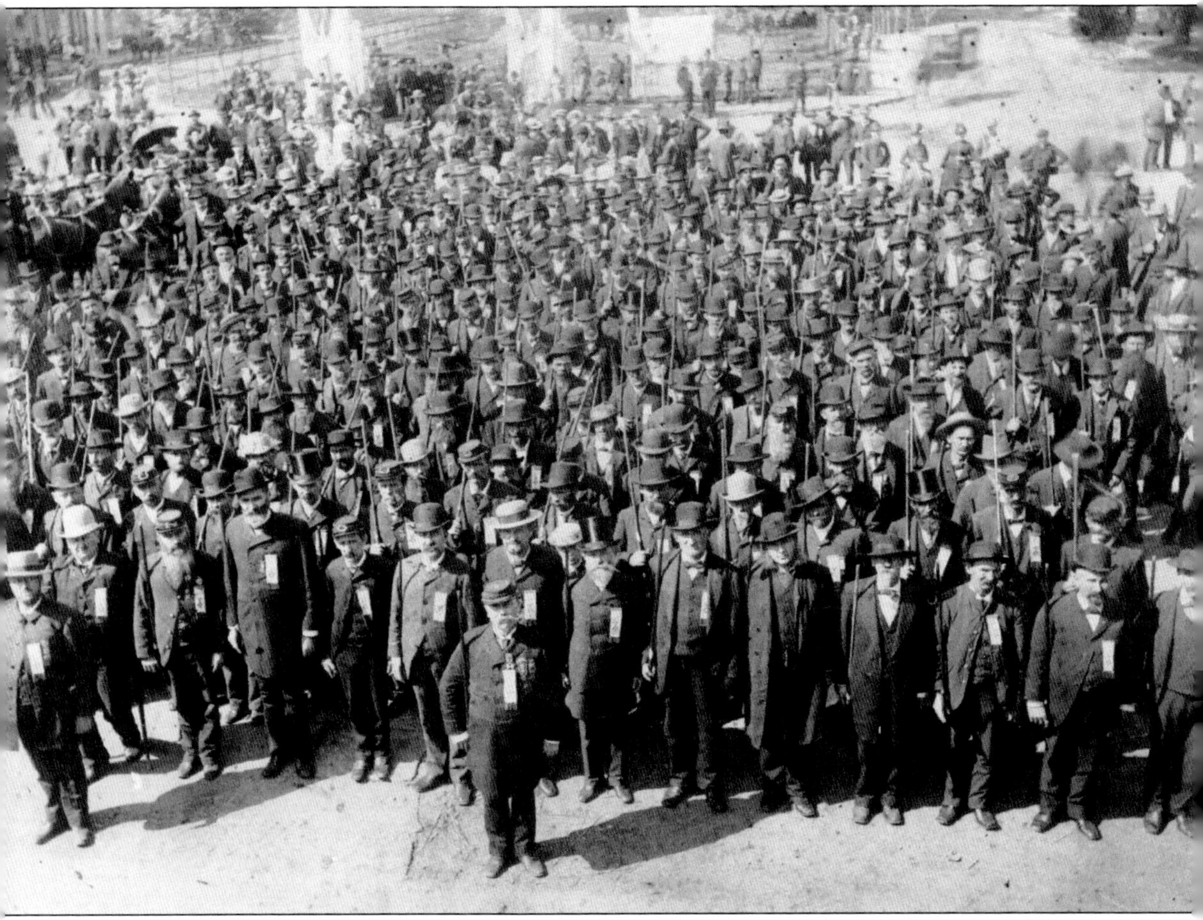

This early-1900 photograph shows a large group of Civil War soldiers standing in the center of town in Sunbury. The men are gathered to remember the war and to honor those from Northumberland County who had died. On the morning of Wednesday, April 17, 1861, a call had been issued for a public meeting in the courthouse at Sunbury and on the evening of that day, a large concourse of people assembled. One camp of Union soldiers was located in East Sunbury, at a large spring in a field south of Market Street and east of the branch road that connected the line of Philadelphia and Erie and Shamokin Valley and Pottsville railroads. On the first day after breaking camp, the company marched as far as Stambach's tavern on the old Reading Road in the village of Paxinos. (Courtesy of NCHS.)

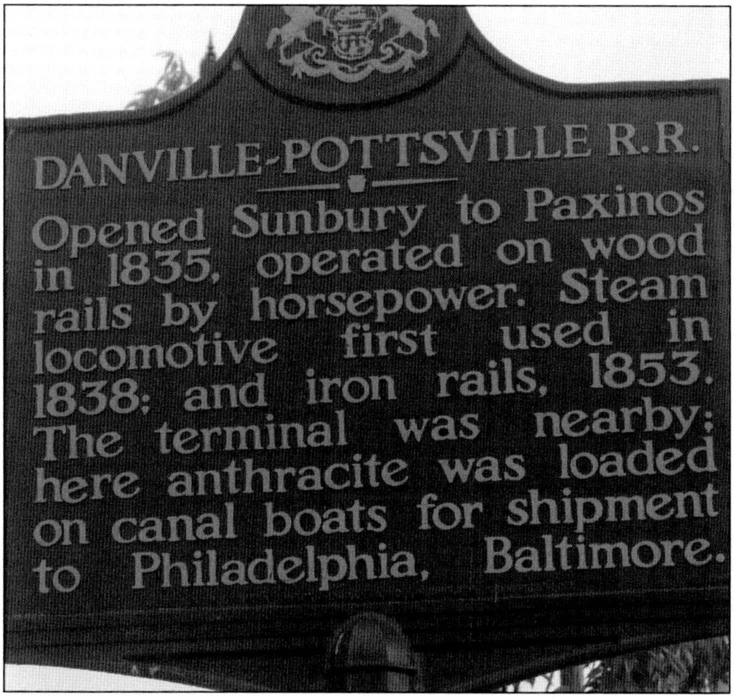

This marker indicates where the Danville-Pottsville Railroad opened in Sunbury in 1835. The line went from the Sunbury to Paxinos, a few miles away. The train ran on wooden rails and was driven by horsepower. It was not until 1838 that the first steam locomotive was used, and iron rails were introduced in 1853. (Courtesy of Klaus Krippendorff.)

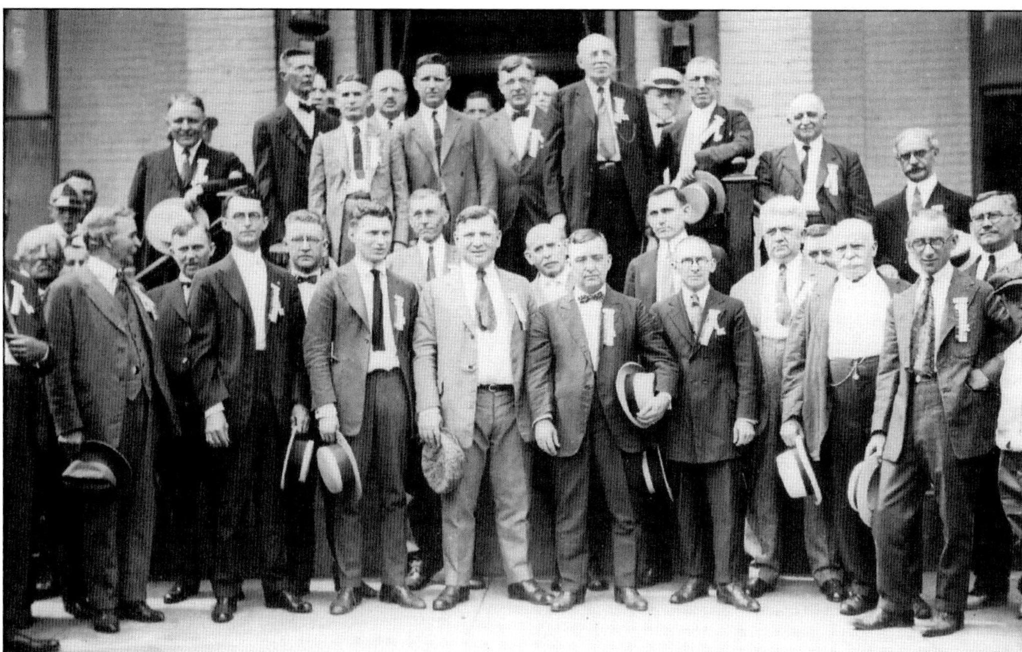

This 1922 photograph shows Sunbury Central Station employees who are assembled for Thomas Edison's visit that year. Early that fall, Edison arrived first in Shamokin, a coal mining town a few miles from Sunbury. There, he met with a group of investors who organized the Edison Electrical Illuminated Company of Shamokin. However, Shamokin would not be the world's first town illuminated by the first three-wire electric light station with overhead conductors. (Courtesy of US Department of the Interior, National Park Service, Thomas Edison National Historical Park.)

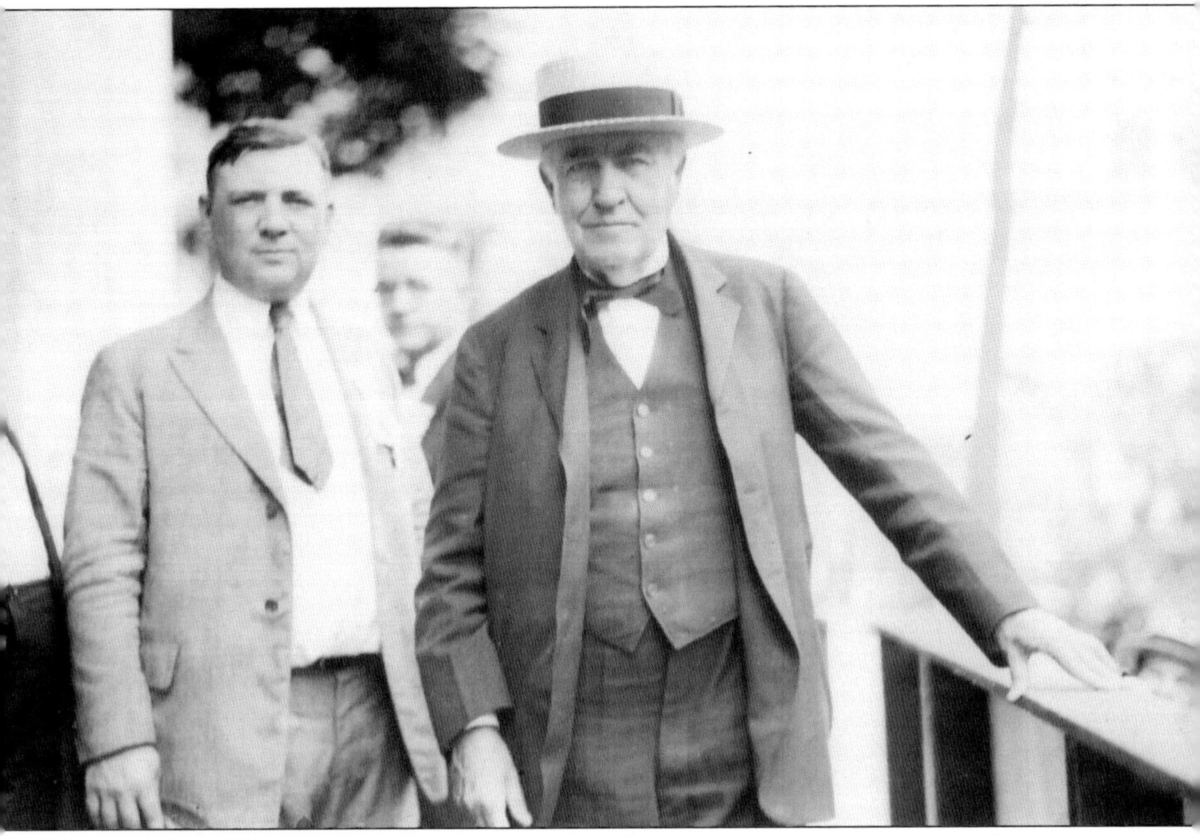

Shortly after his arrival in Shamokin, Thomas Edison licensed an electric company with investors in Sunbury, some 16 miles to the southeast of Shamokin. His plan was to establish the first use of electricity in Shamokin; however, he was convinced to change his plans and move his operation to Sunbury. Shown here in this photograph are Edison (right) and Reed McCarthy of the Sunbury Chamber of Commerce during Edison's visit to Sunbury in 1922. Edison would eventually provide electricity for Shamokin and Williamsport, a town to the north. (Courtesy of US Department of the Interior, National Park Service, Thomas Edison National Historical Park.)

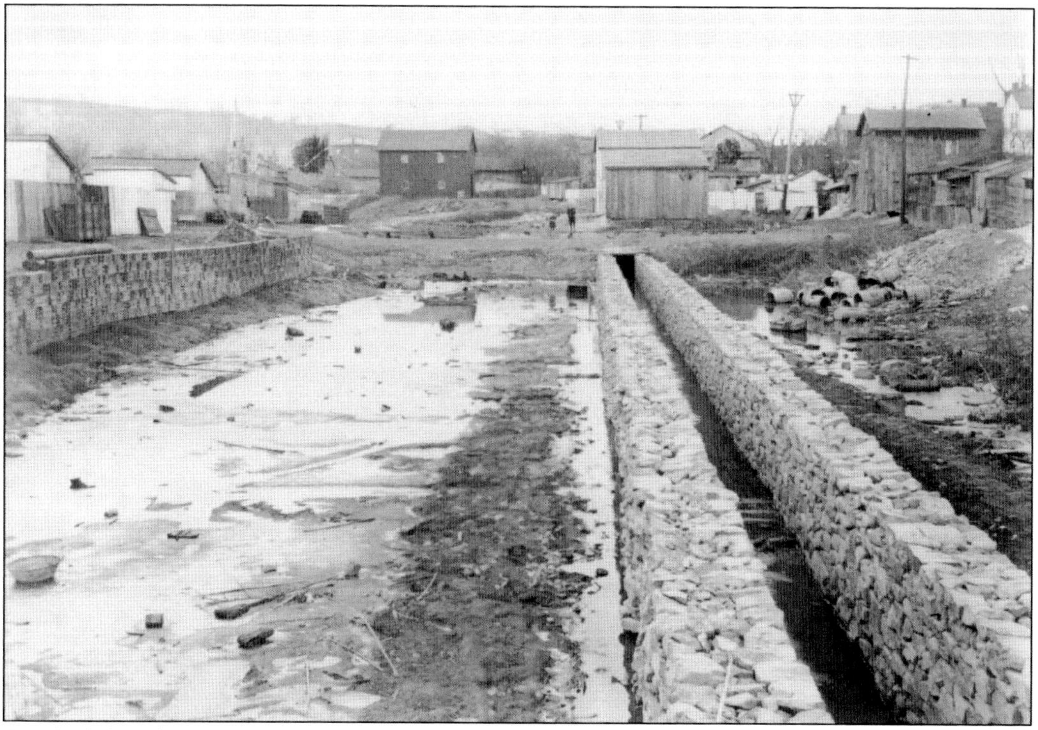

On the left is the vacant lot in Sunbury at Vine and Fourth Streets where Thomas Edison and his engineers planned to build a coal-fired electrical power plant. They built the makeshift structure, shown on the right, in just three weeks; it was where the first pole line was strung on the west side of the street and ran between Race and Arch Streets. Edison knew that, because of Pennsylvania's rich coal deposits, he would find abundant and affordable fuel sources for electrical generating plants. Unfortunately, the building is no longer standing; however, a historical marker indicates the spot where this building stood. (Courtesy of US Department of the Interior, National Park Service, Thomas Edison National Historical Park.)

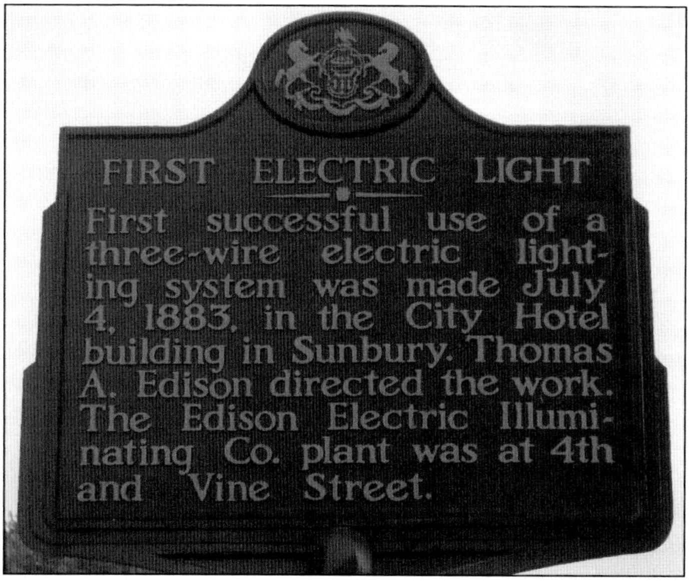

The first use of a three-wire electric light system was made on July 4, 1883, in Sunbury. Thomas A. Edison, as indicated in this historical marker, directed the work from the Edison Electric Illuminating Company. The plant was located at Fourth and Vine Streets. (Courtesy of Klaus Krippendorff.)

Sunbury's Masonic lodge, Lodge No. 22, is located at 220 Market Street, between Center and Second Streets. This lodge is the oldest in northern Pennsylvania and was begun at a meeting at Fort Augusta in 1779. Before settling into the current building in 1908, the Masons met variously in people's home and in the grand jury room of the old courthouse from 1809 to 1866. Freemasonry is a fraternal organization. (Courtesy of Klaus Krippendorff.)

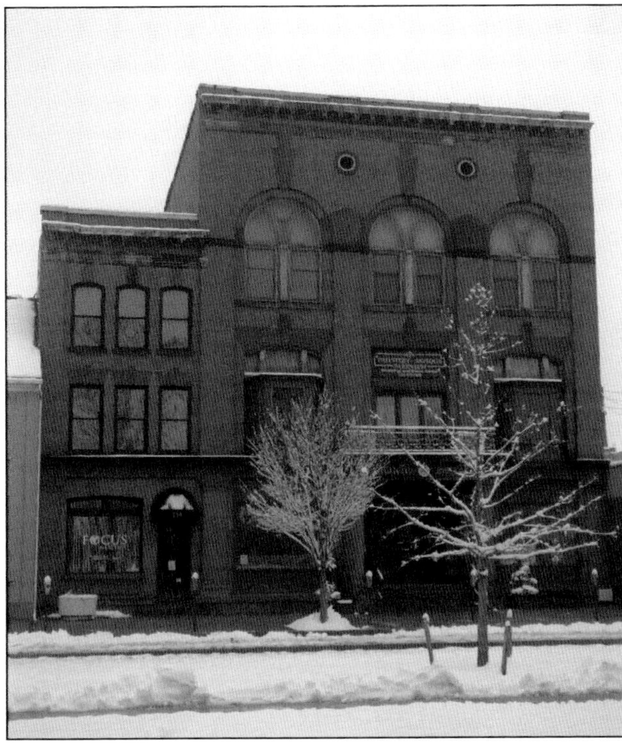

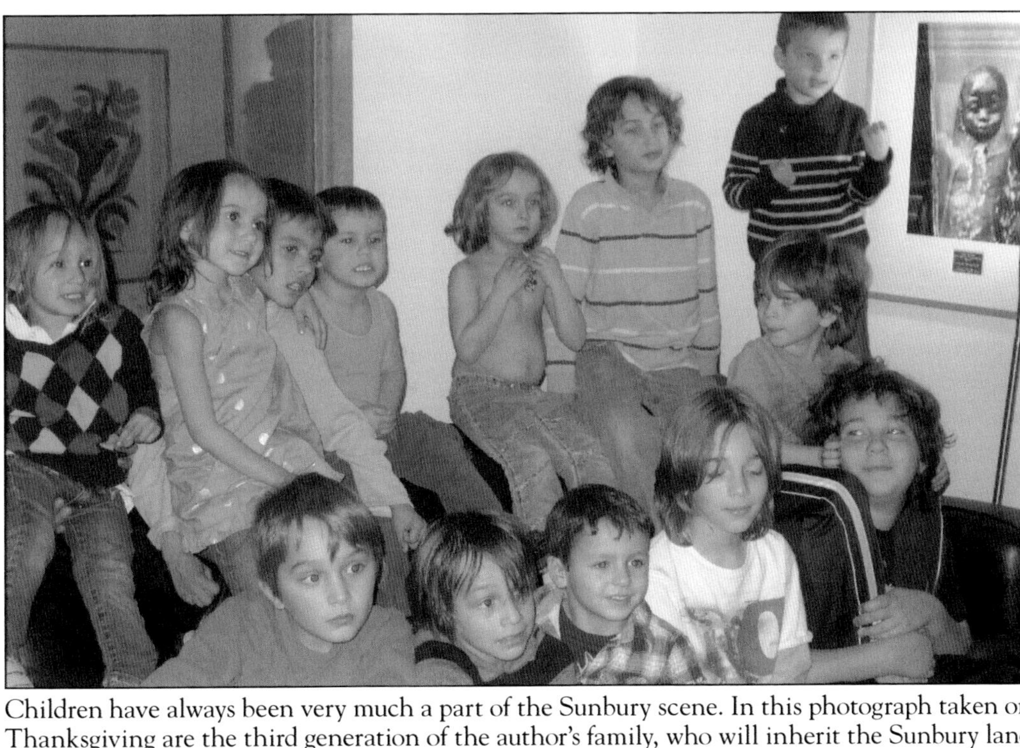

Children have always been very much a part of the Sunbury scene. In this photograph taken on Thanksgiving are the third generation of the author's family, who will inherit the Sunbury land owned by the Krippendorff, Maitin, and Moore families who in the past spent the November holiday there. (Courtesy of Klaus Krippendorff.)

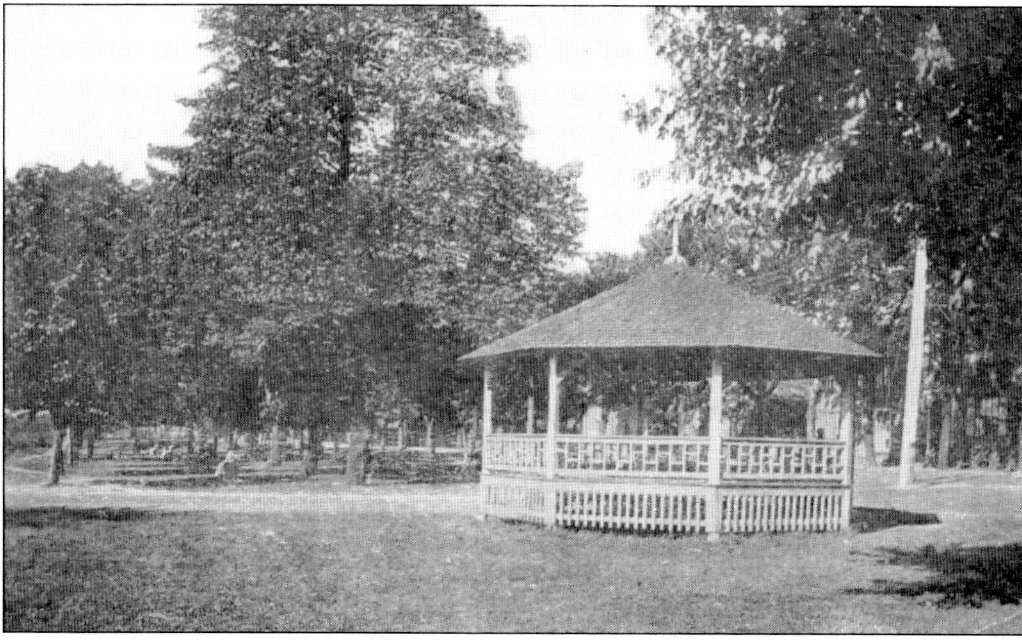

This is a photograph of the bandstand at River Park, located on the Susquehanna River in Sunbury. The bandstand provided entertainment and amusement during the 1900s for the residents of Sunbury. Many famous bands and entertainers came to Sunbury to perform. (Courtesy of David Persing.)

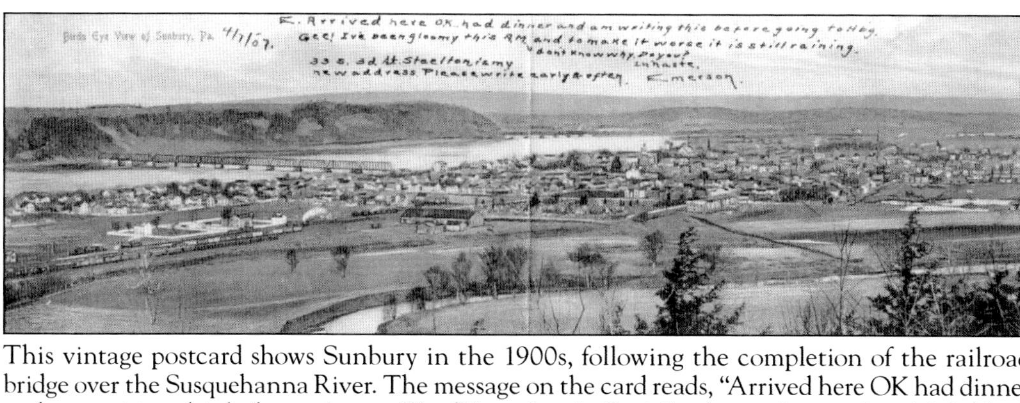

This vintage postcard shows Sunbury in the 1900s, following the completion of the railroad bridge over the Susquehanna River. The message on the card reads, "Arrived here OK had dinner and am writing this before going to Hbg [Harrisburg]. Gee! I've been gloomy this A.M. (don't know why. Do you?) and to make it worse it is still raining." A person named Emerson signed the postcard "in haste." He adds his new address and asks that the recipient "please write early & often." (Courtesy of Tim Auman.)

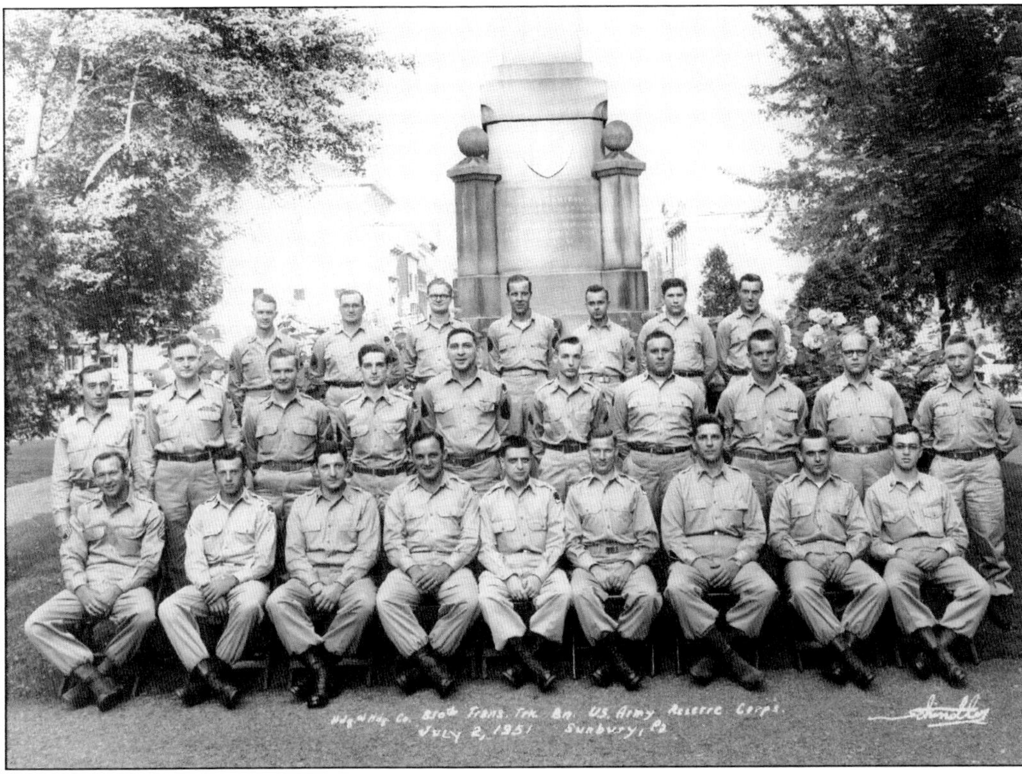

Servicemen gather here in Sunbury in Cameron Park on July 2, 1951. These are members of the 830th Transportation Truck Company, US Army Reserve Corps. It was in July 1951 that the Korean War armistice negotiations began in Kaesong, North Korea. (Courtesy of NCHS.)

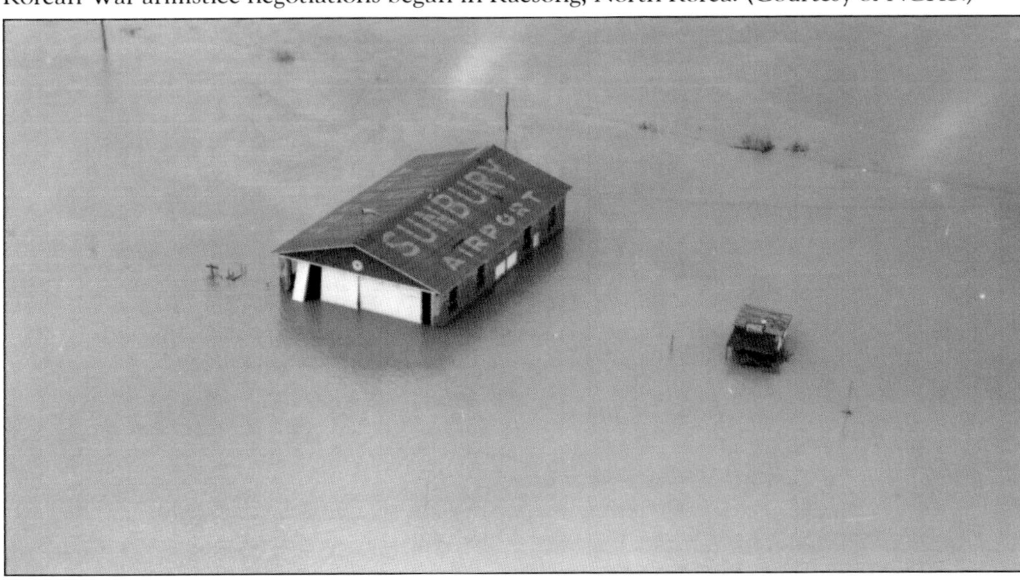

This photograph of a flood in Sunbury shows the Sunbury Airport, located on Packer Island, almost submerged in water. The picture, taken by S.W. Kunnert of Harrisburg, tells the tale of Sunbury's battle with floods. The Sunbury Airport is still operational today and is located two miles northeast of the city. (Courtesy of the Pennsylvania Archives.)

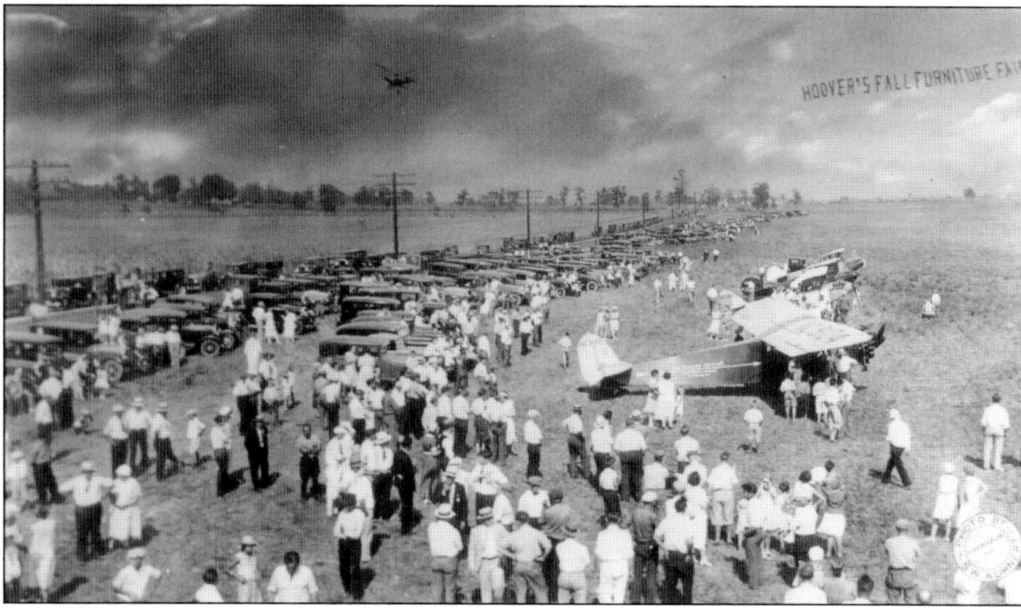

Hoover's Fall Furniture Fair provided vintage airplane rides for residents of Northumberland County and took place at the Sunbury Airport. Hoover's, a housewares and furniture store located a few miles from Sunbury, sponsored the show. Taking a ride in a vintage airplane was always an exciting activity for Sunbury residents. (Photograph by S.W. Kunnert, courtesy of the Pennsylvania Archives.)

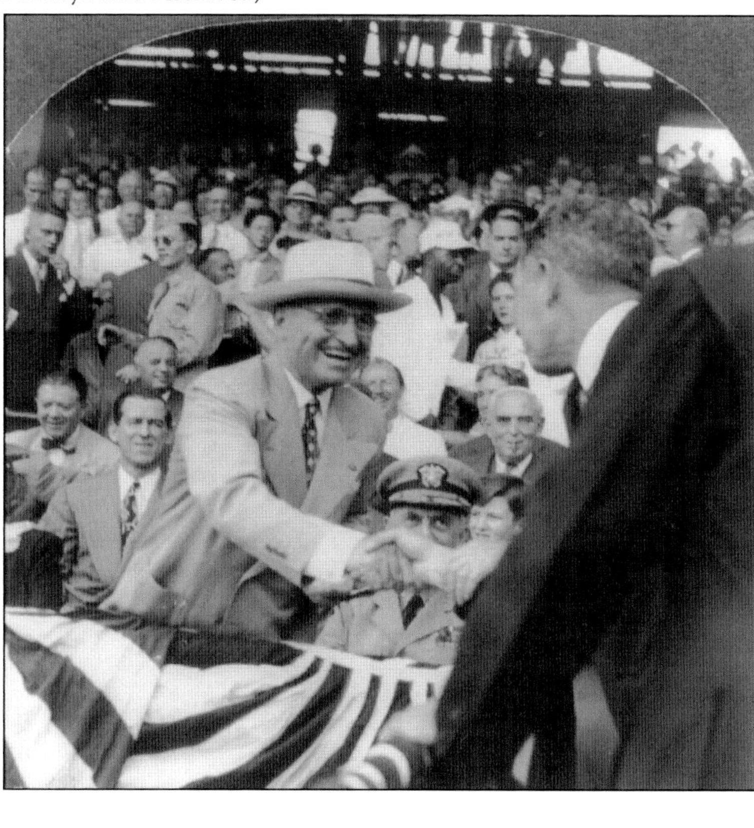

The 33rd president of the United States, Harry S. Truman, came to Sunbury during his second term of office, on the train and made a speech from the business car at the rear of the train and, later, spoke to business leaders. He won his election in 1948 over Thomas E. Dewey, the predicted winner. (Courtesy of the Library of Congress.)

Four

Sunbury in the Postwar Years

Like the rest of the country, Sunbury entered a period of unparalleled economic growth during a post–World War II economic boom. With the onset of the Cold War and decades of fear of communism, Sunbury, for a short time until the 1970s, was a conformist, conservative, materialistic society, with increasing affluence. The Vietnam War would precipitate a change, with the country as well as Sunbury leaning toward becoming more liberal. Sunbury also possessed a conservative social elite and a highly active and prosperous main avenue—Market Street. Many businesses operated up and down Market Street. The first modern credit card was introduced in the 1950s. Harry S. Truman was president, narrowly beating Thomas Dewey, the Republican candidate—both of whom campaigned in Sunbury.

Natural disasters continued to plague the city, with floods and overflowing of the Susquehanna River. There was even an earthquake on May 12, 1964, and 31 tornado events with a magnitude of 2 or higher occurred in or near the city. Hurricane Agnes, in late June 1972, killed four people in the Sunbury area.

The extensive Sunbury Riverfront Park Project created a restraining flood wall protection system, designed and built by the US Army Corps of Engineers in 1951. Additional height was added to the wall in 2003. The system has provided protection from 15 major flood events over the past 50 years.

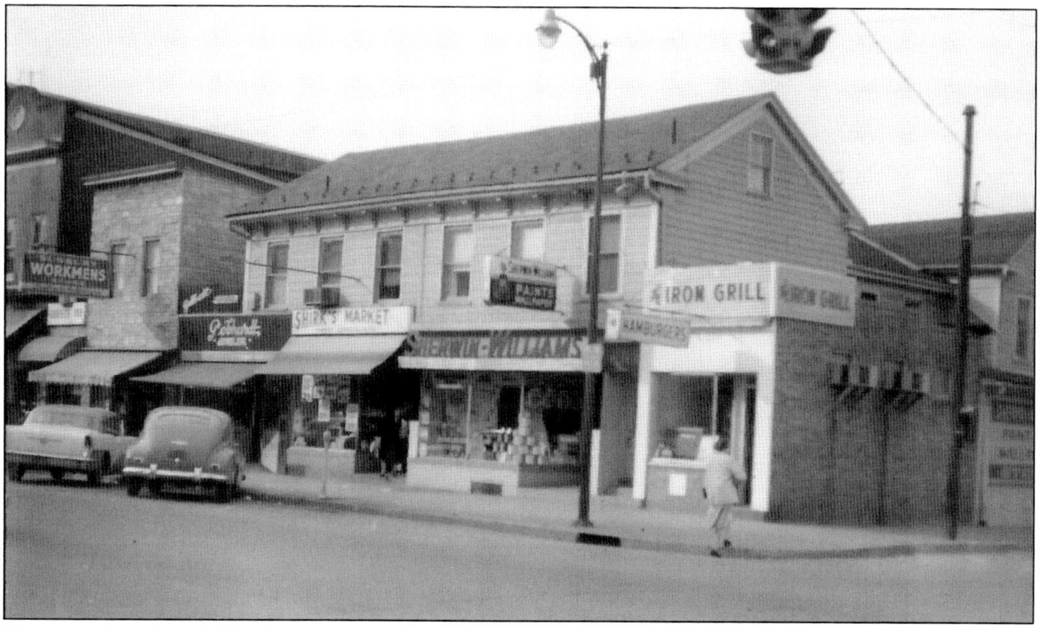

Illustrated in this 1959 photograph of Market Street at Fifth Street are some of the many shops that were once located there. Some of the establishments that were situated on the corner of Fifth Street were the Iron Grill, a small sandwich shop next to the paint store Sherwin-Williams; Shirk's Market; Gebhardt Jewelers; and the Sunbury Workmen's Store, which was above the Squeeze-In luncheonette. (Courtesy of an anonymous donor.)

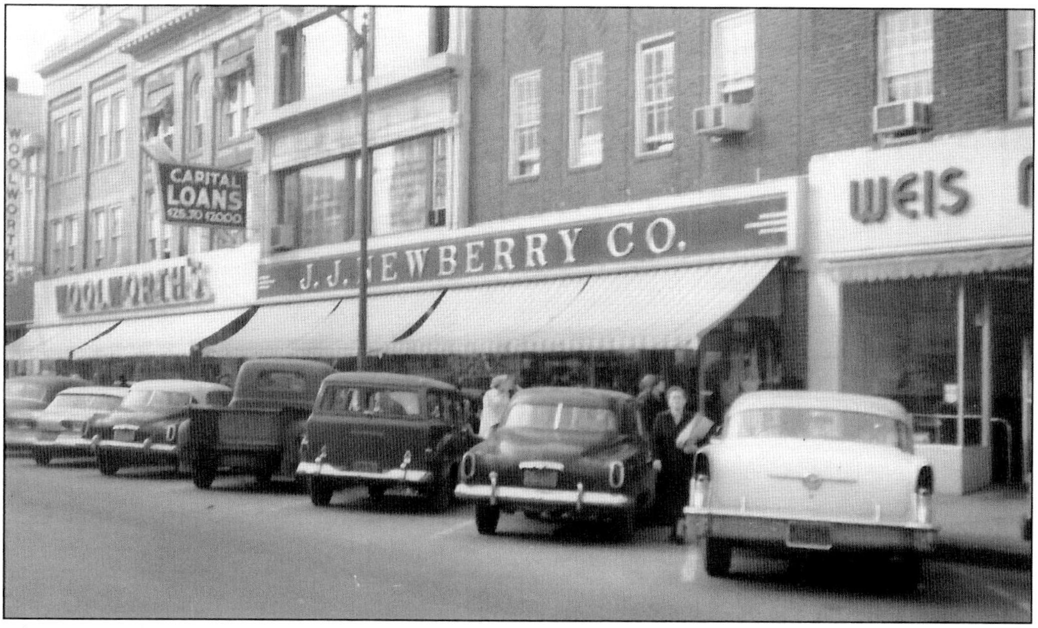

The J.J. Newberry Co. store on Market Street was a Sunbury institution. John Josiah Newberry, the founder of the chain of five-and-dime stores, was born in Sunbury and began his career at the age of 13 as a messenger for the Pennsylvania Railroad. In 1953, sales totaled $173 million. Gov. John S. Fine honored him and made him an ambassador of Goodwill of the State in 1953. (Courtesy of an anonymous donor.)

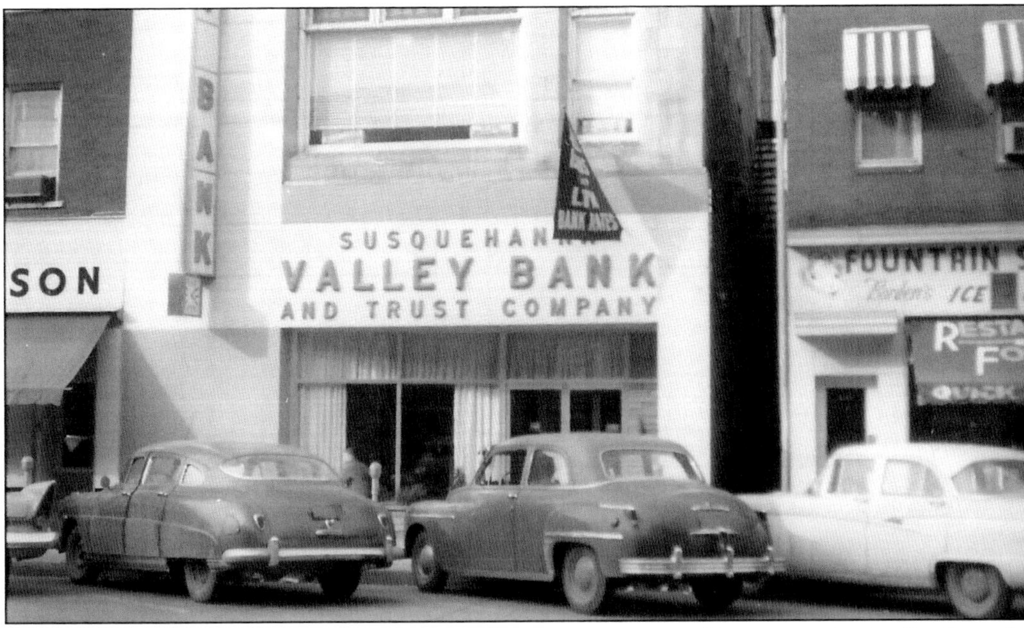

The Susquehanna Valley Bank and Trust Company was a viable institution in Sunbury for many years, loaning money to businesses and providing banking services to the town. Located at 440–442 Market Street between South Fifth and South Fourth Streets, it was established on July 21, 1958. It was acquired by Northern Central Bank and closed on May 3, 1974. (Courtesy of an anonymous donor.)

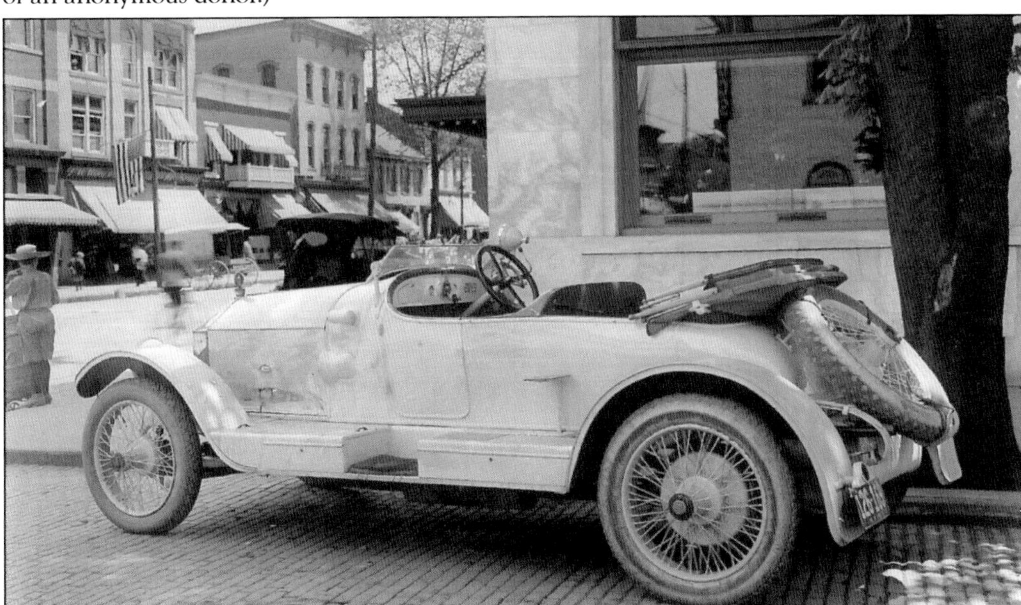

This MG convertible, a TD Midget model, shown in a late 1950s photograph, sits on the corner of South Fourth and Market Streets beside the Edison Hotel. The owner of the automobile is unknown, but this model was produced between 1950 and 1953. The two-door roadster was very popular—MG in England manufactured nearly 30,000 models—and the car became a collector's item over the years. (Courtesy of an anonymous donor.)

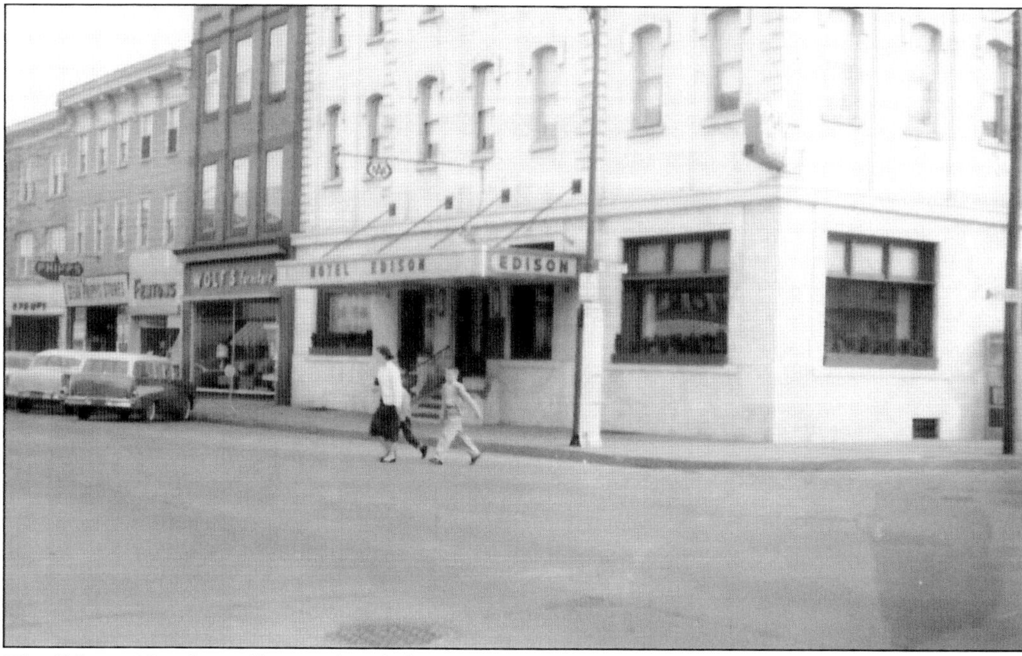

The Edison Hotel is still considered the centerpiece of the downtown area and is still occupied today. An early innovation at the hotel included a hand-operated elevator. Part of the hotel burned in 1914, and when it was renovated, a fourth floor was added. It is said to be haunted by a spirit named Ramona. (Courtesy of an anonymous donor.)

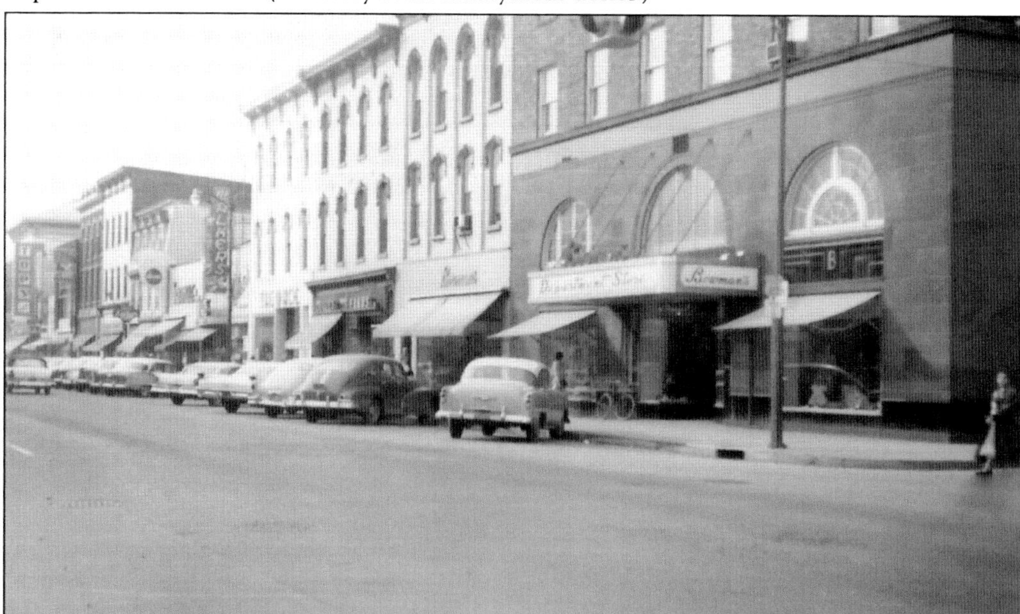

At one time, Bowman's Department Store, once located at 314 Market Street in Sunbury, was one of Harrisburg's two downtown department stores. In the 1950s, Bowman's opened suburban stores and purchased Bittner's Department Sore in Sunbury, creating a division called Bowman's Sunbury, Inc., and gave it the unique name, Bowman's Fashionalia. With the advent of the malls, like many other small department stores, it closed. (Courtesy of an anonymous donor.)

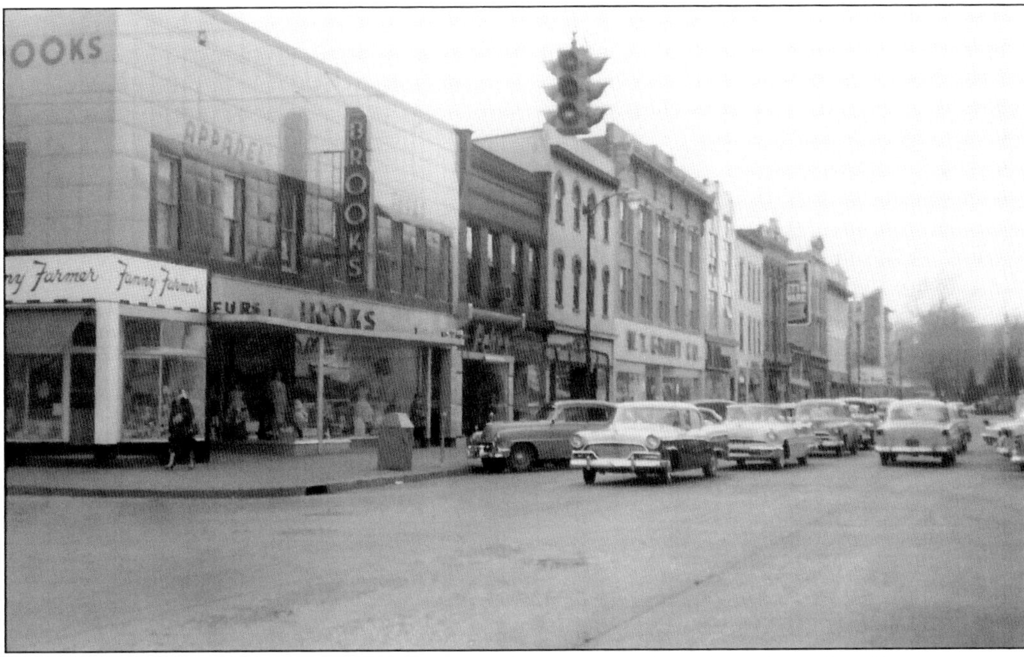

Fanny Farmer, a candy shop, was located on the corner of Fourth and Market Streets, next to Brooks Furs and down the street from the W.T. Grant Company. This was a time when the town's main street was thriving. The candy manufacturer and retailer Fanny Farmer was named after culinary expert Fannie Farmer. (Courtesy of an anonymous donor.)

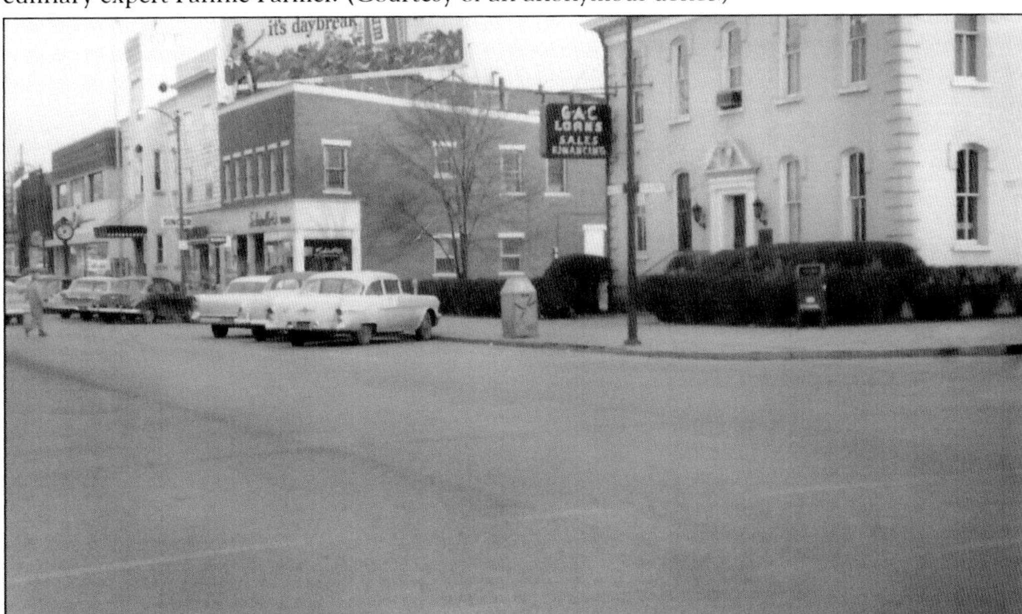

GAC Loans, situated on the corner of South Fifth at Market Street, was one of the many loan companies opening up in Northumberland County and elsewhere in the 1950s, as credit cards were instituted and buying on credit was becoming the American way. In 1951, the first bank credit card appeared in New York's Franklin National Bank for loan customers. (Courtesy of an anonymous donor.)

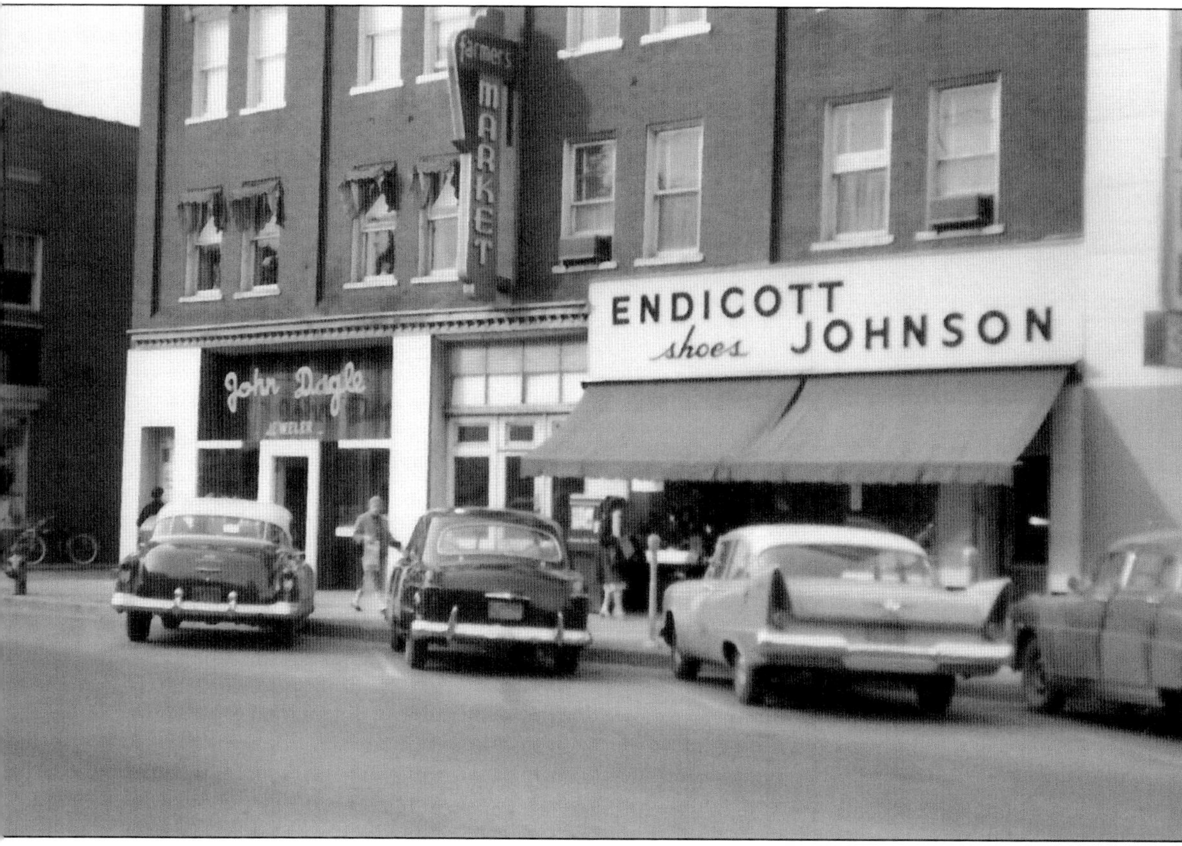

The Endicott Johnson Shoe Company, founded in 1881, was one of the country's largest and most prosperous shoe manufacturers. EJ, as it was often called, opened a store in Sunbury on Market Street. (Courtesy of an anonymous donor.)

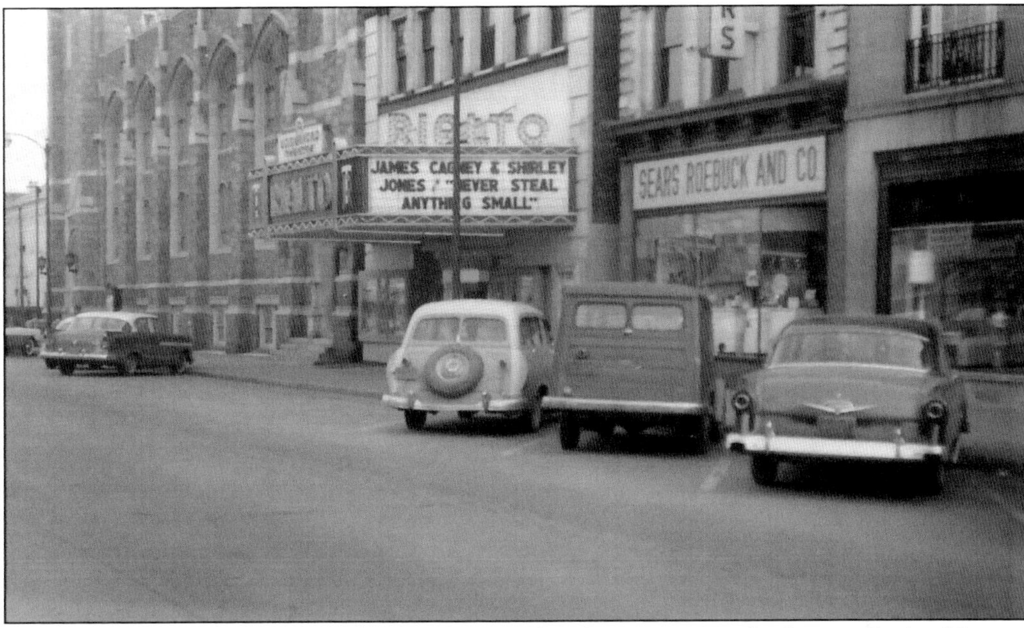

Sears, Roebuck & Company had a store on Market Street next to the famous Rialto Theatre, which, in this image, is showing *Never Steal Anything Small* with James Cagney. The Rialto Theatre was a small movie theater built without a balcony but was considered a showcase theater for an extended area run of *The Sound of Music*. The theater was destroyed by fire in 1978. (Courtesy of an anonymous donor.)

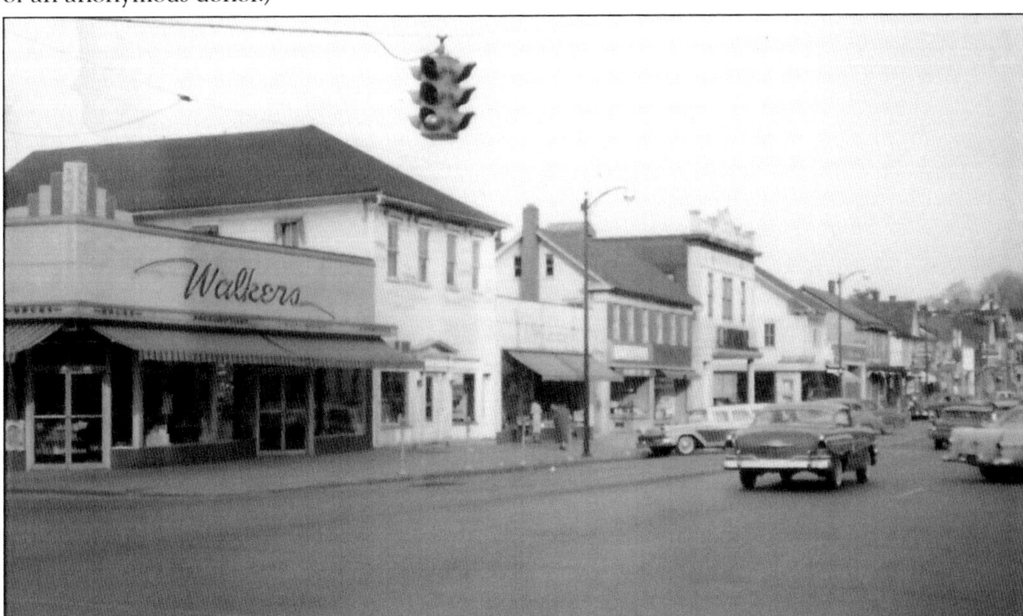

Walker's drugstore, at Fifth and Market Streets, was the local pharmacy for many years for the residents of Sunbury. Eventually, as in the case of many towns, the large chains came in, and some of these smaller drugstores were forced to close down. A few area pharmacists, such as George Albert Rossman, were trained at the Philadelphia College of Pharmacy, as reported in *The First Century of the Philadelphia College of Pharmacy: 1821–1921*. (Courtesy of an anonymous donor.)

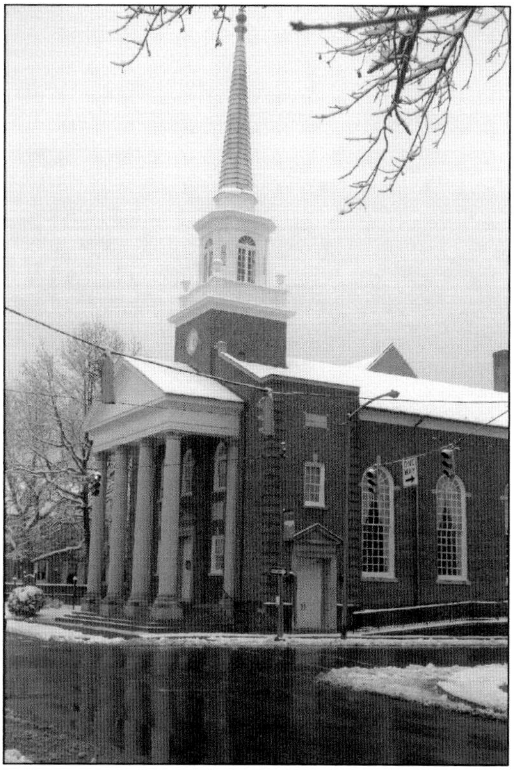

At the corner of Second Street on Chestnut Street stands the United Church of Christ (First Reformed Church), which was begun by Pennsylvania Germans and Scots-Irish settlers. A congregation was formed in Sunbury as early as 1776, and in 1784, it received its corporate seal. During that same year, a route was organized for a traveling preacher, Rev. Jonathan Rahauser, to journey from town to town, making periodic stops in Sunbury. (Courtesy of Klaus Krippendorff.)

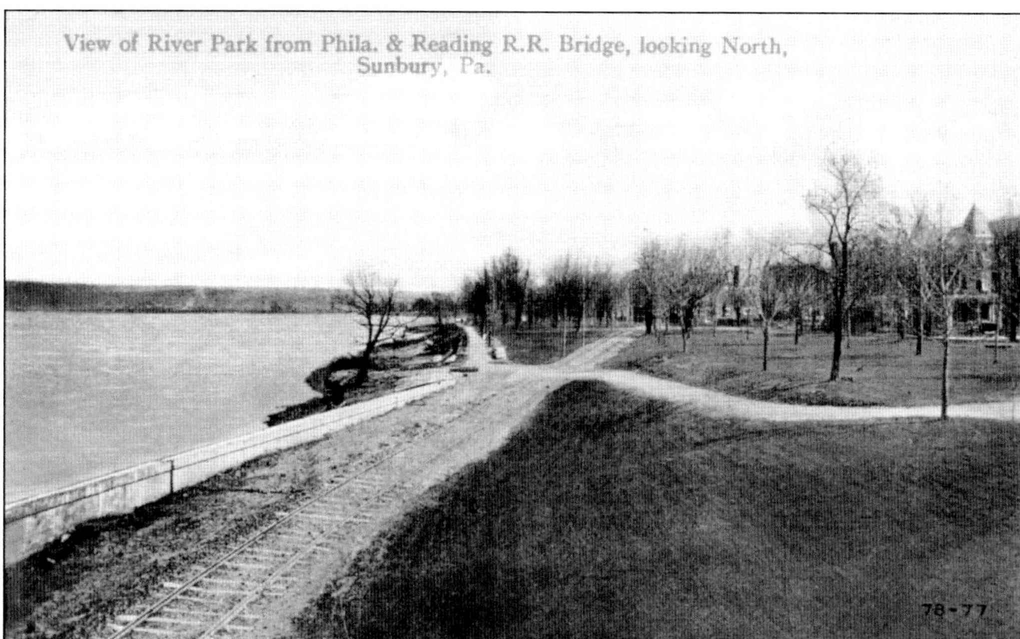

This postcard depicts a view of the Sunbury Riverfront Park from the Philadelphia & Reading Railroad Bridge, looking north. It shows the railroad tracks and a relatively low river wall, which was created to protect the city from floods. It did not, however, do a very good job of protecting Sunbury from the ravages of the overflowing river. (Courtesy of Tim Auman.)

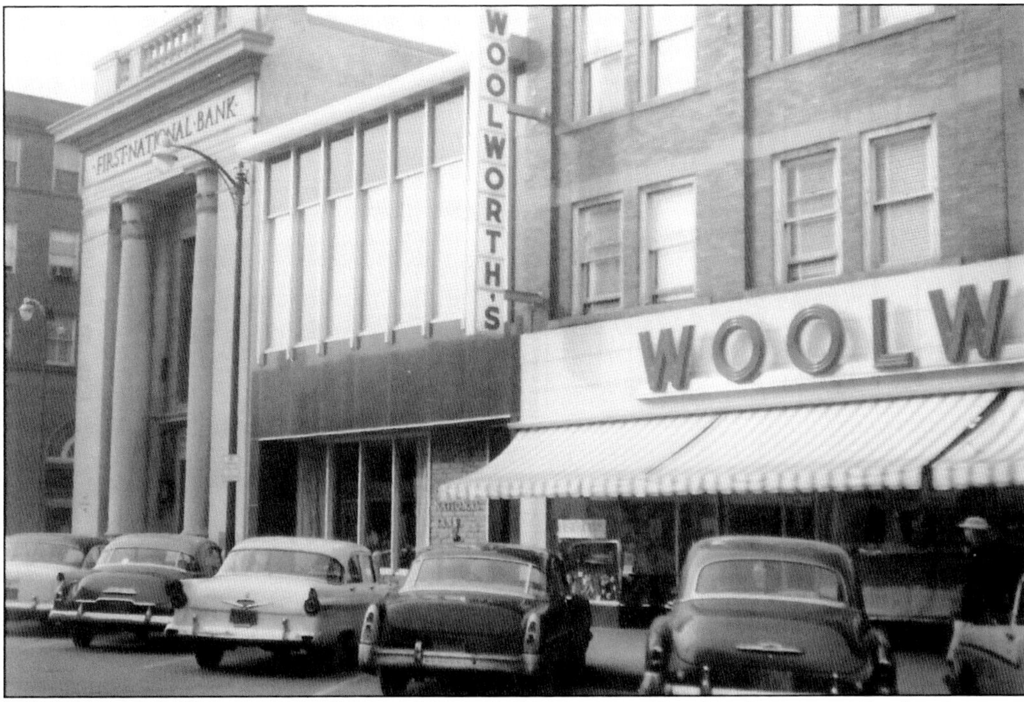

F.W. Woolworth Company, the famous five-and-dime store, maintained a presence in the town—as it did all across the United States. On the same block as the First National Bank at Fourth Street on Market Street for many years, it was a mecca for shoppers and a reliable employer for the townsfolk for over 25 years. (Courtesy of an anonymous donor.)

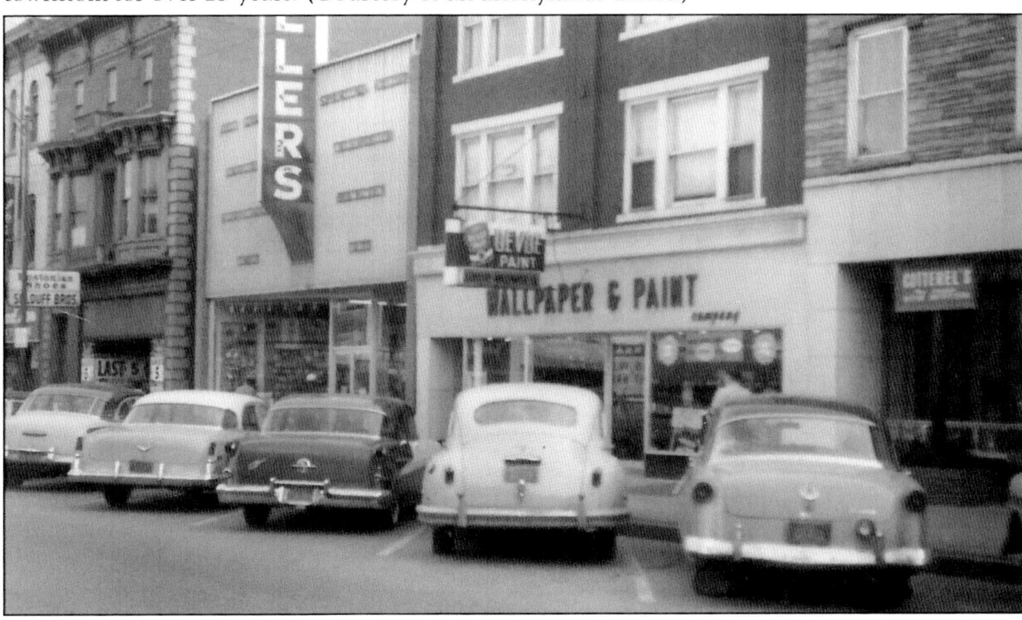

The Wallpaper & Paint Company on Market Street sold Devoe, a paint brand from 1754 that sold exclusively through independent paint dealers. As Sunbury continued to grow and build during the 1950s and 1960s, a wallpaper and paint shop was a necessity. (Courtesy of an anonymous donor.)

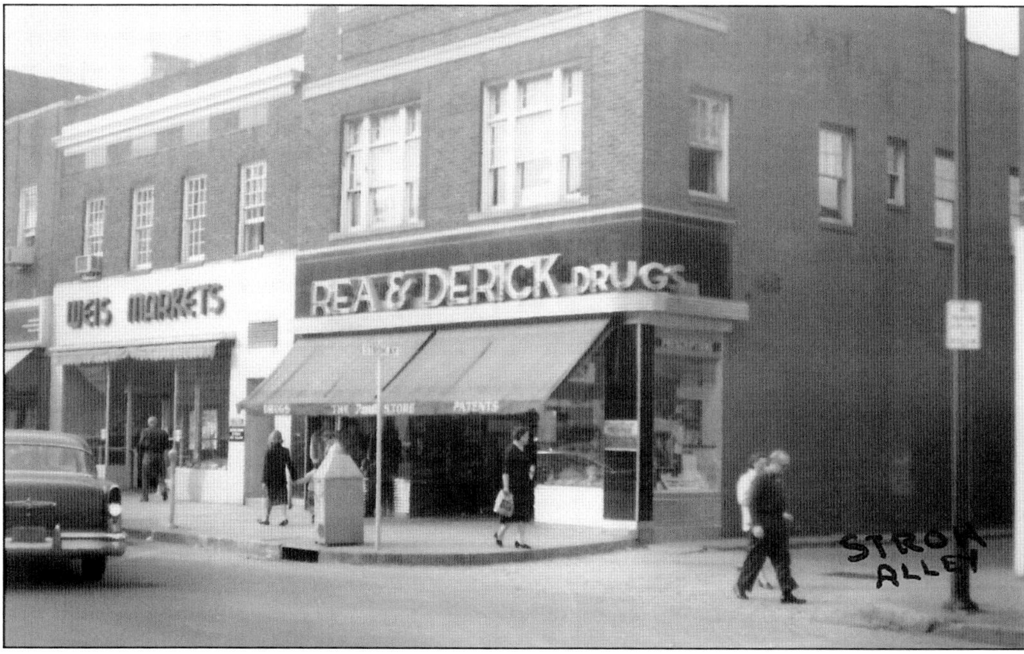

Rea & Derick Drugs stood at the corner of Market Street and Stroh Alley. On July 2, 1970, the store celebrated the 50th anniversary of the opening of its first store in Sunbury. Opened by two pharmacists, Scott C. Rea and George C. Derick, the first store was at 430 Market Street—eight more stores soon followed. (Courtesy of an anonymous donor.)

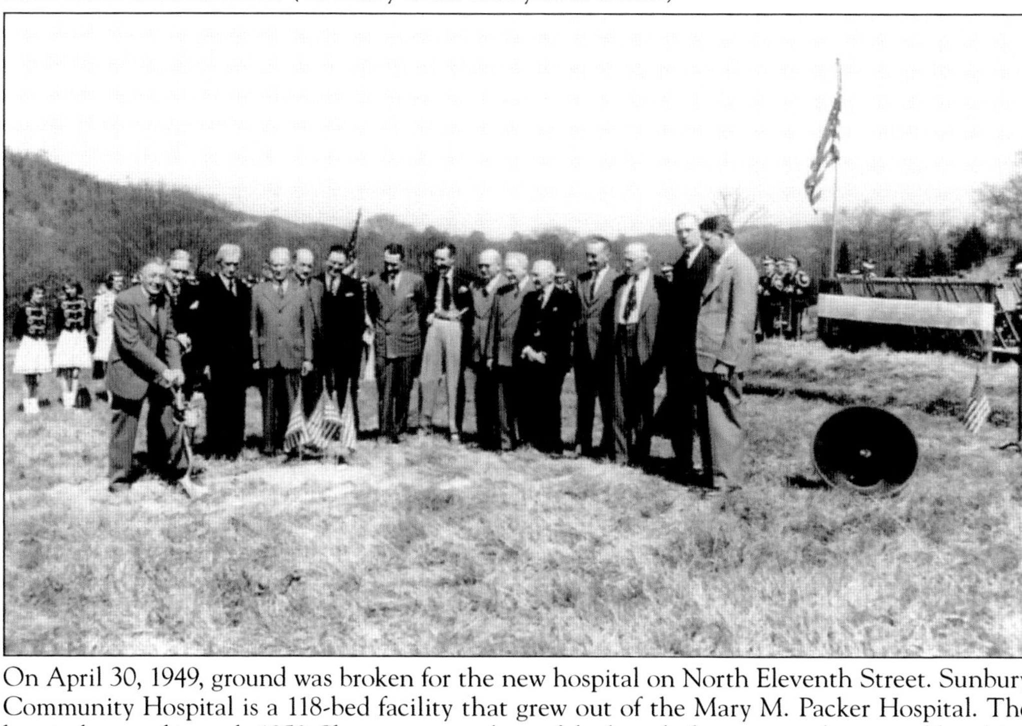

On April 30, 1949, ground was broken for the new hospital on North Eleventh Street. Sunbury Community Hospital is a 118-bed facility that grew out of the Mary M. Packer Hospital. The hospital opened in early 1950. Shown are members of the board of trustees at the ground-breaking ceremony. (Courtesy of Sunbury Community Hospital.)

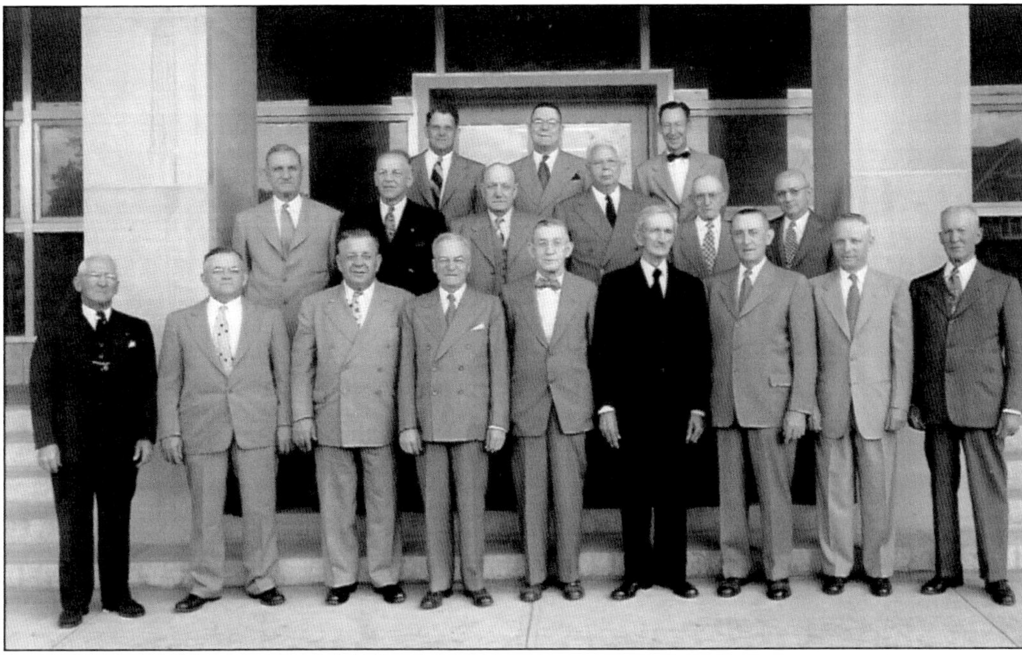

Shown here in this 1950s photograph are members of the board of trustees of the Sunbury Community Hospital during their first inspection of the building. Today, the 118-bed hospital has a dedicated team of nurses, staff, volunteers, and more than 40 physicians representing general family medicine and specialty care. (Courtesy of Sunbury Community Hospital.)

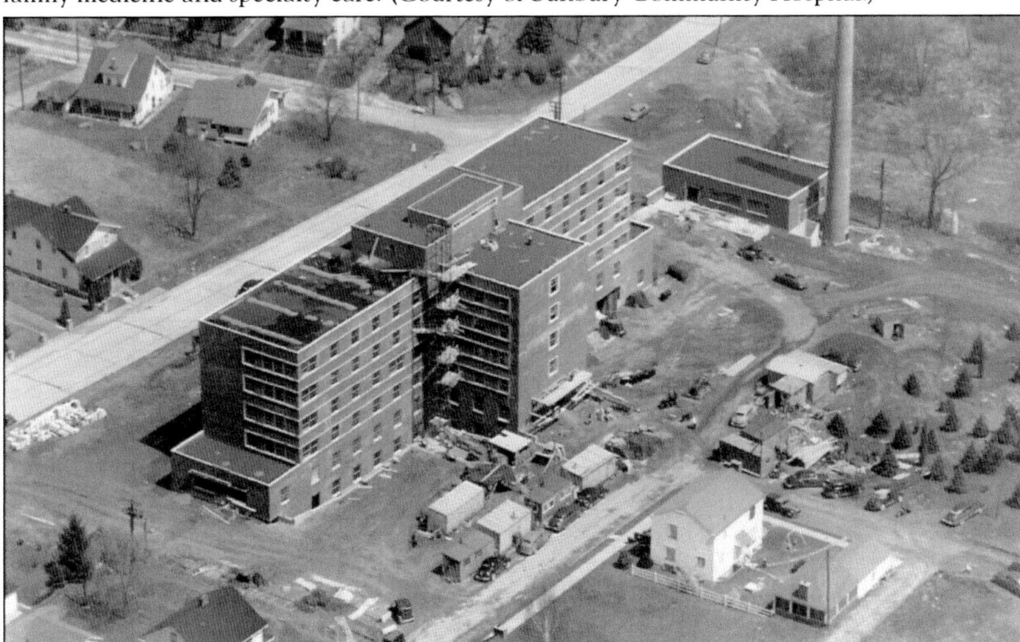

This 1950 aerial view shows the construction site of the Sunbury Community Hospital. Once completed, the new hospital would double the capacity of the Mary M. Packer Hospital at a cost of $1.5 million. The new hospital would provide maximum sunlight in all rooms. (Courtesy of Sunbury Community Hospital.)

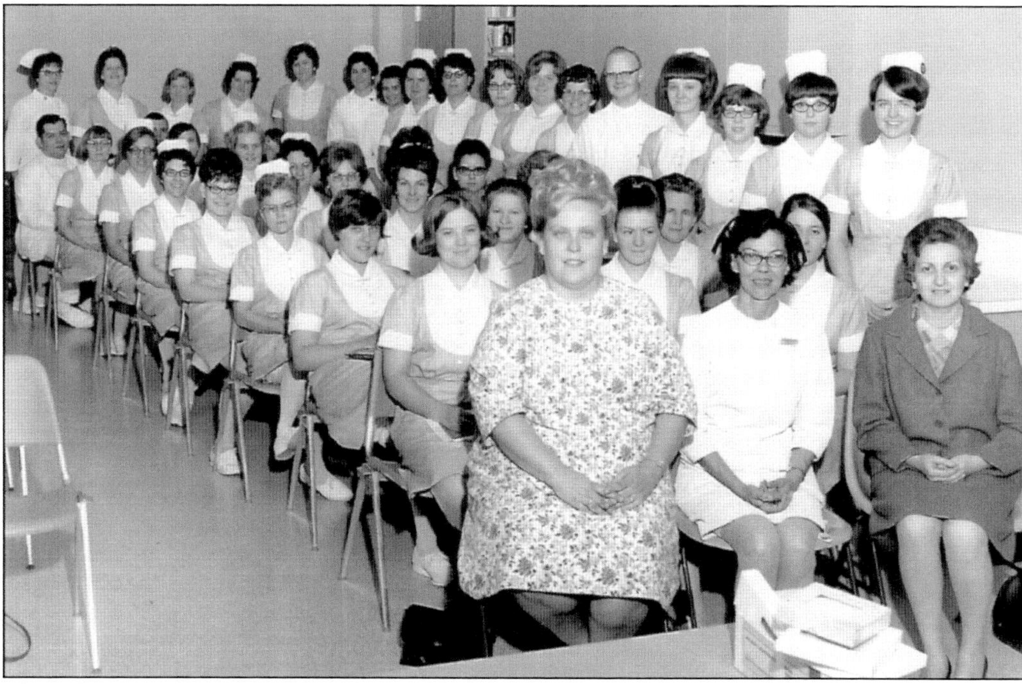

This photograph is of a group of nurses in 1966. These dedicated men and women made the patients comfortable and helped to make their experience as patients as pleasant as possible. (Courtesy of Sunbury Community Hospital.)

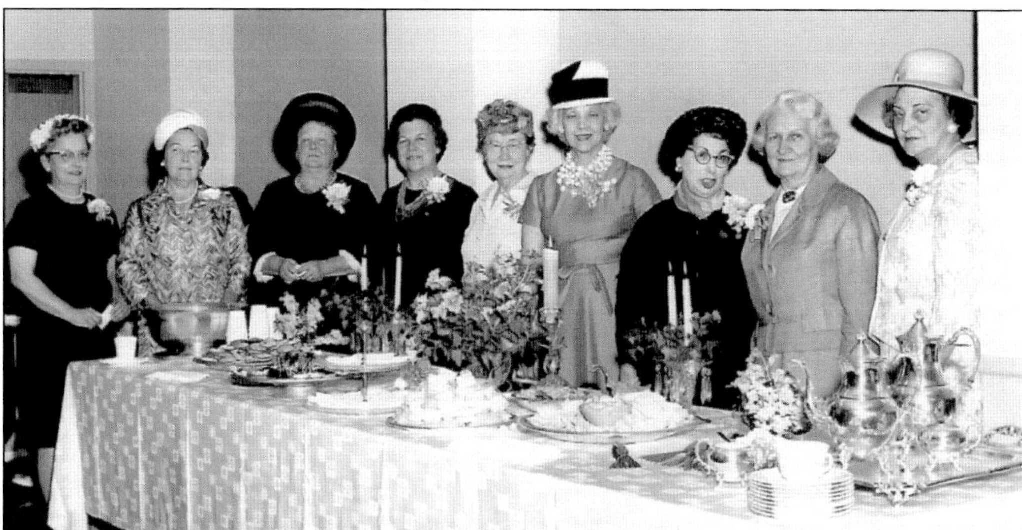

Ladies' aid societies were formed in the late 1890s and have always worked diligently for every hospital project, in every building campaign, and for each special event in Sunbury. Before the turn of the 20th century, Mary Derr Rockefeller, junior aid, and the Senior Aid Auxiliary of Sunbury Hospital, shown here in 1952 at their annual banquet, worked to build and sustain the hospital. The Ladies Auxiliary engages in fundraising for the hospital. Mary Derr, born on October 4, 1871, married Charles W. Rockefeller on June 8, 1892. They were both important civic leaders of Sunbury. (Courtesy of Sunbury Community Hospital.)

This 1960s photograph illustrates the work of a dietician at the Sunbury Community Hospital. Here, she is weighing food to make sure that her patients have the correct volume of nutriment for hospital patients. (Courtesy of Sunbury Community Hospital.)

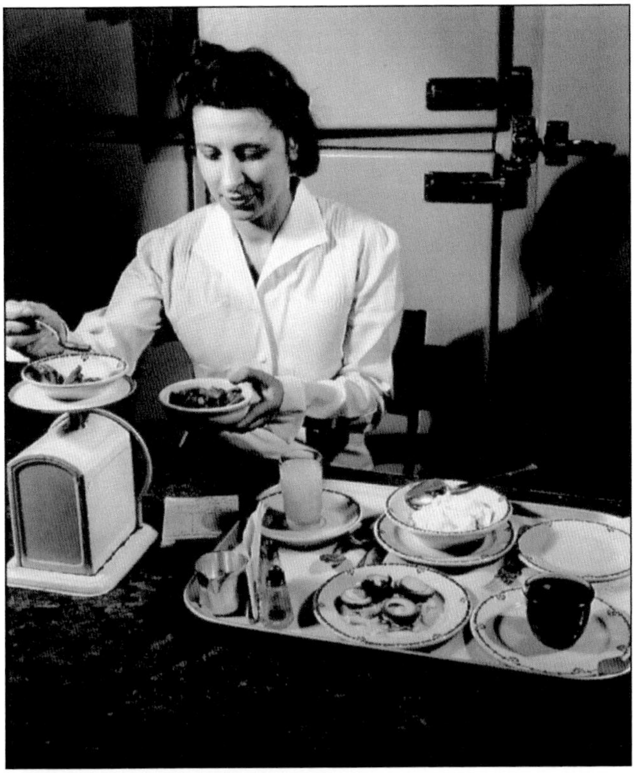

This photograph of the admitting desk of the Sunbury Community Hospital was taken during the early years of the hospital. Shown in the background is information about the Blue Cross Insurance plan. (Courtesy of Sunbury Community Hospital.)

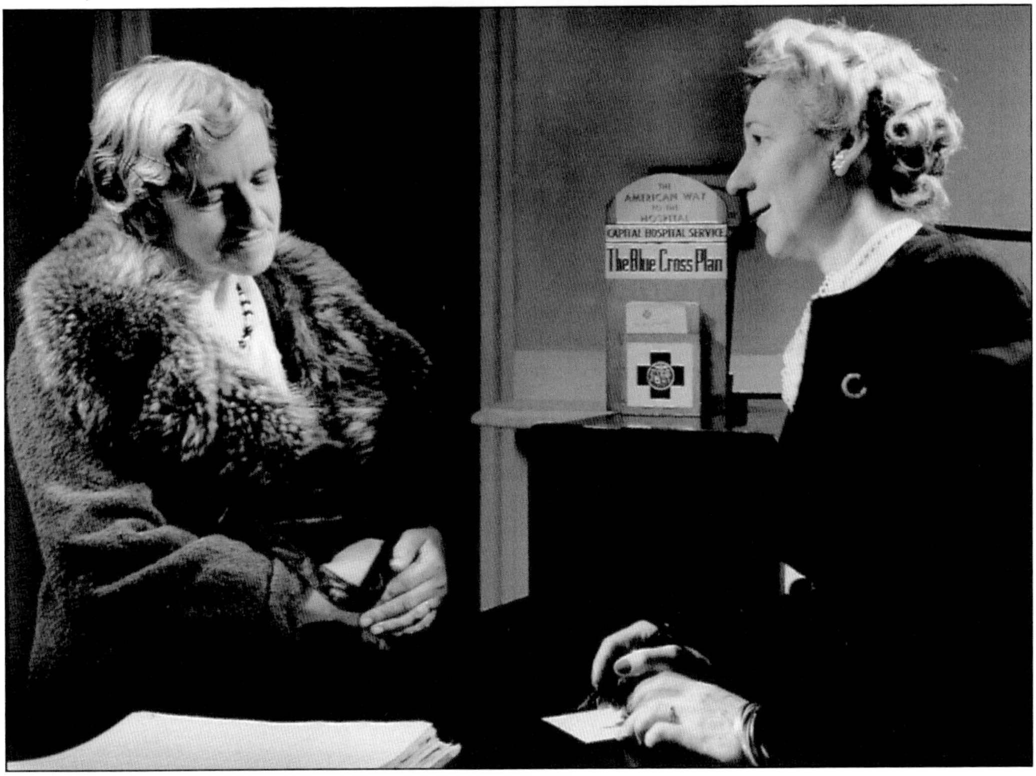

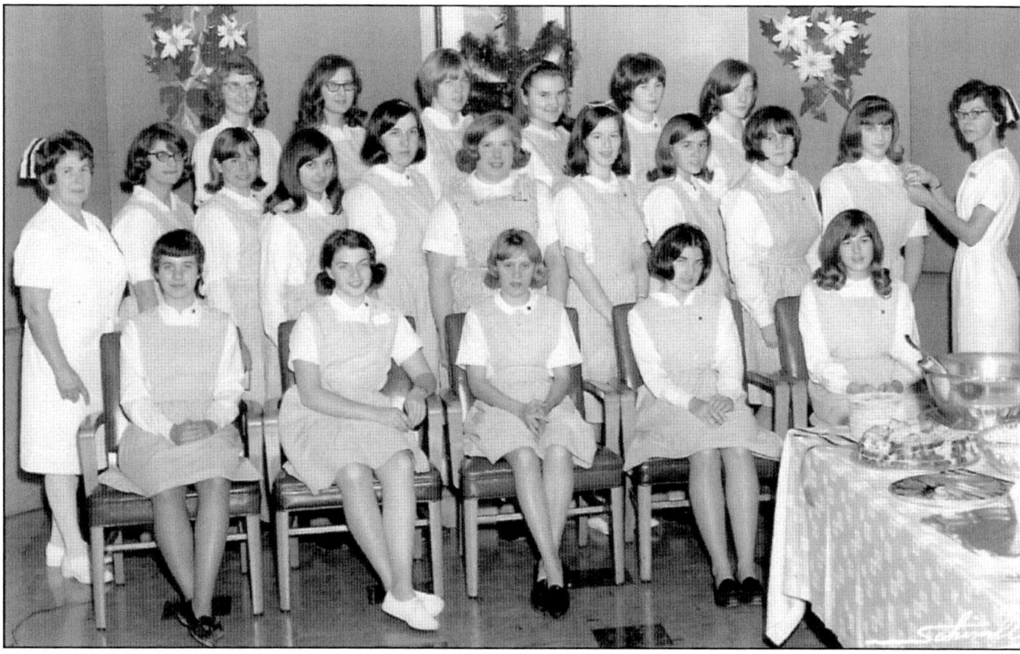

The candy stripers of the Sunbury Community Hospital are shown here in the summer of 1975 at their orientation banquet. Candy stripers perform needed services on hospital floors, providing water to patients, putting flowers in vases, and escorting patients from their rooms to various services within the hospital. (Courtesy of Sunbury Community Hospital.)

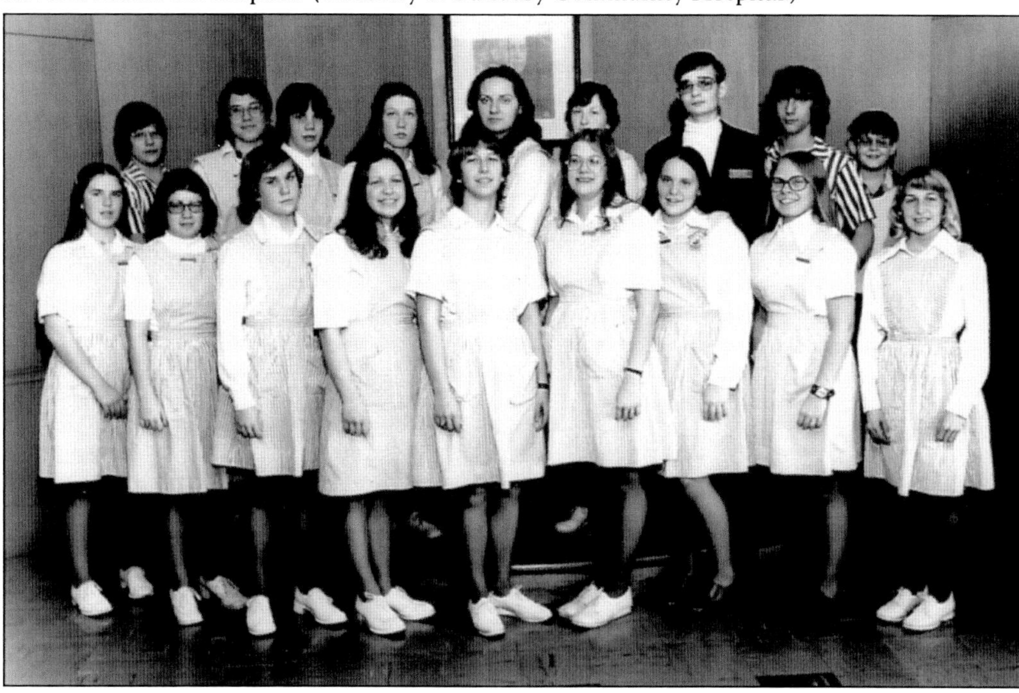

This is another group of young people celebrating their graduation from training as candy stripers at the Sunbury Community Hospital. Not only do they help the hospital, but also they learn skills and also whether they want careers in medicine. (Courtesy of Sunbury Community Hospital.)

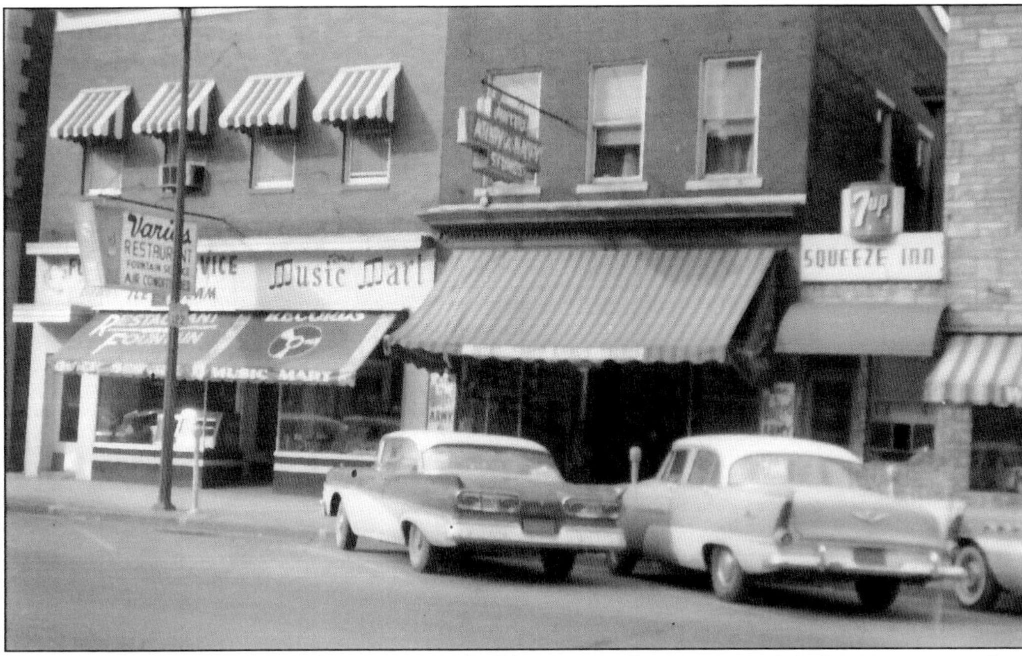

The Squeeze Inn, a tiny luncheonette crushed between other stores on Market Street, is indeed a place where one has to squeeze in. It was established at a time when Sunbury had a bustling downtown area—before people migrated away from Sunbury's main street to shop at the malls across the river. (Courtesy of an anonymous donor.)

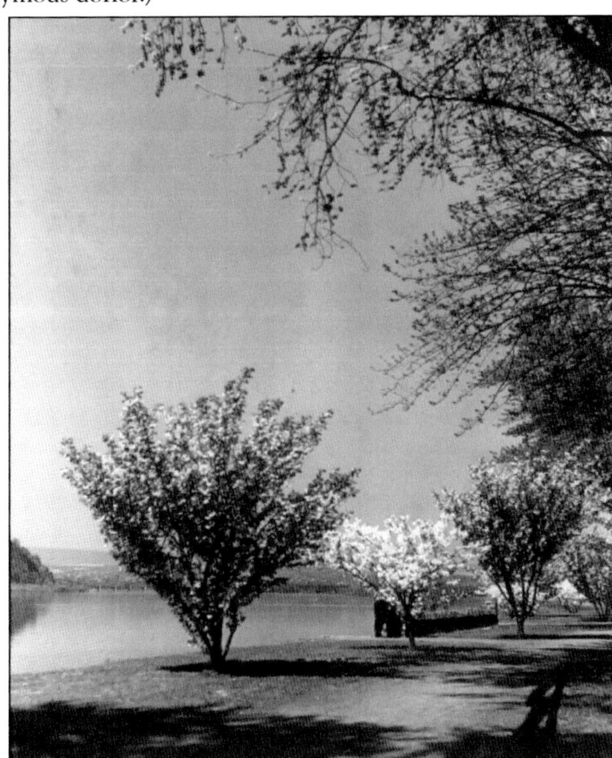

This lovely picture of Sunbury in the spring shows a parklike setting with benches for enjoying the cool breezes off the Susquehanna River as well as a path. The blooming trees add to the pleasurable view of the day. (Courtesy of NCHS.)

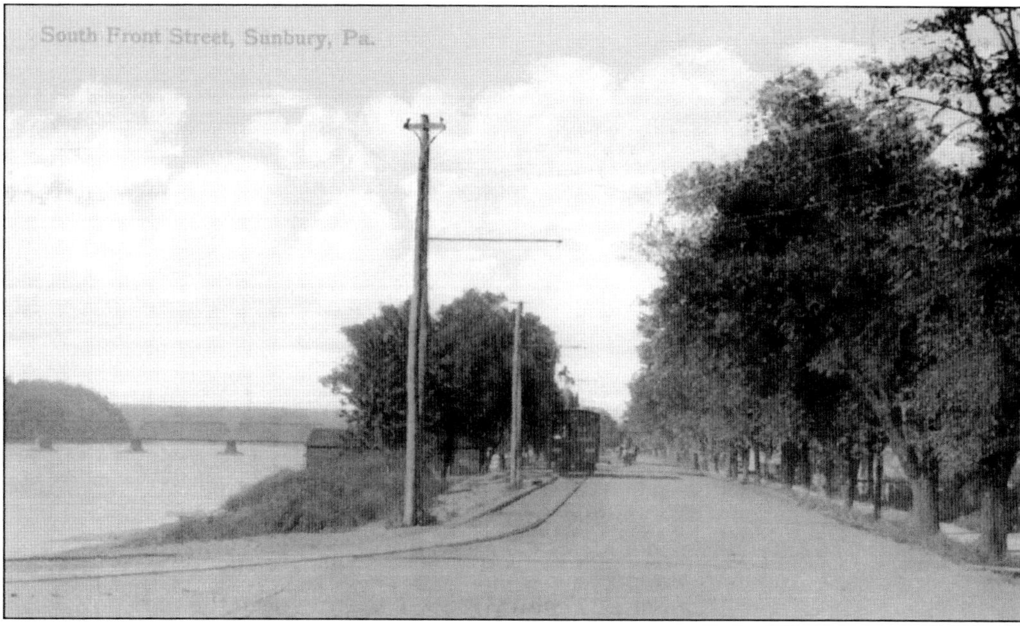

This scenic view of South Front Street shows a tram running along the street beside the Susquehanna River. In the early days, there were many horse races in town. Horses from all the neighboring towns were brought here on those occasions. There were two courses—one was on Front Street, from the corner of Spruce Street down to the two trees, or the dam. (Courtesy of Tim Auman.)

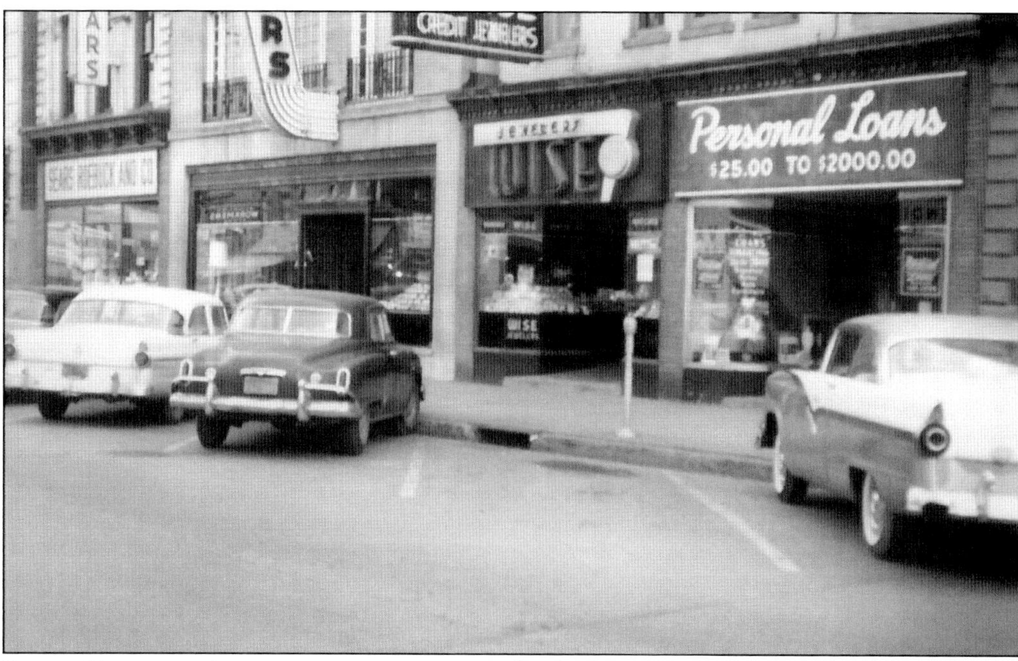

Personal loans were becoming very necessary in the prosperous 1950s, as many people were buying on credit following World War II. The country and Sunbury were energetic, and many people were using newly established credit cards. This photograph also shows a jewelry store and other businesses on Sunbury's popular Market Street. (Courtesy of an anonymous donor.)

Five

Sunbury and Its Industries

Many industries have supported Sunbury's economy through the years. Sunbury has been both industrious and economically solvent, beginning with the farms, small markets, barbershops, blacksmiths, weavers, nailers, tannery shops, and saddlers. Later, with the creation of a system of canals followed by the railroads, Sunbury became an important transportation hub, adding boatbuilding as an industry in the city. The Sunbury & Shamokin Railroad was opened in 1936, and other lines soon followed.

Politics and the hospitality industry also figured prominently in the development of Sunbury. In *Reminiscence of Sunbury*, J.C. Irwin writes, "The bar-rooms were regular rendezvous on Sundays for a talk over matters of the preceding week. Of course, large hogs and politics were the principal topics discussed." Other professions were also ably represented in Sunbury, such as law, medicine, education, and journalism. Coal mining, while not undertaken in Sunbury proper, also drove the economy because of Sunbury's transportation system, which supplied the East Coast with coal by rail, especially during the Civil War. Later, the textile industry, and even wine making, would become important industries in Sunbury.

Sports and the arts were also important components of Sunbury, and while there was no formal theater in Sunbury, plays and other forms of entertainment were produced in the courthouse, hotel lobbies, and dining rooms for many years. Eventually, there would be an opera house, followed later by two theaters, the Rialto and Strand Theatres, where many live performances and films could be seen. Sunbury is also known for its early creation of magnificent architecture, which can still be seen today.

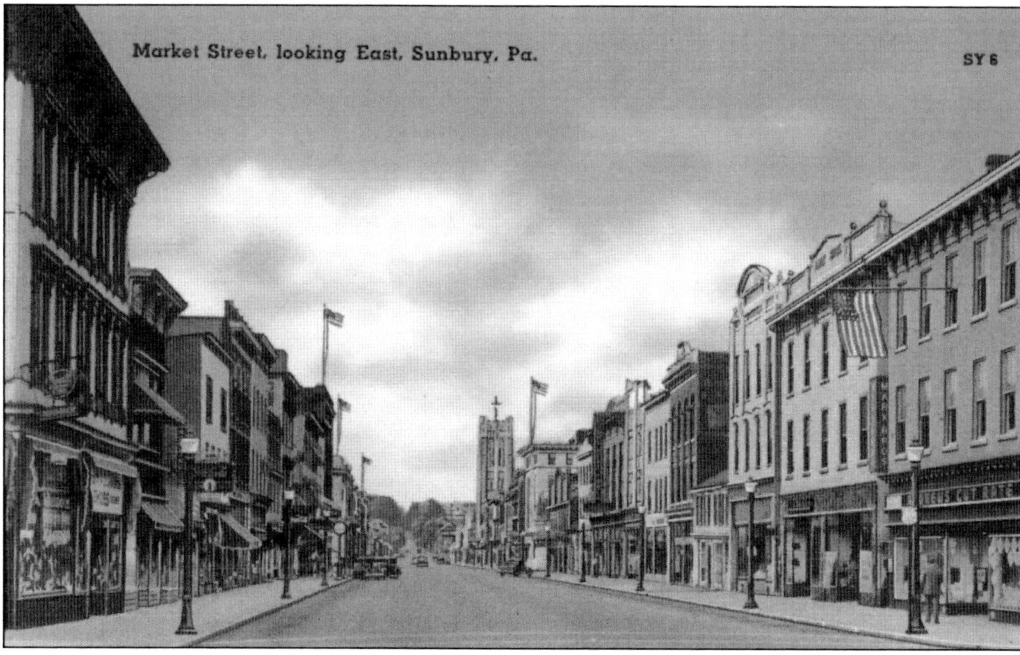

In the 1800s, Front, Market, and Chestnut Streets were mainly residential, with frame and log houses, barns, and stables. In the early 1830s, streets were green with grass, and sheep, geese, ducks, and cows pastured wherever they chose. Pictured above is Market Street, in a view looking east that shows the changes made over the years. Below is an older image of East Market Street, with trees and homes visible, but note that animals no longer roamed the street at that time. (Both, courtesy of David Persing.)

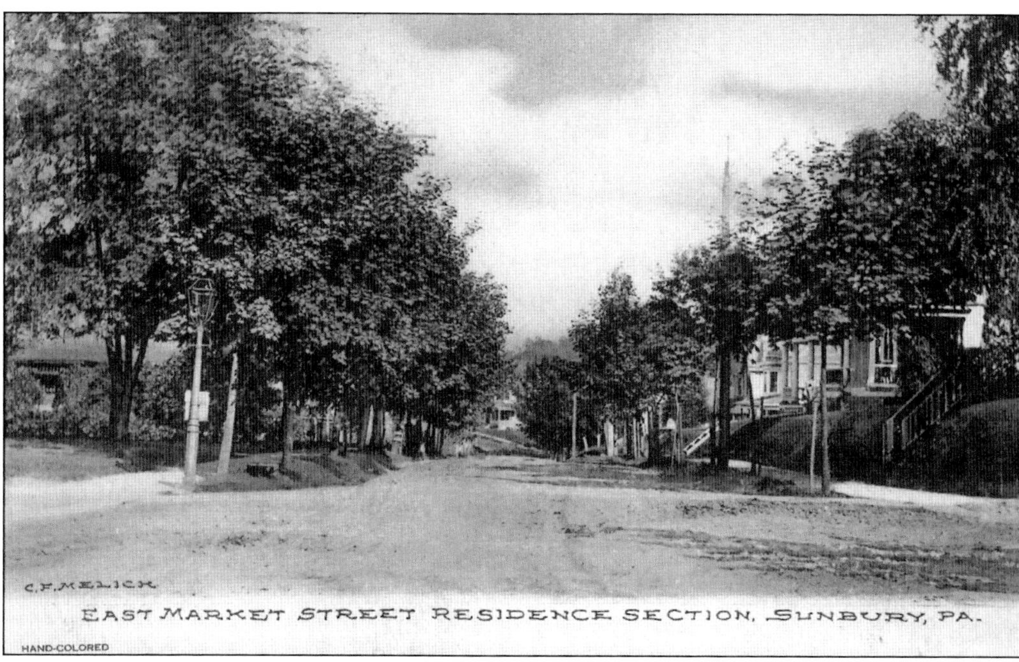

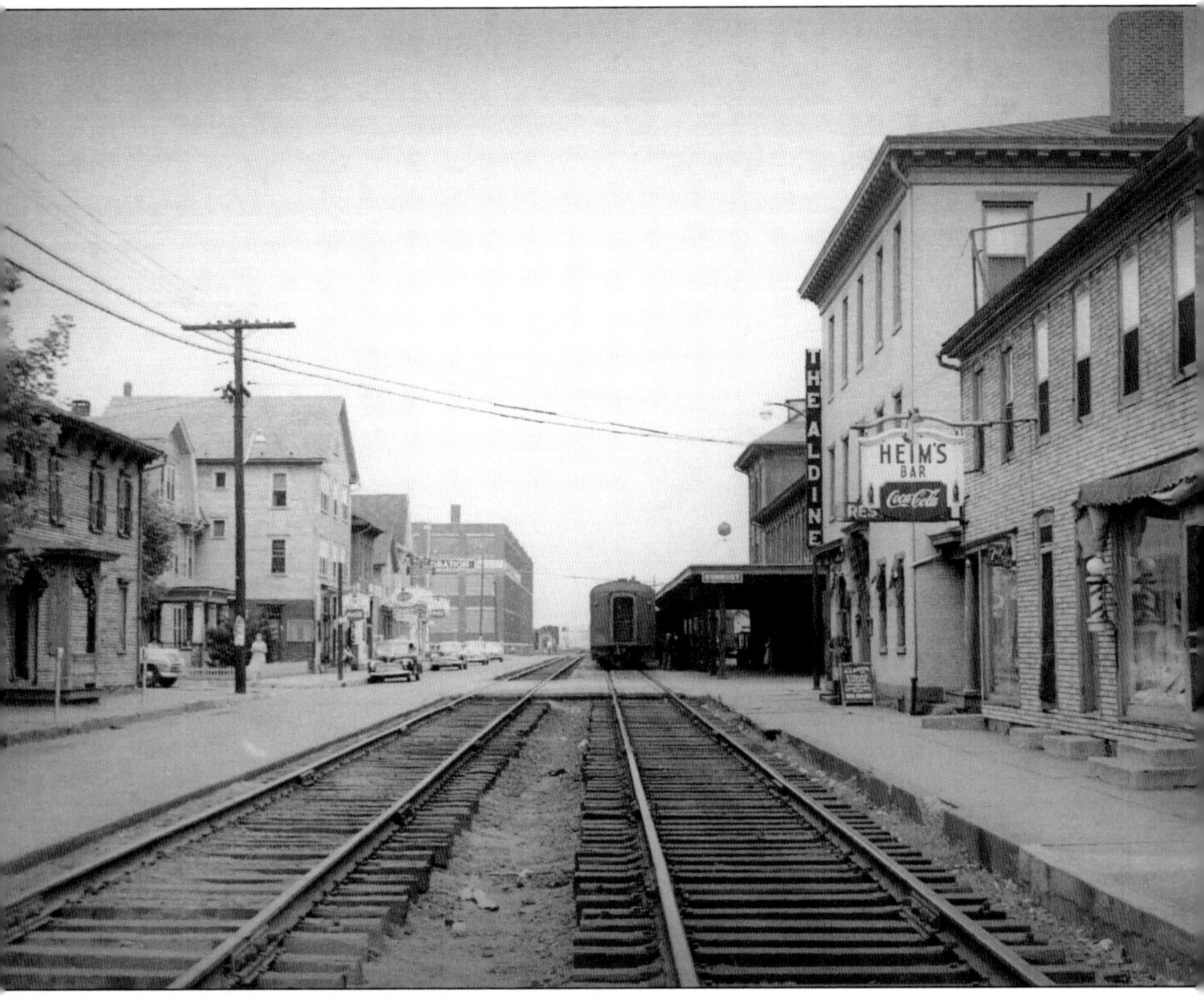

When the railroads were introduced, they went right through the center of town, and their tracks were very close to homes and businesses. This photograph is of the corner of Arch and Third Streets, showing the Pennsylvania Railroad Station on the right in the distance. Note the track runs down one side of the street, occupying approximately half of the roadway. All told, there were 14 streets with railroad crossings. Sunbury is still served by train service at two stations. (Courtesy of NCHS.)

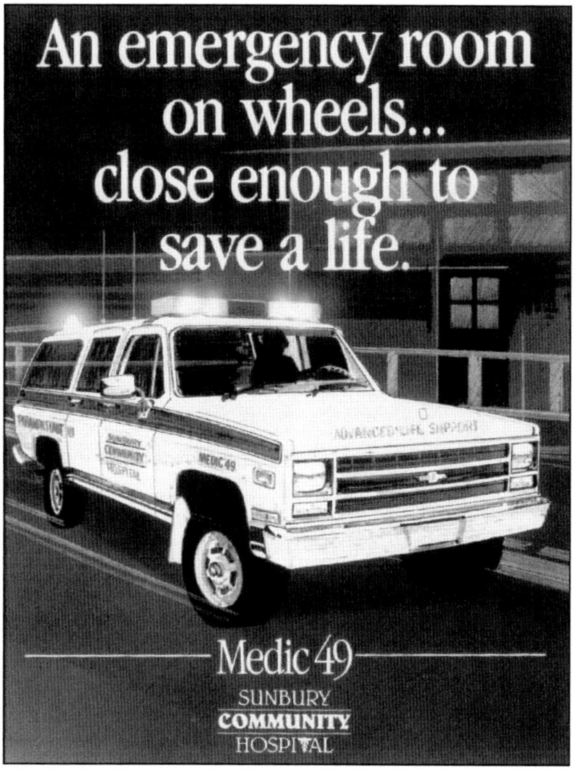

This poster announces the new ambulance service for the Sunbury Community Hospital, which was inaugurated in 1960. "An emergency room on wheels . . . close enough to save a life" was important to the people of Sunbury. Prior to this, the hospital used the fire company rescue truck. (Courtesy of Sunbury Community Hospital.)

The Sunbury Pennsylvania Railroad (PRR) station was built around 1872. The small Sunbury and Erie Railroad quickly faced the same trials and tribulations as many other railroads created in the 19th century. It was often difficult for small railroads to receive funding from the larger companies such as the Pennsylvania Railroad. Its completion was delayed until it received financial backing from the PRR, and it was constructed as the Philadelphia & Erie Railroad. (Courtesy of NCHS.)

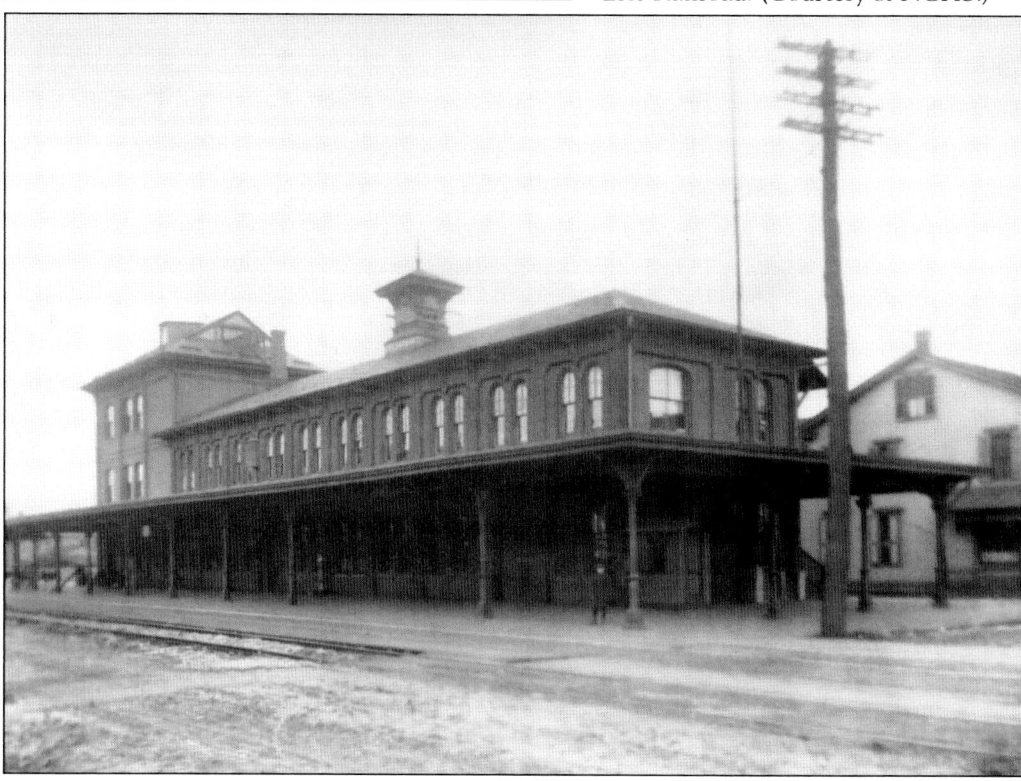

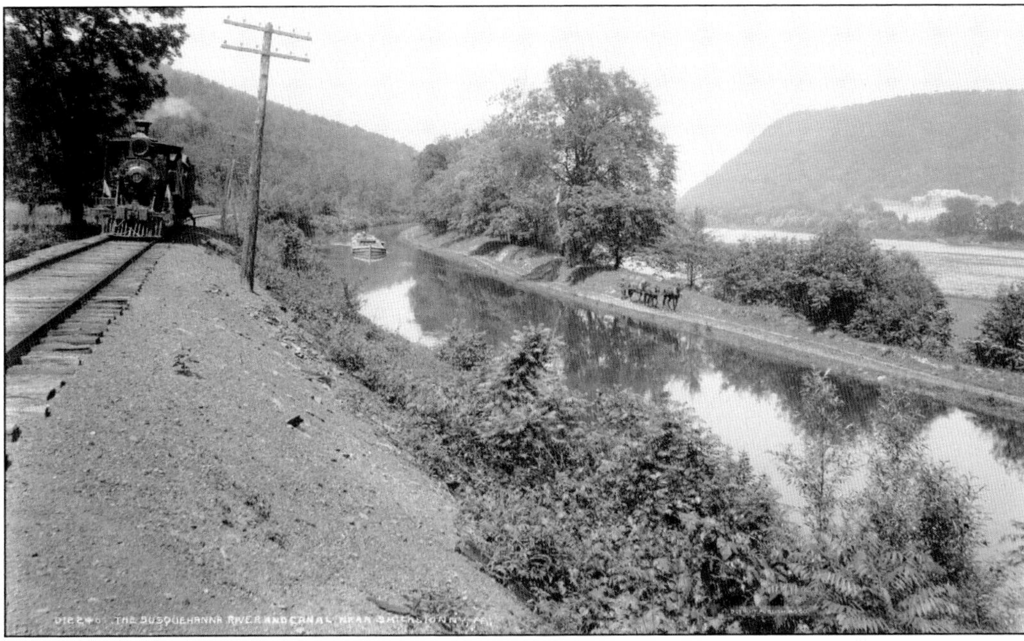

A port on the Pennsylvania Canal and a major railroad center, Sunbury bustled with the activity of many successful industrial ventures, which also spawned a thriving business district as well as residential growth. By the 1800s, there was a canal boom in the United States, with the canals of the Susquehanna River valley helping to drive industry. (Courtesy of the Library of Congress.)

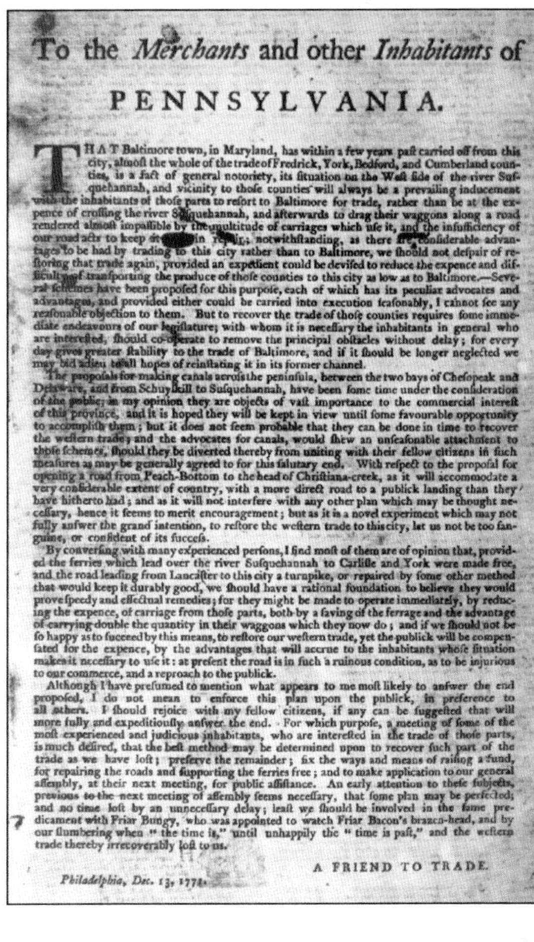

To the *Merchants* and other *Inhabitants* of

PENNSYLVANIA.

THAT Baltimore town, in Maryland, has within a few years past carried off from this city, almost the whole of the trade of Fredrick, York, Bedford, and Cumberland counties, is a fact of general notoriety, its situation on the West side of the river Susquehannah, and vicinity to those counties will always be a prevailing inducement with the inhabitants of those parts to resort to Baltimore for trade, rather than be at the expence of crossing the river Susquehannah, and afterwards to drag their waggons along a road rendered almost impassible by the multitude of carriages which use it, and the insufficiency of our road acts to keep it [illegible] in repair; notwithstanding, as there are considerable advantages to be had by trading to this city rather than to Baltimore, we should not despair of restoring that trade again, provided an expedient could be devised to reduce the expence and difficulty of transporting the produce of those counties to this city as low as to Baltimore.—Several schemes have been proposed for this purpose, each of which has its peculiar advocates and advantages, and provided either could be carried into execution seasonably, I cannot see any reasonable objection to them. But to recover the trade of those counties requires some immediate endeavours of our legislature; with whom it is necessary the inhabitants in general who are interested, should co-operate to remove the principal obstacles without delay; for every day gives greater stability to the trade of Baltimore, and if it should be longer neglected we may bid adieu to all hopes of reinstating it in its former channel.

The proposals for making canals across the peninsula, between the two bays of Chesopeak and Delaware, and from Schuylkill to Susquehannah, have been some time under the consideration of the public; in my opinion they are objects of vast importance to the commercial interest of this province, and it is hoped they will be kept in view until some favourable opportunity to accomplish them; but it does not seem probable that they can be done in time to recover the western trade; and the advocates for canals, would shew an unseasonable attachment to those schemes, should they be diverted thereby from uniting with their fellow citizens in such measures as may be generally agreed to for this salutary end. With respect to the proposal for opening a road from Peach-Bottom to the head of Christiana-creek, as it will accommodate a very considerable extent of country, with a more direct road to a publick landing than they have hitherto had; and as it will not interfere with any other plan which may be thought necessary, hence it seems to merit encouragement; but as it is a novel experiment which may not fully answer the grand intention, to restore the western trade to this city, let us not be too sanguine, or confident of its success.

By conversing with many experienced persons, I find most of them are of opinion that, provided the ferries which lead over the river Susquehannah to Carlisle and York were made free, and the road leading from Lancaster to this city a turnpike, or repaired by some other method that would keep it durably good, we should have a rational foundation to believe they would prove speedy and effectual remedies; for they might be made to operate immediately, by reducing the expence, of carriage from those parts, both by a saving of the ferrage and the advantage of carrying double the quantity in their waggons which they now do; and if we should not be so happy as to succeed by this means, to restore our western trade, yet the publick will be compensated for the expence, by the advantages that will accrue to the inhabitants whose situation makes it necessary to use it: at present the road is in such a ruinous condition, as to be injurious to our commerce, and a reproach to the publick.

Although I have presumed to mention what appears to me most likely to answer the end proposed, I do not mean to enforce this plan upon the publick, in preference to all others. I should rejoice with my fellow citizens, if any can be suggested that will more fully and expeditiously answer the end. For which purpose, a meeting of some of the most experienced and judicious inhabitants, who are interested in the trade of those parts, is much desired, that the best method may be determined upon to recover such part of the trade as we have lost; preserve the remainder; fix the ways and means of raising a fund, for repairing the roads and supporting the ferries free; and to make application to our general assembly, at their next meeting, for public assistance. An early attention to these subjects, previous to the next meeting of assembly seems necessary, that some plan may be perfected; and no time lost by an unnecessary delay; least we should be involved in the same predicament with Friar Bungy, who was appointed to watch Friar Bacon's brazen-head, and by our slumbering when " the time is," until unhappily the " time is past," and the western trade thereby irrecoverably lost to us.

A FRIEND TO TRADE.

Philadelphia, Dec. 13, 1771.

Dated December 13, 1771, this proposal requesting funds, which had been for some time under the consideration of the public, was sent to merchants and inhabitants of Pennsylvania in order to create canals across the peninsula between the two bays of Chesapeake and Delaware and from the Schuylkill to Susquehanna Rivers. (Courtesy of the Library of Congress.)

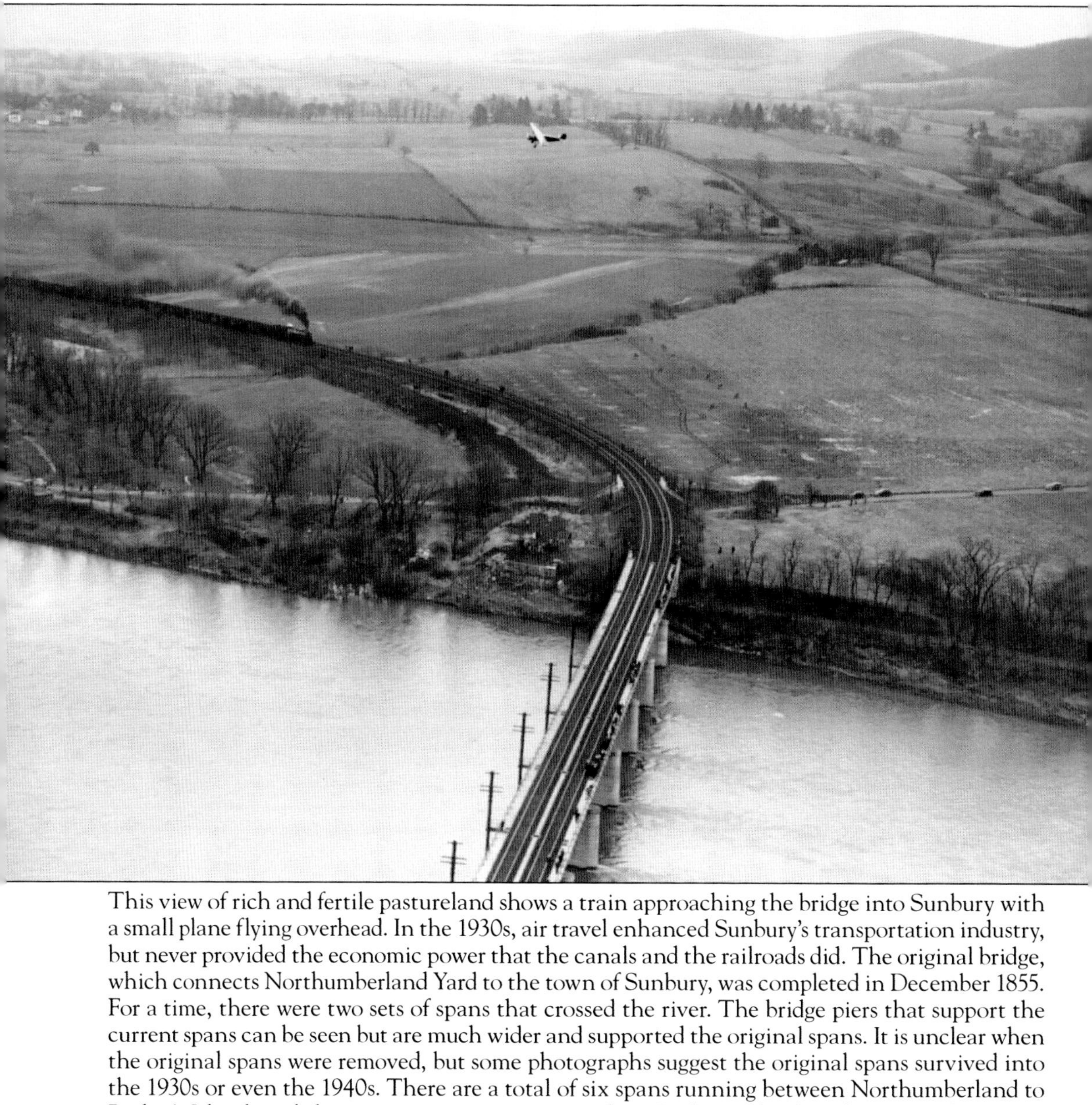

This view of rich and fertile pastureland shows a train approaching the bridge into Sunbury with a small plane flying overhead. In the 1930s, air travel enhanced Sunbury's transportation industry, but never provided the economic power that the canals and the railroads did. The original bridge, which connects Northumberland Yard to the town of Sunbury, was completed in December 1855. For a time, there were two sets of spans that crossed the river. The bridge piers that support the current spans can be seen but are much wider and supported the original spans. It is unclear when the original spans were removed, but some photographs suggest the original spans survived into the 1930s or even the 1940s. There are a total of six spans running between Northumberland to Packer's Island, and then six spans again crossing from Packer's Island to the town of Sunbury itself. (Courtesy of the Pennsylvania Archives.)

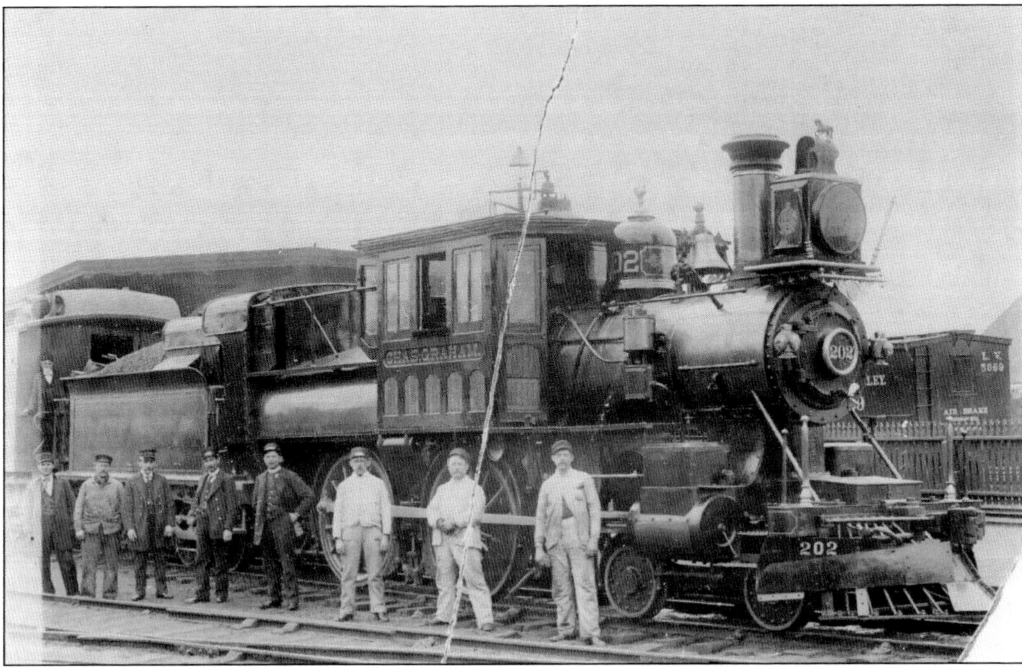

These photographs of train workers show engineers standing in front of their train and workers possibly waiting to be assigned rail work of some kind. At one time, with six rail lines traveling through and maintained by Sunbury, transportation was economically important for the town. These trains carried not only passengers throughout the state but also coal from the anthracite regions. Over 100 trains passed through Sunbury each day. (Both, courtesy of NCHS.)

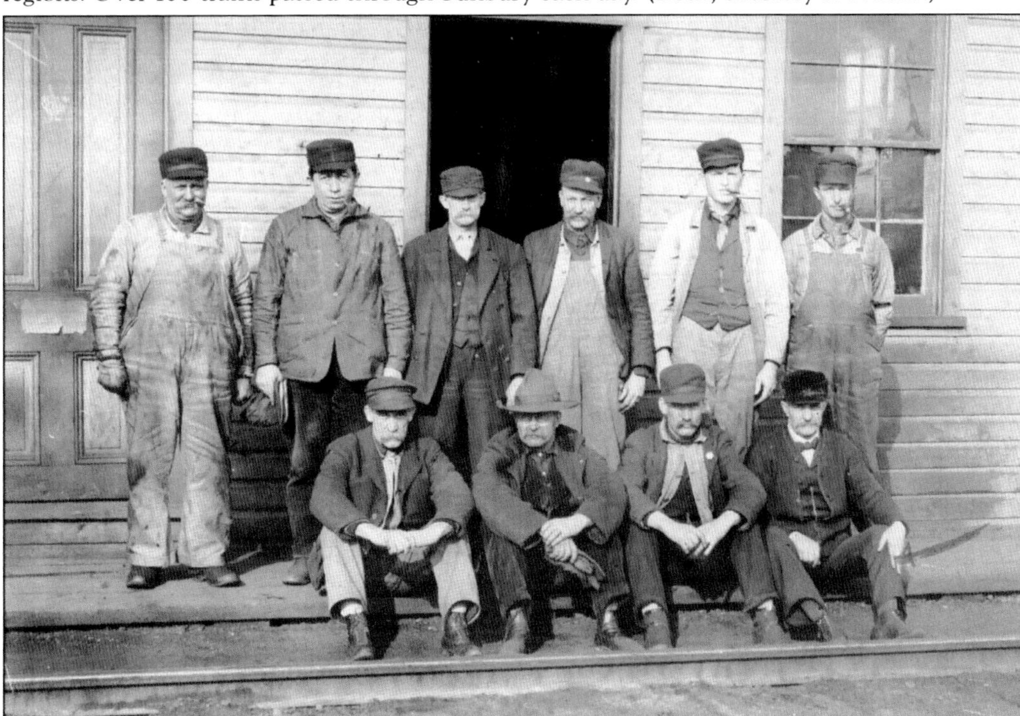

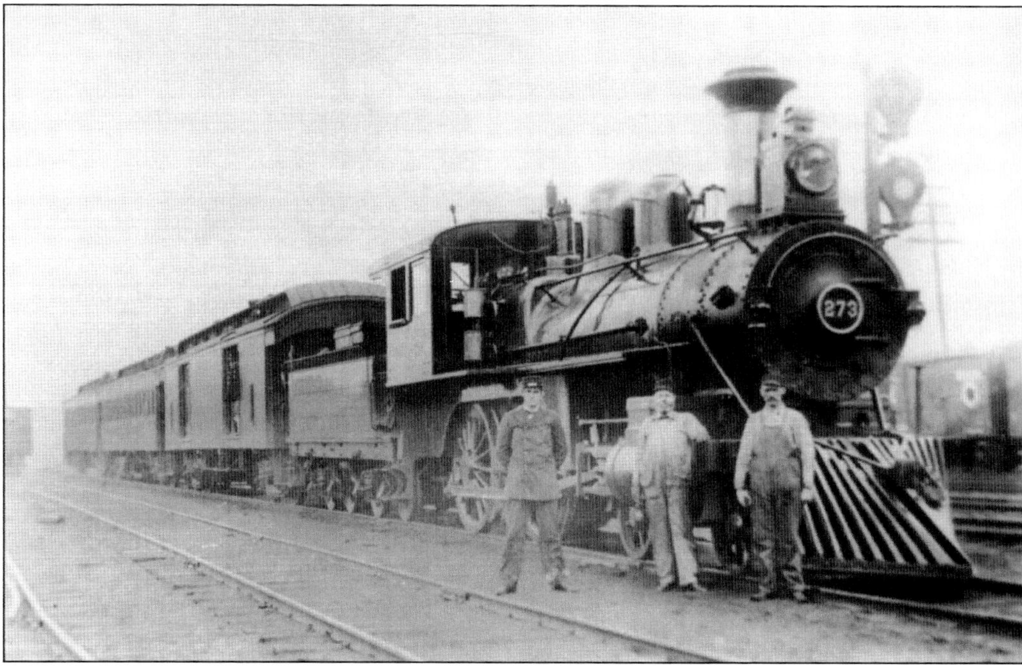

Photographed here are train workers, including, from left to right, a conductor, engineer, and fireman, from train No. 273. The history of rail transportation in the county began with the opening of the Philadelphia & Erie Railroad on Monday, September 24, 1855, with passenger travel established between the borough of Northumberland and Williamsport, Pennsylvania. The Susquehanna River Bridge was erected in late fall of 1855, and the first train to Sunbury passed over it on January 7, 1856. (Courtesy of NCHS.)

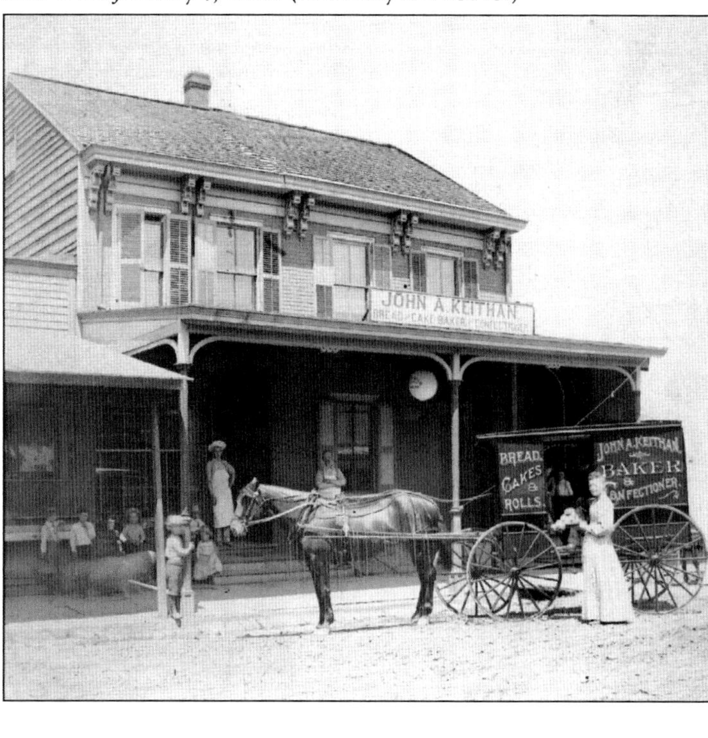

Not all industry had to do with the railroads. Shown here is the store of John A. Keithan, who made bread, rolls, cakes, and other confections on the premises. The building was once owned by John Boulton, who kept a hotel called the Red Lion Inn Tavern on the north side of Market Street between Third and Fourth Streets. Keithan's wares were sold both from this building and from his horse-drawn buggy. (Courtesy of NCHS.)

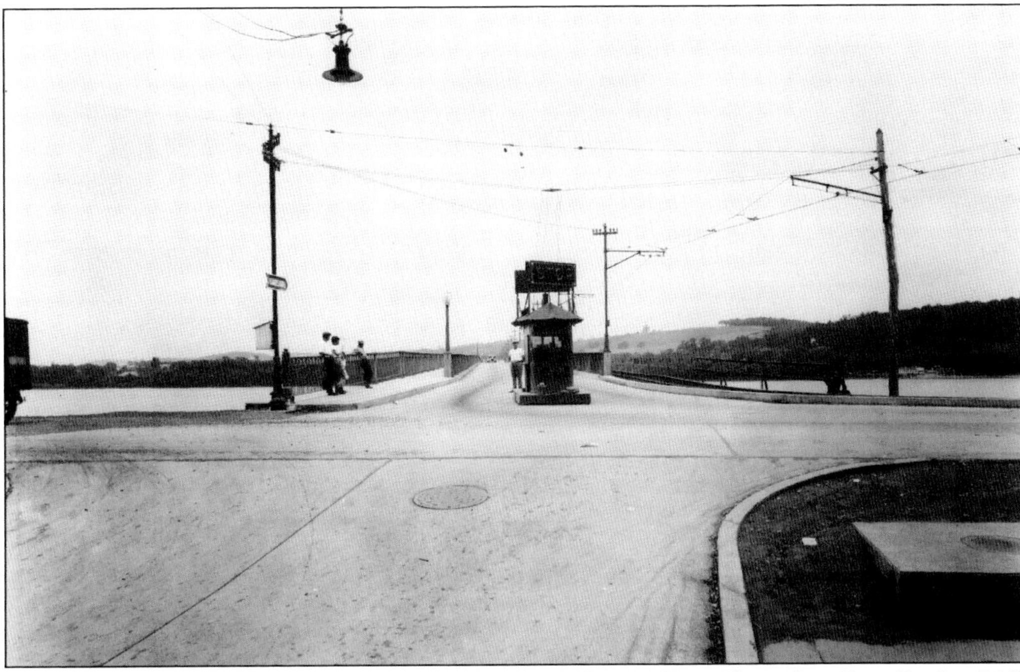

The 1908 Sunbury tollhouse was at the entrance to the Sunbury-Shamokin Dam Bridge. Tolls were collected on the right side of the building, while on the left was a store selling small travel items. The toll collector lived on the second floor. It has been said that there was a beautiful view up and down the river from the second floor. Pictured below is the tollgate over the old Bainbridge Bridge across the Susquehanna River. The railroad bridges were for trains only. A small rectangular sign at the entrance of the railroad bridge prohibits pedestrians from walking across the bridge. The sign states, "Notice, all persons are forbidden to cross this Bridge." (Above, courtesy of NCHS; below, courtesy of Tim Auman.)

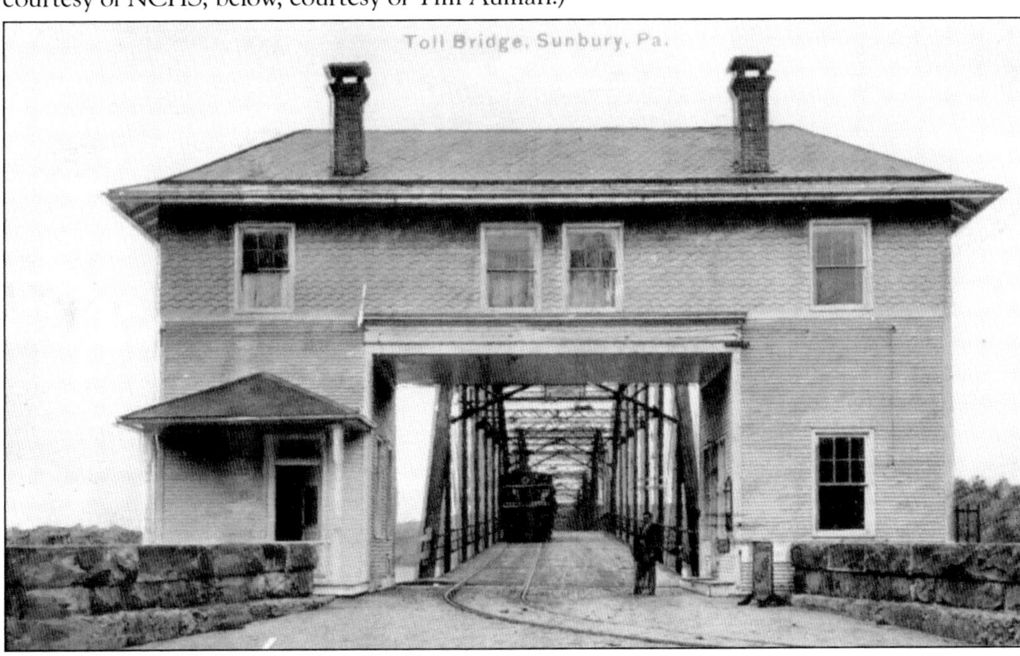

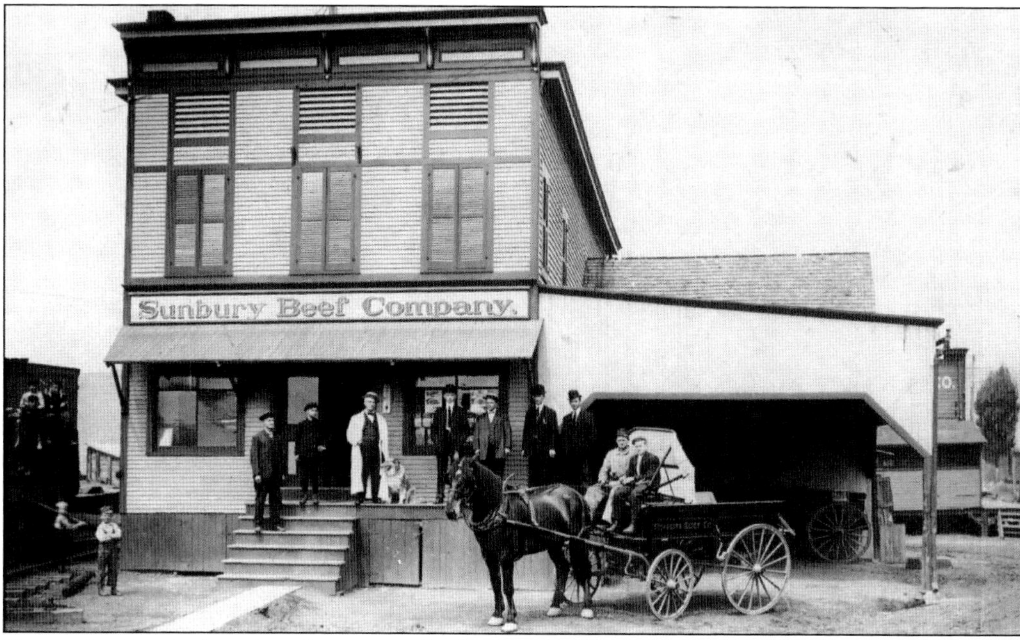

Pictured is the Sunbury Beef Company. In front is a delivery wagon taking merchandise to homes in Sunbury. It was not one of the many food wagons seen at sporting or military events around the county. It did, however, provide meats of all kinds to Sunbury residents from the store, which provided beef, fish, and poultry and engaged in meat processing. At the time of this early-1900s photograph, there were a number of butchers. (Courtesy of NCHS.)

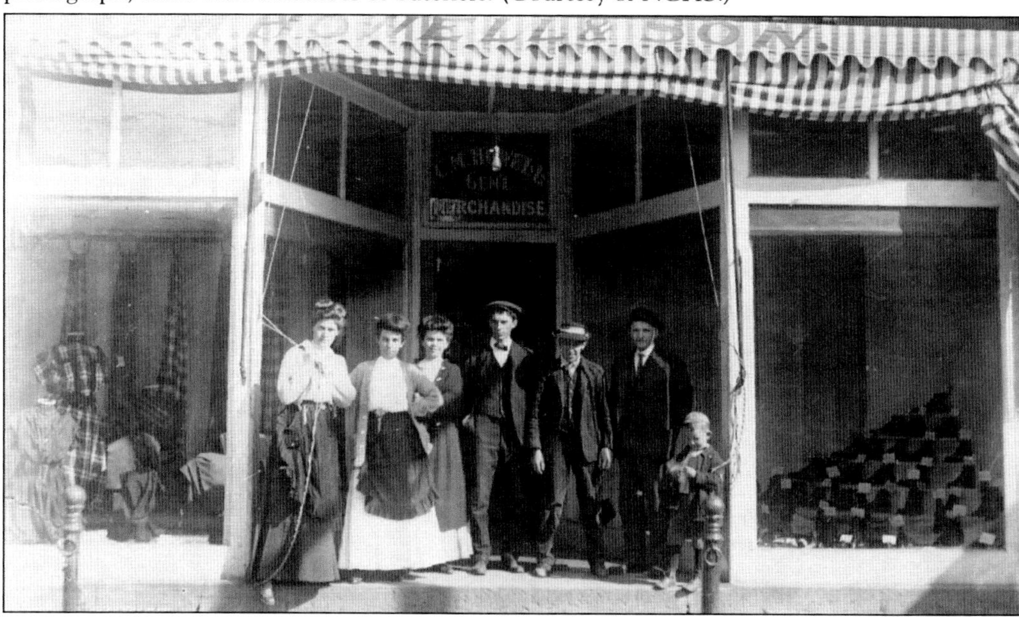

The C.M. Howell & Sons store sold general merchandise and hardware and had one of the most profitable businesses in Sunbury. Howell (center) was also considered one of the foremost men of his day. He is pictured with several salespeople and a young boy. The store sold clothing for men and women and other items for household use, such as equipment for the kitchen and garden. (Courtesy of NCHS.)

This photograph provides a detailed view of truss-end bearings of the Pennsylvania Railroad's Selinsgrove Bridge, which spanned the Susquehanna River. The women pictured are engineering students from Susquehanna College. Many of the bridge's wrought-iron Pratt through truss spans date back to 1888, and there were significant alterations made to the bridge in 1901, 1925, and 1930. (Courtesy of the Library of Congress.)

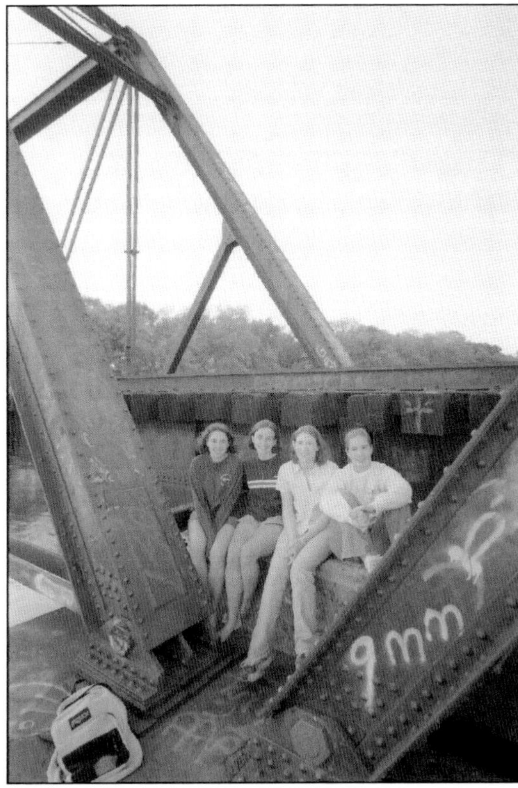

This photograph shows the staff with students of Sunbury High School, as pictured in the May 1912 issue of the class yearbook, the *Sunburian High*. The principal at the time was Harry C. Henry (first row, center), and the vice principal John J. Houtz (first row, right). The public school system in Sunbury was established in 1834, with the first school being built on land owned by Susan Giberson. The first principal of the Sunbury schools was David Trites, whose monthly salary was $27. (Courtesy of the Degenstein Community Library.)

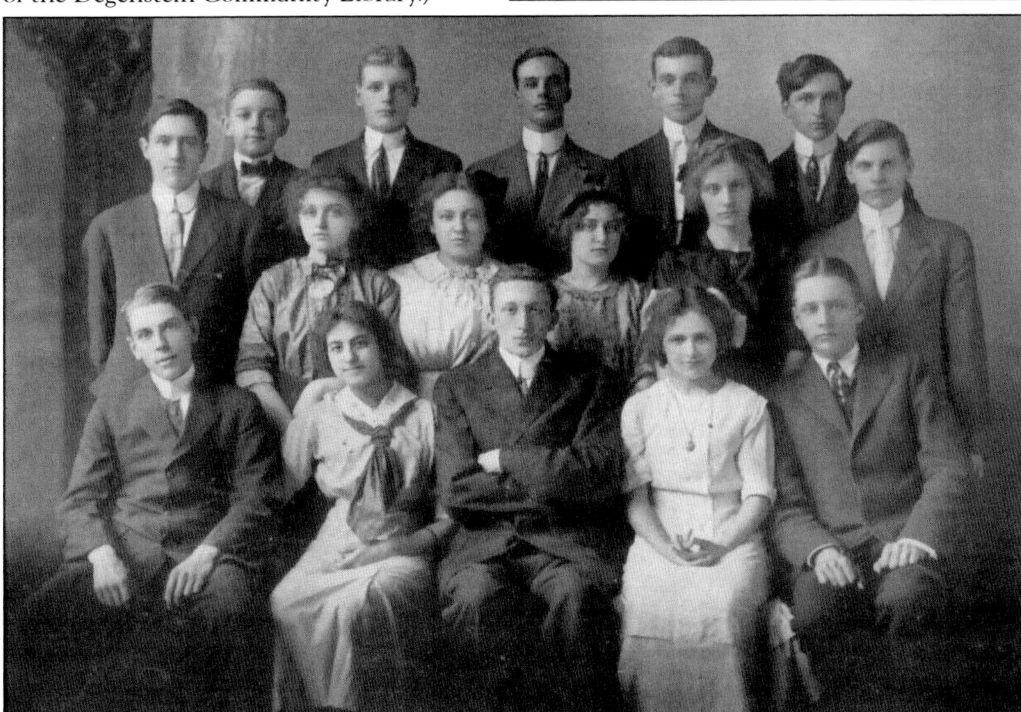

STAFF OF SUNBURIAN HIGH, 1912

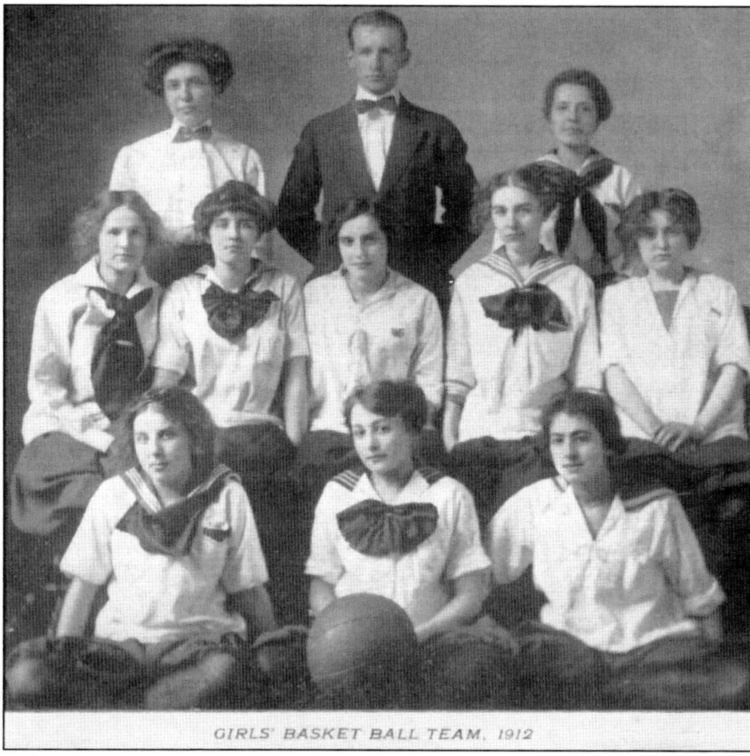

The girls' basketball team of Sunbury High School is shown in this 1912 photograph with their coach, R.A. Hufford, who was also the athletic director of the high school. Athletics for girls was strongly encouraged by the school administration; however, girls were required to wear bulky uniforms that somewhat impeded their athletic abilities. (Courtesy of the Degenstein Community Library.)

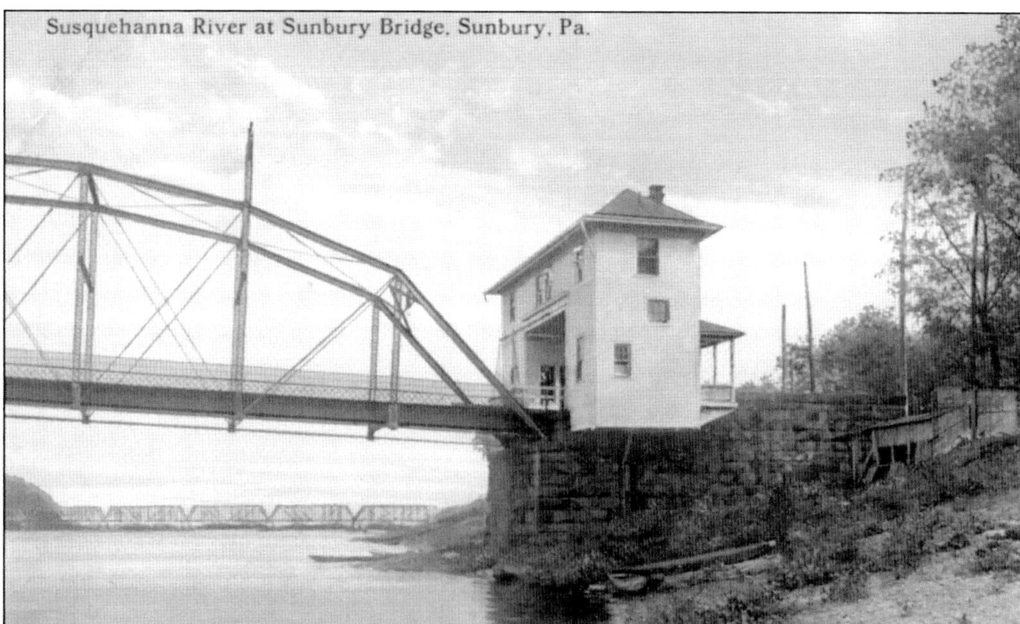

This is a view of the Susquehanna River at the Sunbury Bridge. It opened for pedestrians at 6:00 p.m. on October 5, 1907, and for horse and buggy at 4:00 a.m. on October 7, 1907. Traffic was estimated at 7,500 yearly in 1911, 11,000 daily in 1957, and 15,000 to 18,000 during Northumberland bridge reconstruction and detour in 1956. Tolls were abolished on replacement of the bridge in 1957. (Courtesy of Tim Auman.)

Cornelius McGillicuddy Sr., better known as "Connie Mack," was the owner of the Philadelphia Athletics. Mack's minor-league team was one of the Sunbury teams that played professional minor-league baseball in Sunbury for approximately 11 years. On his visit to Sunbury in 1936, Mack walked through the town with baseball fans. (Courtesy of the Library of Congress.)

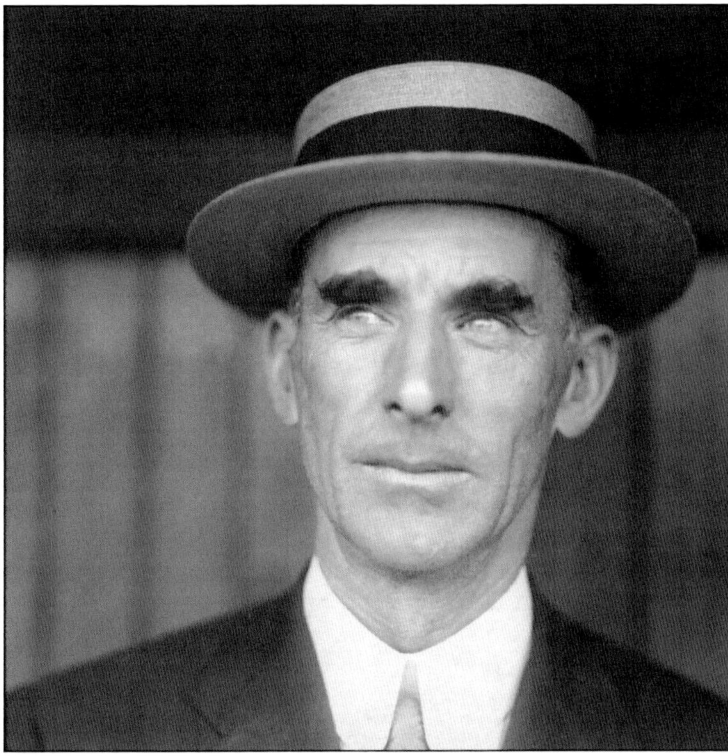

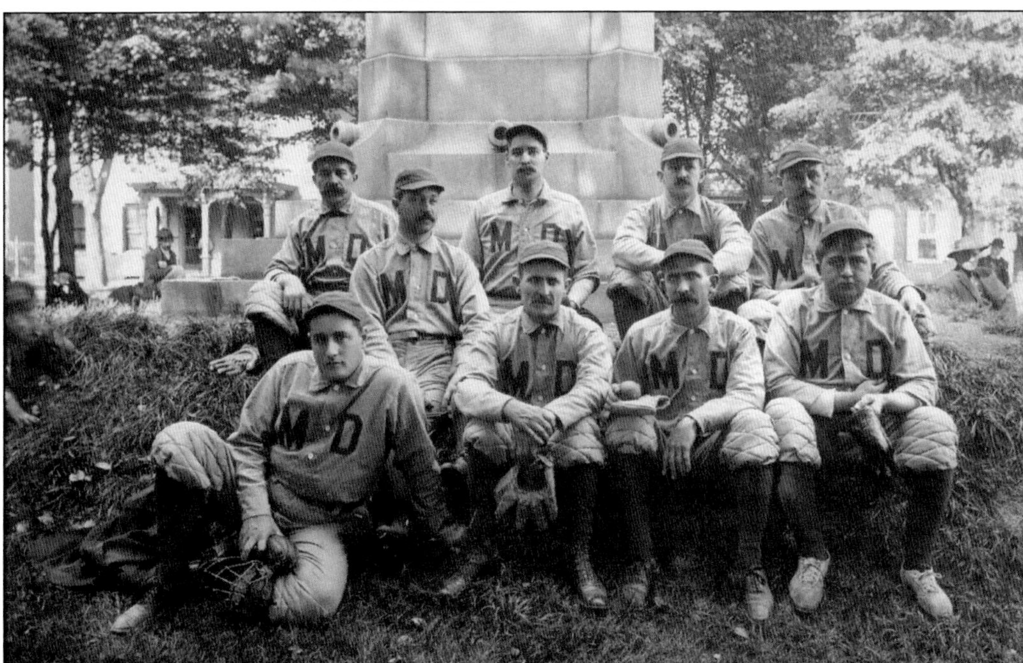

Sunbury residents enjoyed their baseball. Here, an unidentified baseball team poses in Cameron Park before the monument honoring Civil War soldiers. Baseball has been a popular sport in Sunbury for many years. (Courtesy of NCHS.)

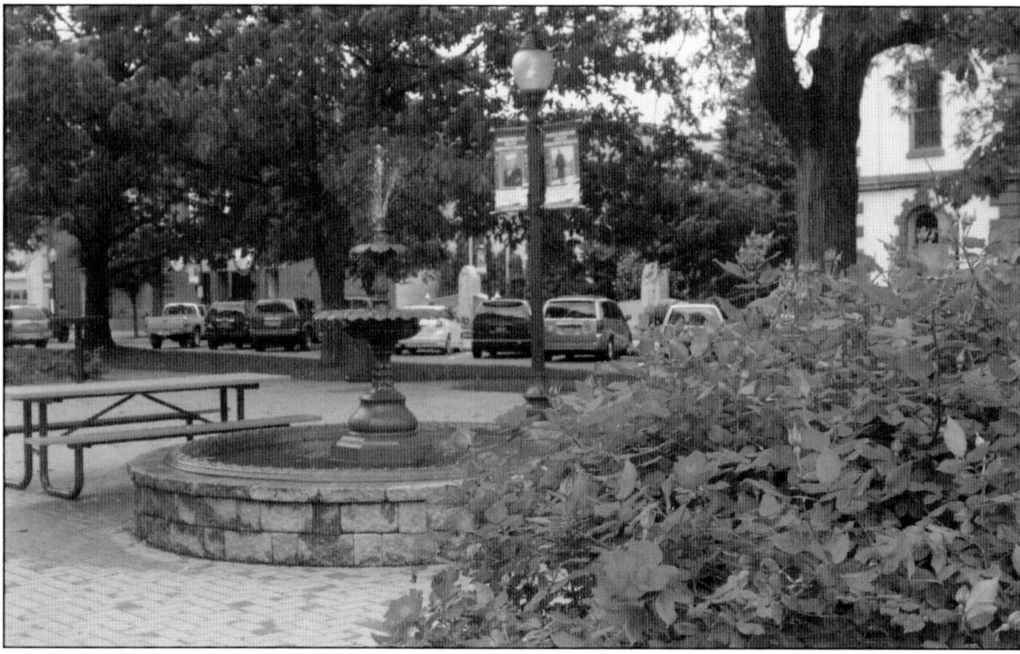

This is a photograph of the fountain constructed in the early 1900s and assembled in Cameron Park, which was designed by William Maclay. In Sunbury for about a century, the fountain has been recently restored so that the water is flowing and on display. (Courtesy of Klaus Krippendorff.)

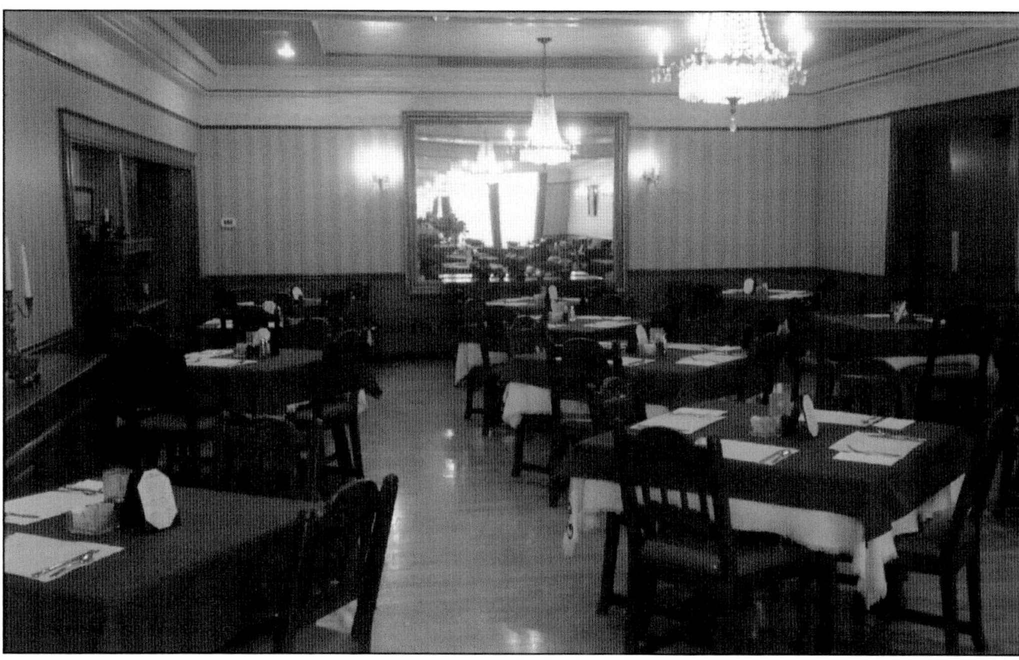

This is the current dining room of the historic Edison Hotel. The hotel and its dining room are the center of activity on Market Street. As in yesteryear, when the hotel first opened, it is known for fine dining and lodging. The lobby of the hotel contains a portrait of Thomas A. Edison as well as photographs, correspondence, and memorabilia. (Courtesy of Klaus Krippendorff.)

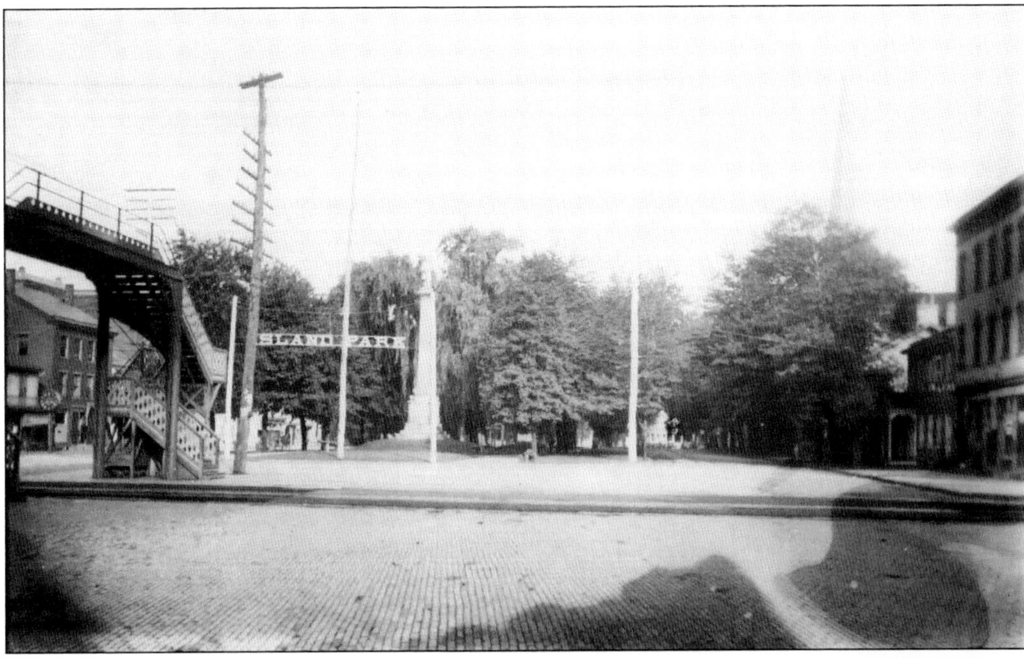

The old trolley stop at Cameron Park was used by fun-seekers traveling Island Park, the county's amusement park, which began operation in 1900. Parks along railroad lines began to crop up as a way to bring into town more people during the weekends and summer months—the slowest times for the railroad. With the construction of the railway through Sunbury, it was only natural that a park would be promoted along the way. The amusement park was located on Packer Island. (Courtesy of NCHS.)

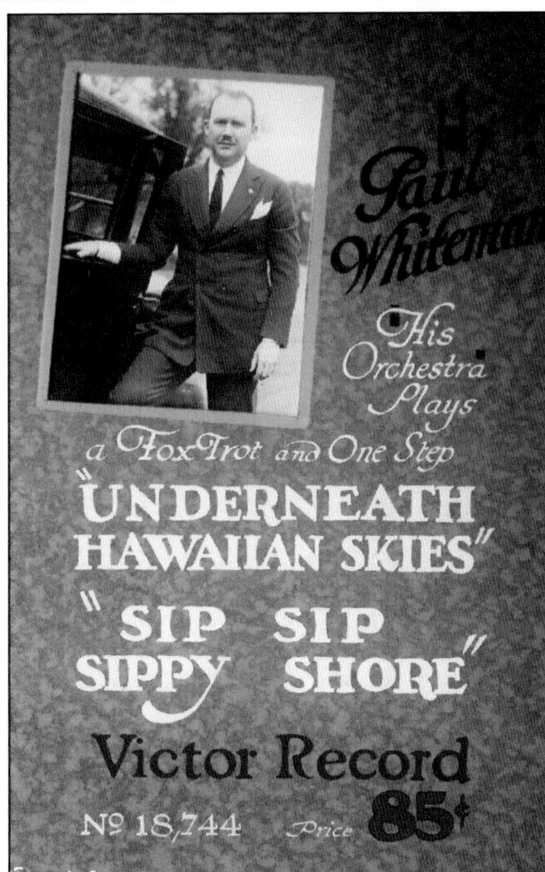

Paul Whiteman, billed as "the King of Jazz" by a clever press agent, played at the dance pavilion at Island Park. His first-issued records, "Whispering" and "Japanese Sandman," ushered in a new style of dance music. Shown here is an advertisement for his record, which cost 85¢. (Courtesy of the Library of Congress.)

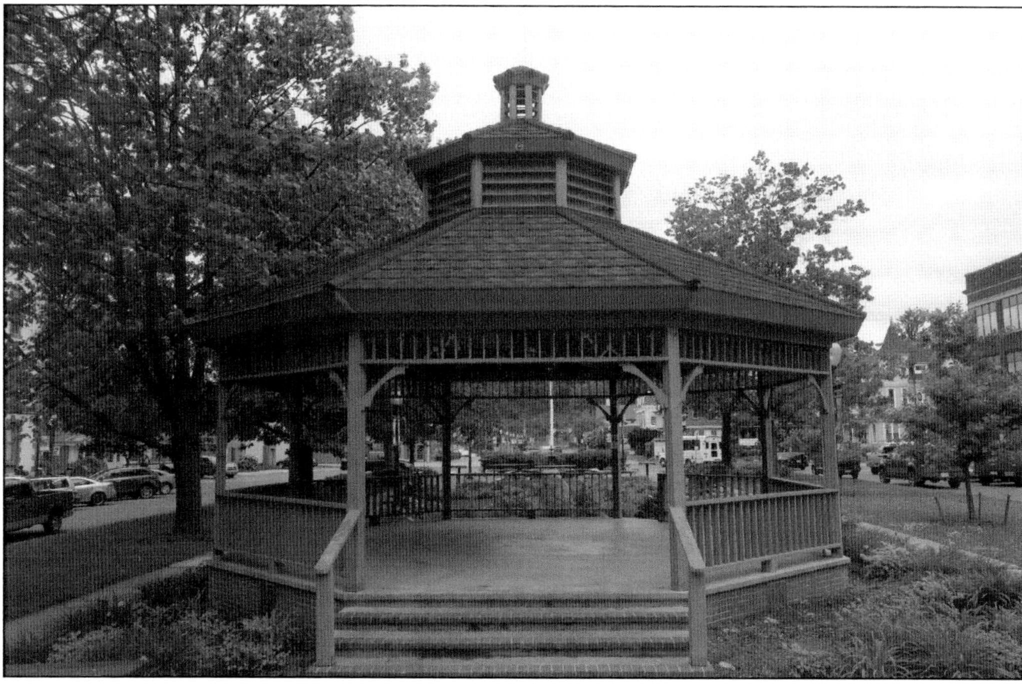

A gathering place for Sunbury residents, the newly built gazebo in Cameron Park is reminiscent of Sunbury's Victorian days. The park is the scene of many activities, and the gazebo hosts musical events as well as puppet shows for the children. (Courtesy of Klaus Krippendorff.)

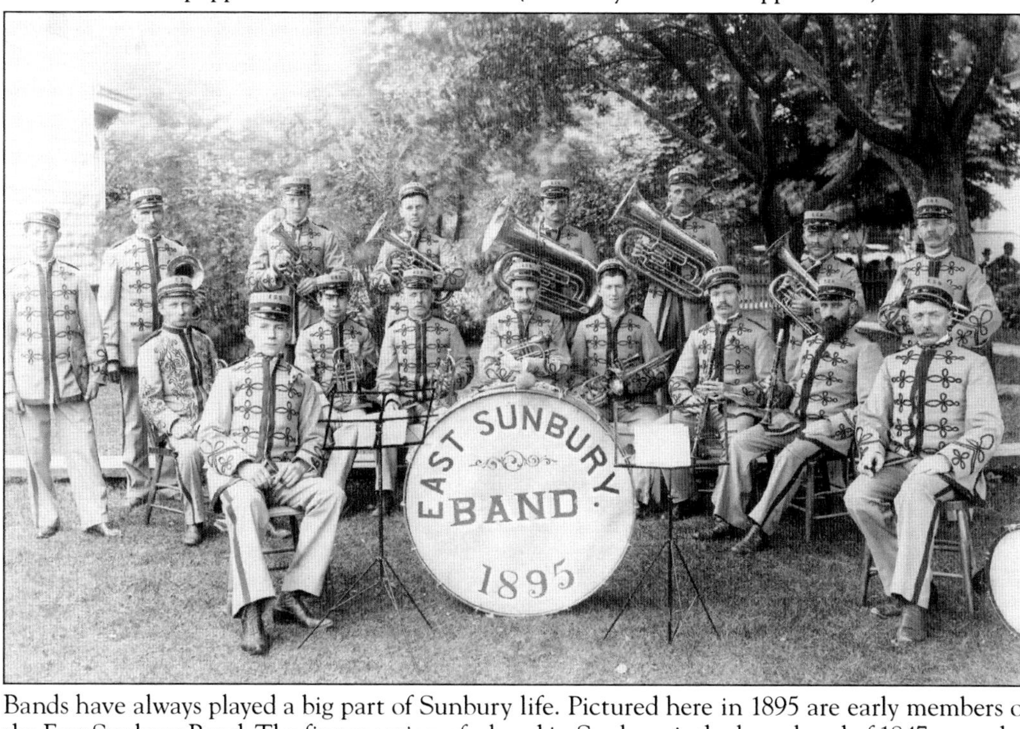

Bands have always played a big part of Sunbury life. Pictured here in 1895 are early members of the East Sunbury Band. The first mention of a band in Sunbury is the brass band of 1847, recorded in J.C. Irwin's *Reminiscences of Sunbury.* (Courtesy of NCHS.)

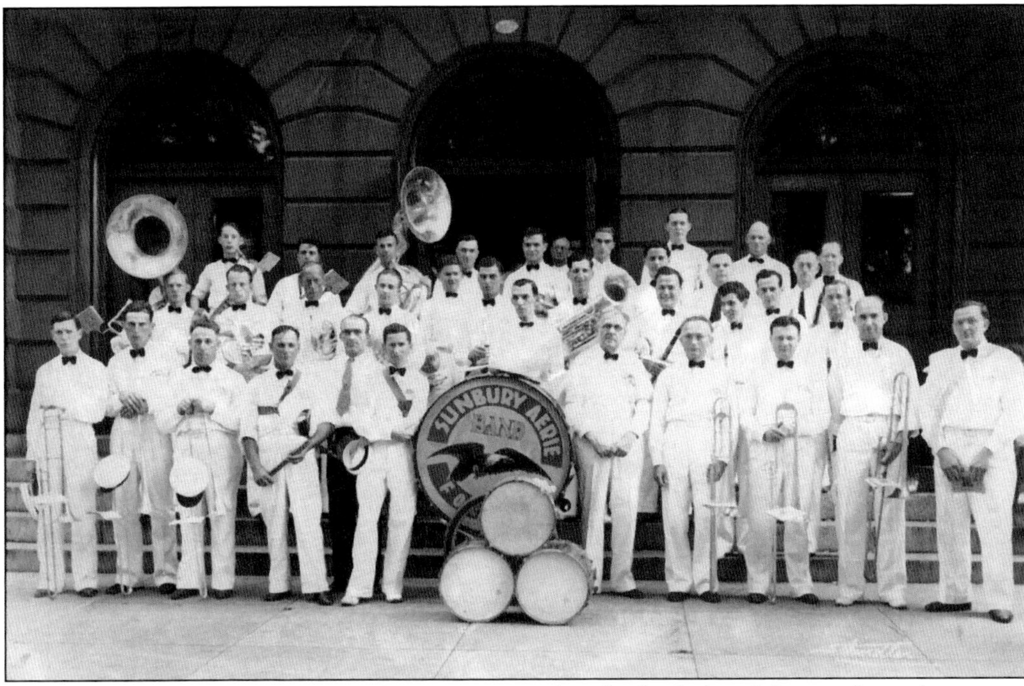

The Fraternal Order of Eagles, Sunbury Aerie No. 503 also had a band that performed at various venues around the county. The Sunbury Eagles currently operate a social room at 33 South Third Street for members and guests. The national Eagles organization was founded in 1898 and was initially open to men only. Now, membership is open to both men and women. (Courtesy of NCHS.)

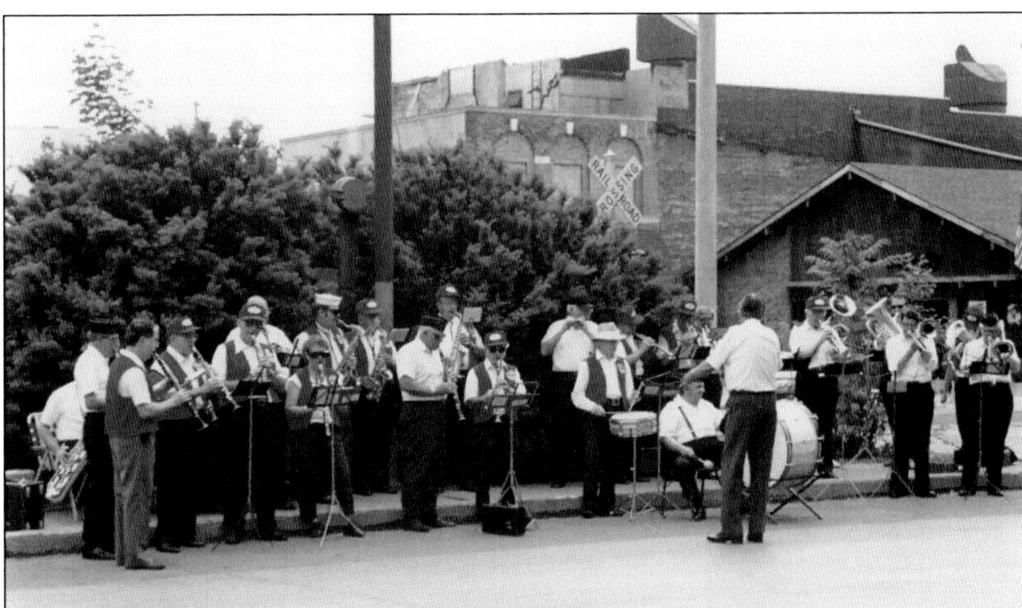

Pictured here is another of Sunbury's many musical ensembles playing in front of the Sunbury railroad station. Sunbury has a long musical history, with many bands taking part in parades and providing entertainment throughout the city. (Courtesy of NCHS.)

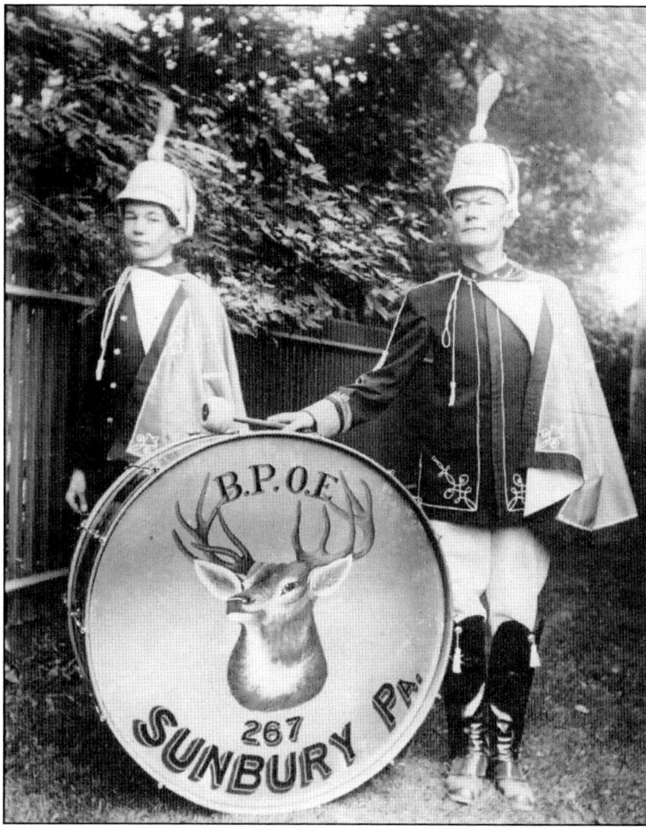

The Benevolent and Protective Order of Elks is a national civic organization that was founded on February 16, 1868. Members of the Sunbury Lodge No. 267 are shown here in ceremonial dress. They began organizing in 1893 and were officially granted a charter on June 14, 1894. William Cairns served as exalted ruler. Originally, the group met in the rooms of the Independent Order of Odd Fellows, but shortly after its founding, it moved to the Oppenheimer Building, where it continued to meet for 25 years. (Courtesy of NCHS.)

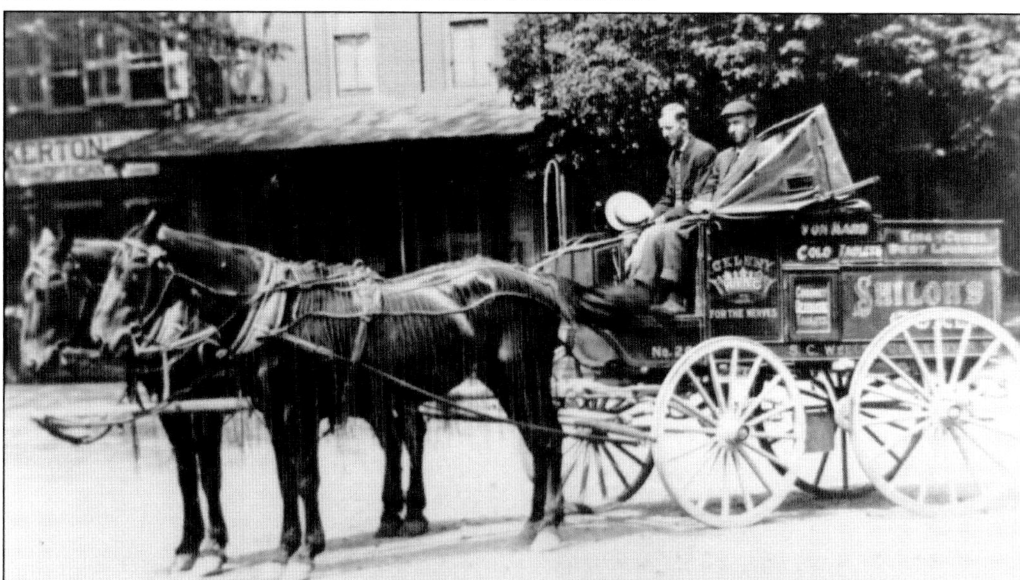

Not all business in Sunbury was conducted by rail or canal. Many small shop owners sold their wares via horse and buggy. Here, Shiloh's wagon, a pharmacy of sorts, stands in front of Keithan's store. According to the advertisement, the men are selling products for nerves, cold tablets, and sleeping draughts. (Courtesy of NCHS.)

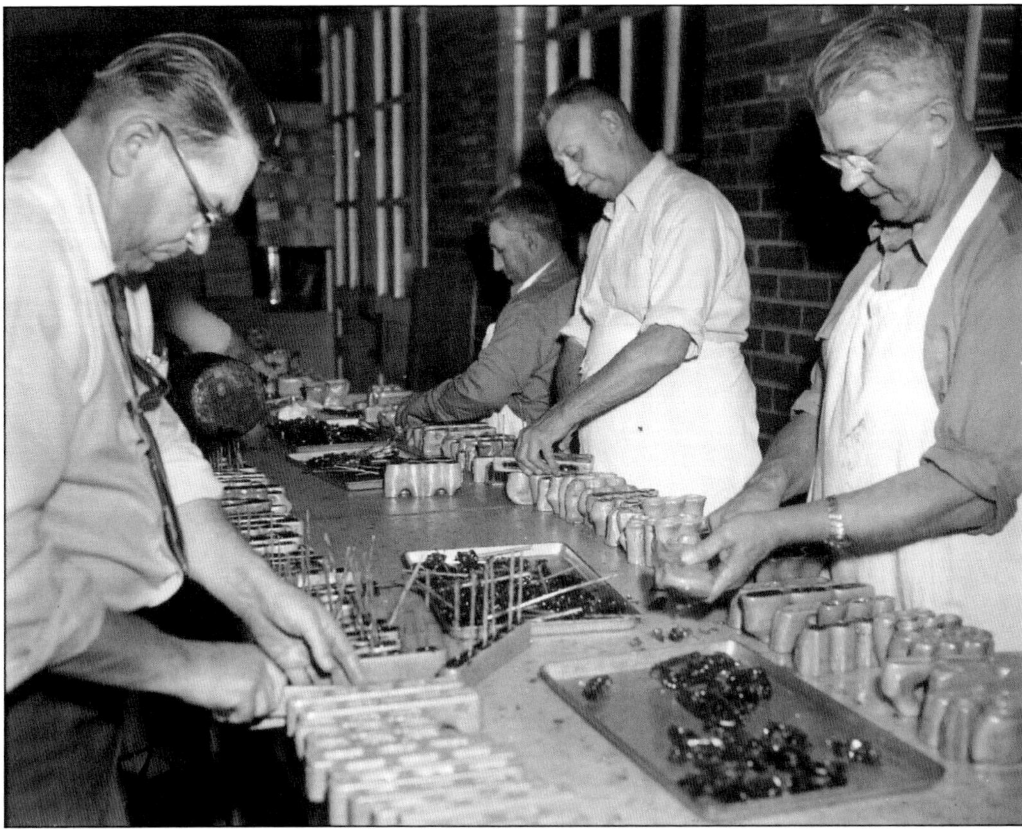

German confectioner John A. Keithan used candy molds from Germany because he considered those in the United States to be inferior. Shown here in this 1960 photograph are, from left to right, Dave Fegley, Frank dePhillips, J. William Keithan, and Charles Keithan. (Courtesy of NCHS.)

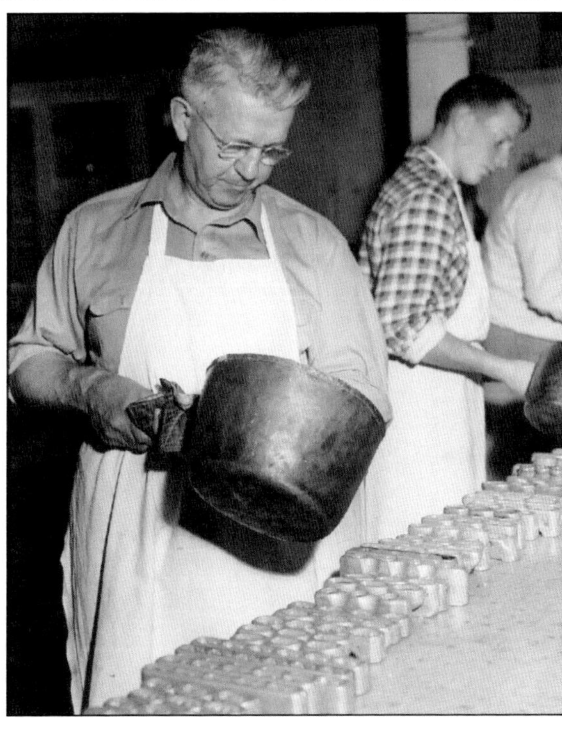

This is another view of the inside of John A. Keithan's shop. Charles Kethan is shown in the foreground, holding the large pot as he prepares hard candies for the holiday season. Note the molds are in various shapes, including those of reindeer, Santa, bells, and so on. (Courtesy of NCHS.)

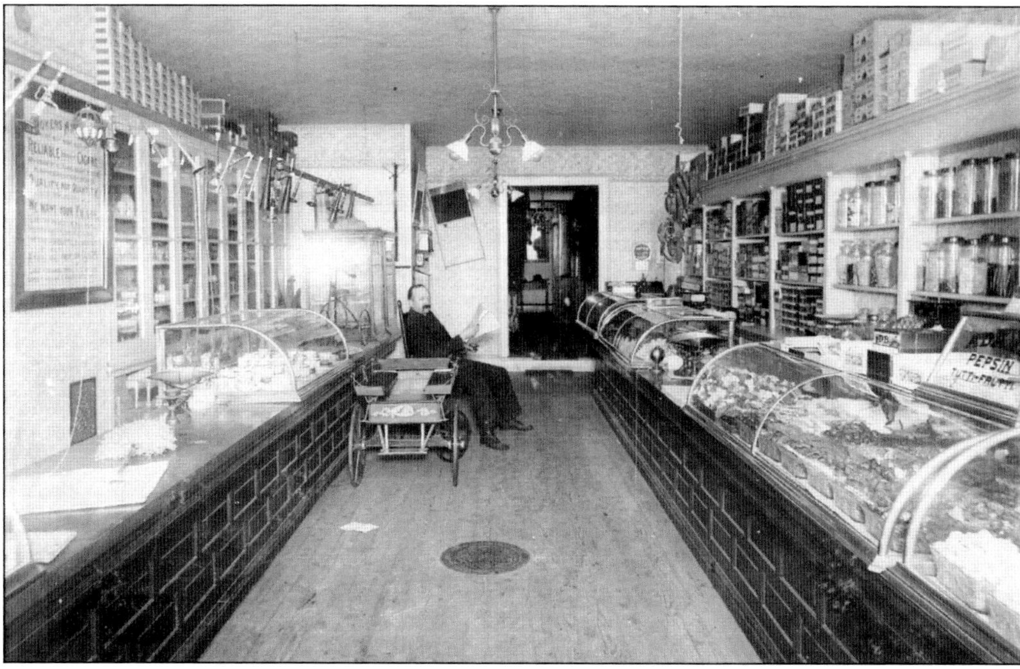

This 1908 photograph shows the inside of John Keithan's store, which at the time was located at 340 Market Street. An unidentified man is reading a newspaper. Keithan's store sold all kinds of confectioneries, such as candies, breads, cakes, and cookies. (Courtesy of NCHS.)

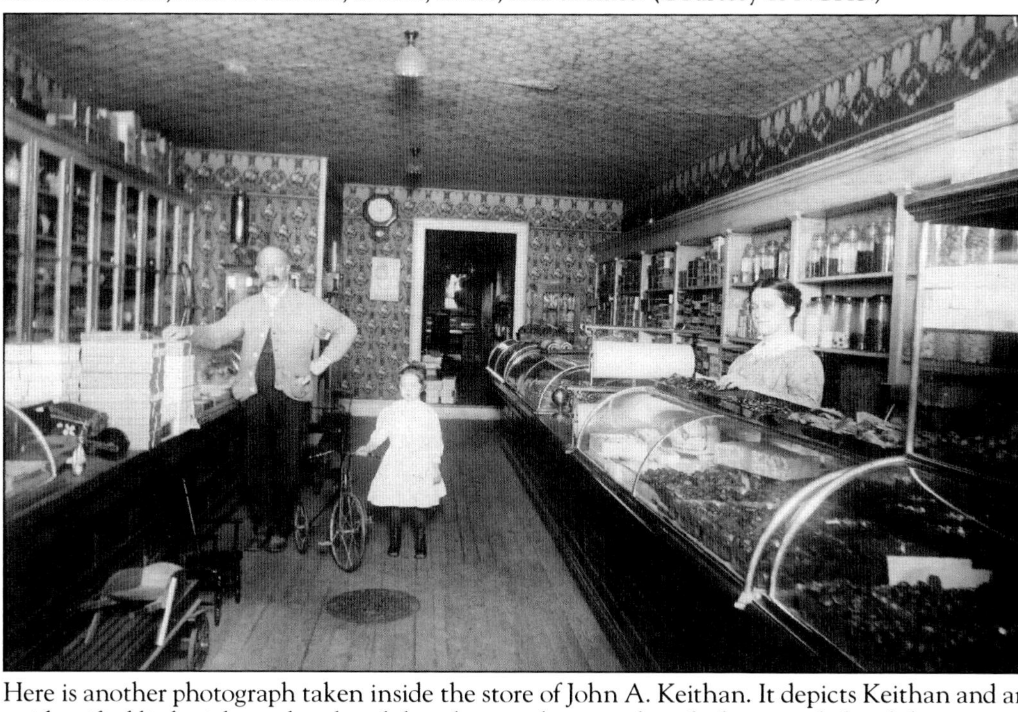

Here is another photograph taken inside the store of John A. Keithan. It depicts Keithan and an unidentified little girl standing by a bike, along with an unidentified woman behind the counter, ready to serve customers. The Keithans were an old and established Sunbury business family. (Courtesy of NCHS.)

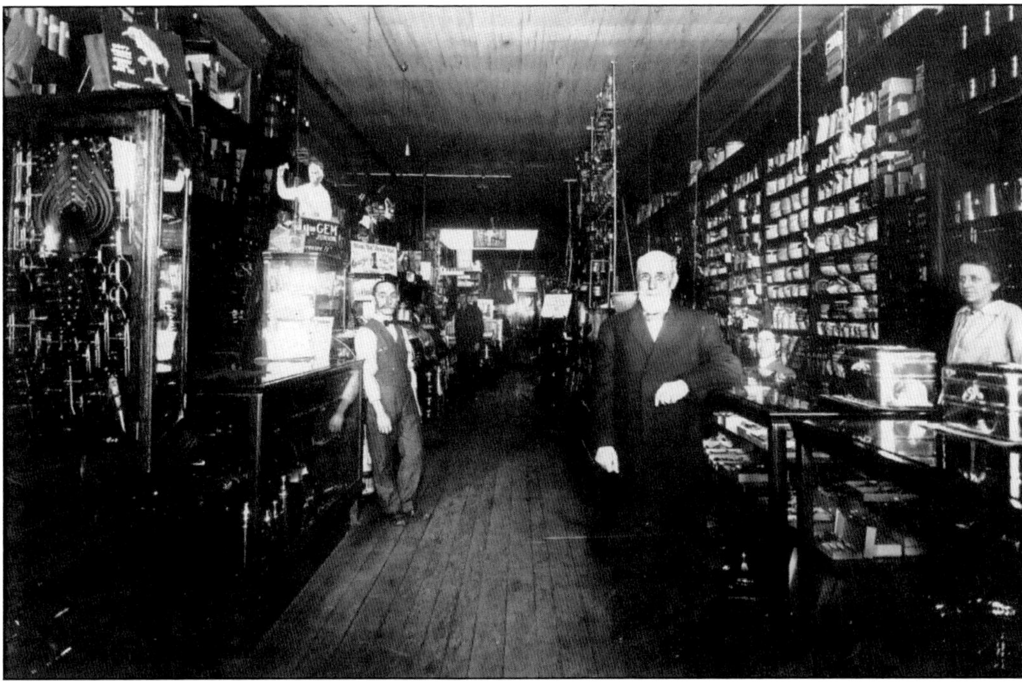

Hackers Hardware Store, which was located in the 300 block of Market Street, was a popular establishment for residents of Sunbury. Shown here are the proprietor of the shop in a dress suit and a salesman standing before the counter. Hacker's sold everything for the sportsman or the fixer-upper and was an important component of the commercial area of Sunbury in the early 1900s. (Courtesy of NCHS.)

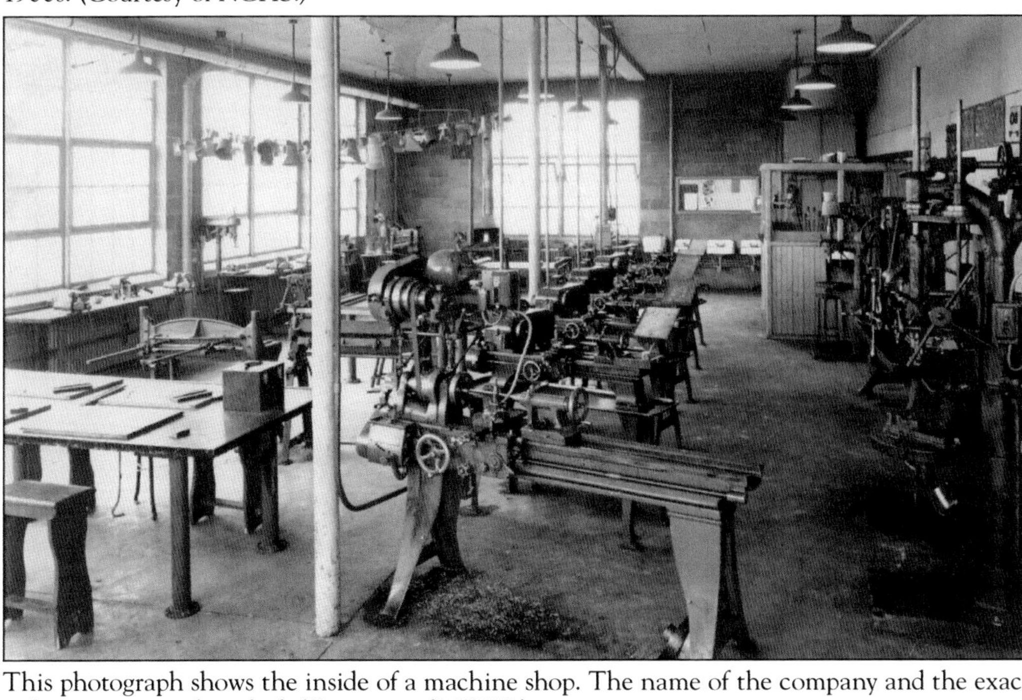

This photograph shows the inside of a machine shop. The name of the company and the exact industry are not identified. (Courtesy of NCHS.)

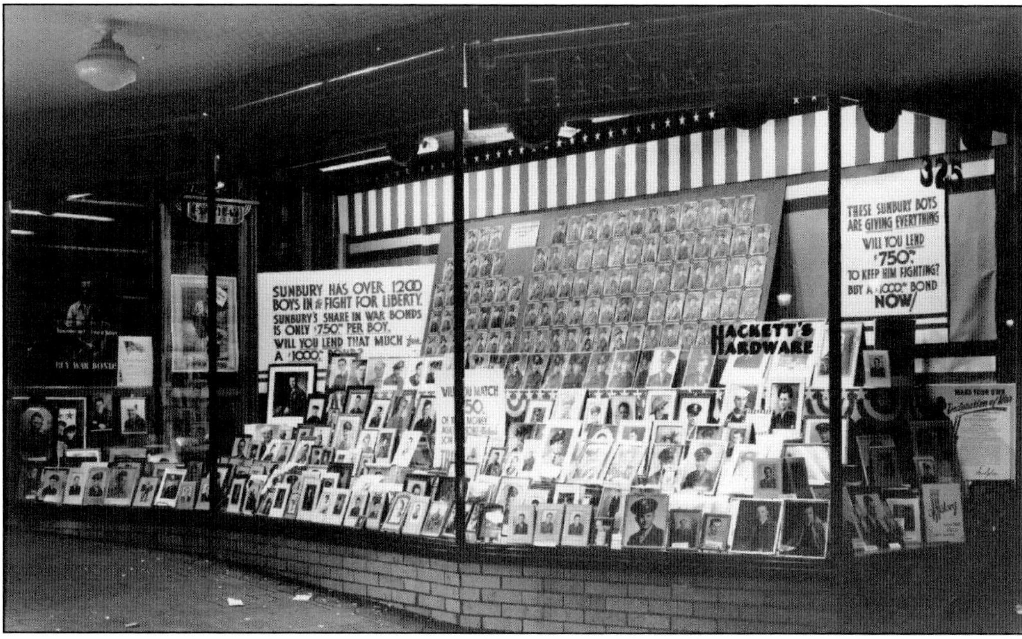

This unidentified storefront on Market Street shows pictures of the men serving in World War II. One sign in the window states the following: "Sunbury has over 1200 boys in the fight for liberty. Sunbury's share in war bonds is only $750.00 per boy. Will you lend that much for a $1000.00 bond?" (Courtesy of NCHS.)

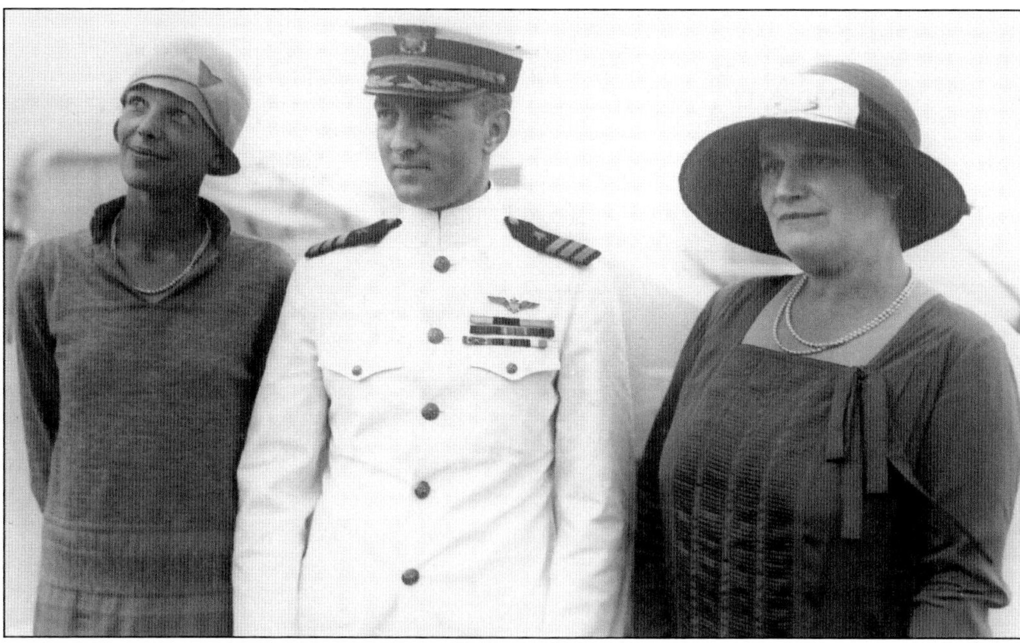

In this 1932 photograph following her successful transatlantic flight, which did make one stop in Sunbury, Amelia Earhart (left) is standing with Elizabeth Guest, an Englishwoman who backed the transatlantic flight of the *Friendship,* and Comdr. Richard E. Byrd. Earhart wrote, "We crossed the Hudson River, went a little south initially at 2,500 then up to 8,500 for smooth air, with a head wind all the way to Sunbury." (Courtesy of the Free Library of Philadelphia.)

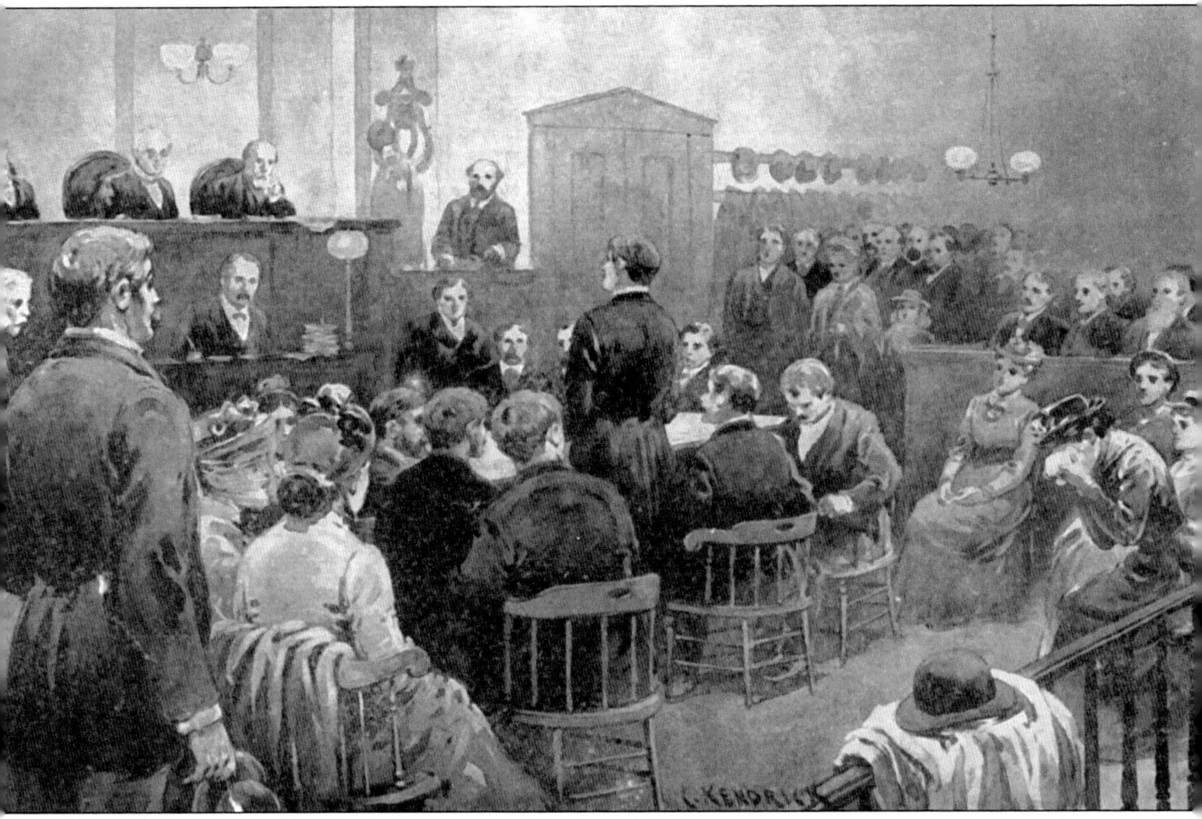

The Molly Maguires was an organization of Irish and Irish American coal miners working the anthracite mines as early as the Civil War. Miners earned very little, while the mine owners became rich. Members wanted to rectify this situation and did so by becoming vigilantes. They were accused of murder, kidnapping, arson, and other crimes, based on allegations by a Pinkerton detective. Many of the members of this organization were rounded up, tried and convicted, and put to death. One such accused was Peter McManus, the last of the Molly Maguires to be tried and convicted for murder, at the Northumberland County Courthouse in 1878. It is debatable how much of the widespread violence in the area was actually carried out by the Molly Maguires. (Courtesy of the Free Library of Philadelphia.)

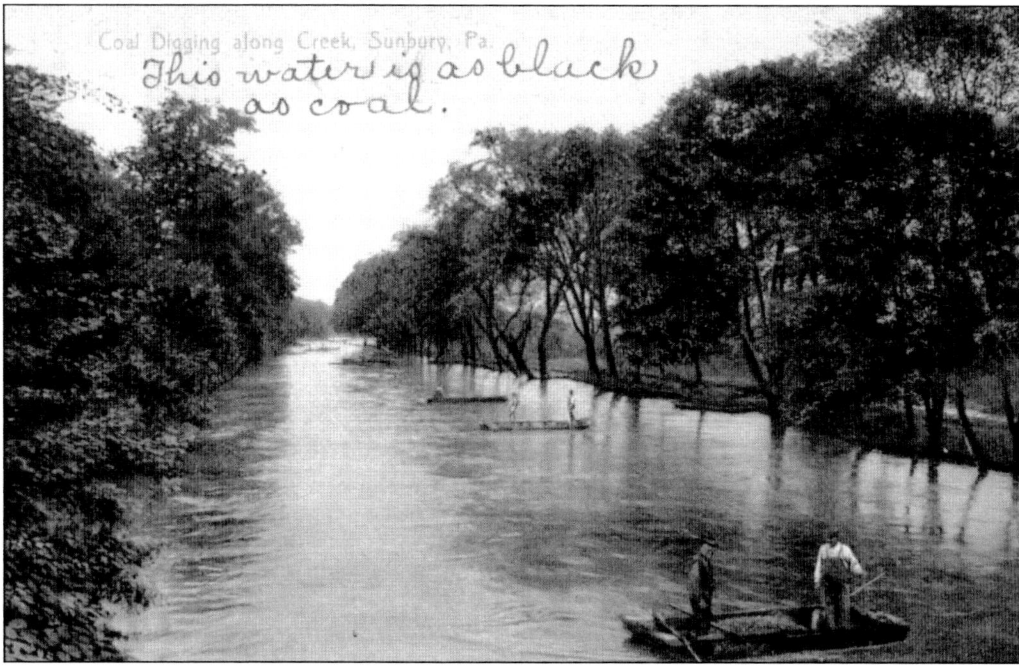

The bucolic nature of Sunbury in its formative years is evident in this early postcard; it shows men on a barge floating down a creek and looking for sites to dig for coal. On the postcard, someone has written, "This water is as black as coal." In the postcard of the west end of Cameron Park, one sees the village of Sunbury following a snowstorm. The scene depicts the loveliness of Sunbury's architecture. Nothing could be more beautiful than these images of both summer and winter in the early days of Sunbury. (Both, courtesy of Tim Auman.)

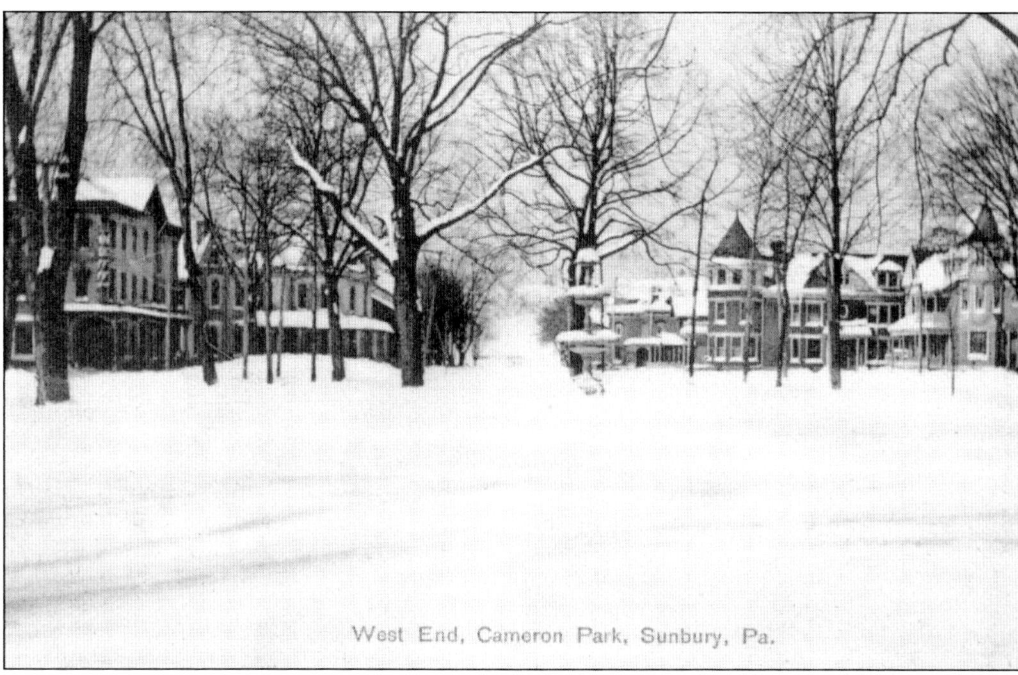

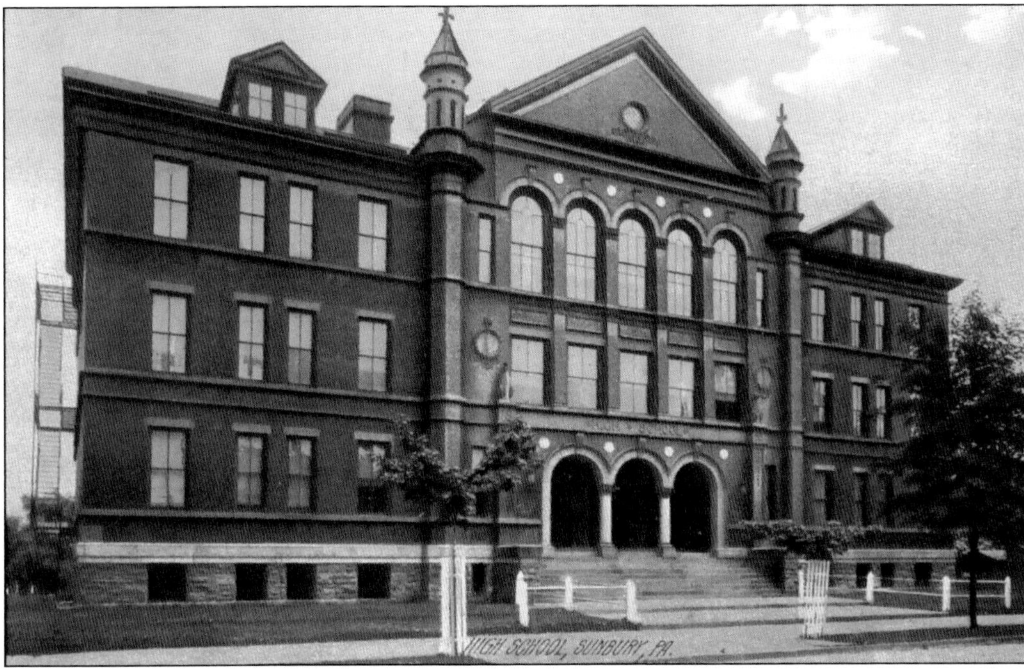

Shown here is the old Sunbury High School, which has now been replaced by the post office building. Many students from the high school still remember fondly their days at the school. Also shown is a view of the 1936 flood that virtually covered the town of Sunbury in water. This was one of the last floods the city experienced. At much cost, the city built a flood wall that contained the rising waters. (Both, courtesy of David Persing.)

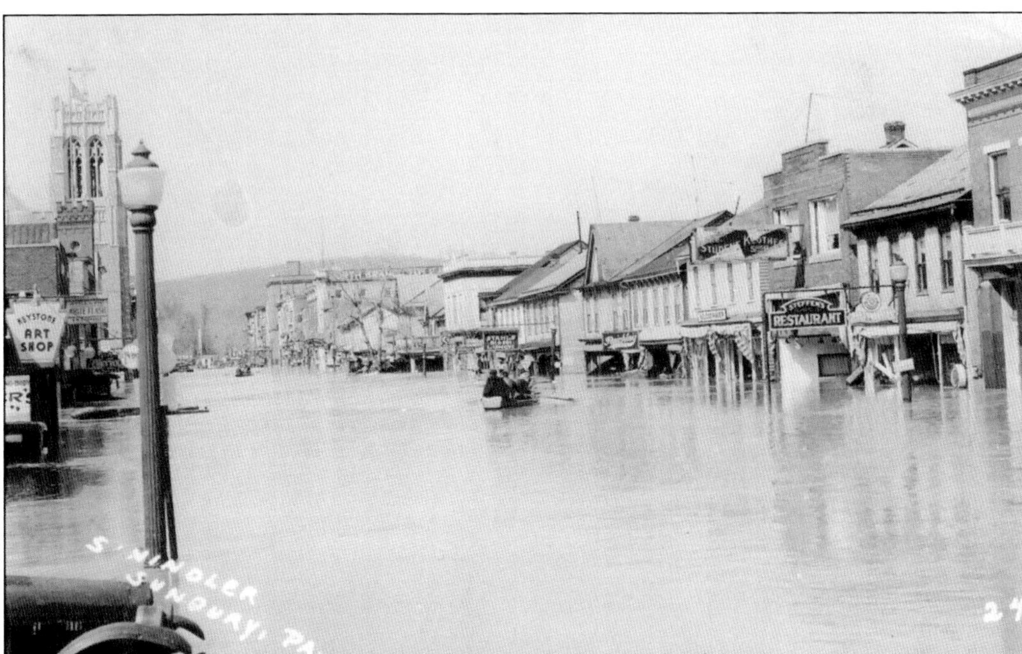

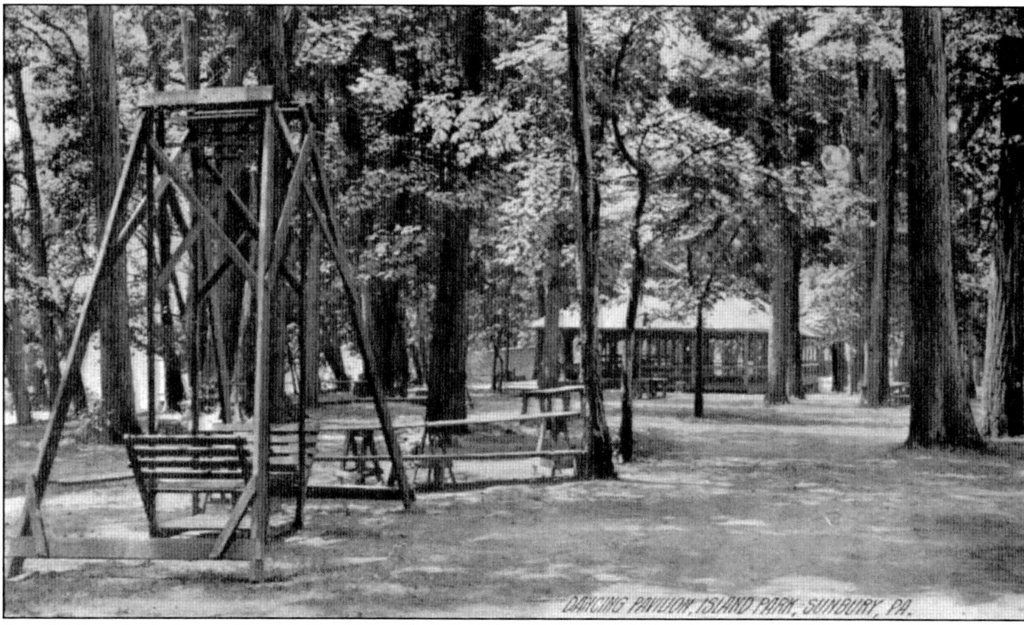

In 1925, a dance pavilion was erected on Packer Island. Some of the nation's big-name bands, including those led by Paul Whiteman, Fred Waring, and Joe Nesbit, played here for dancing. During the flapper era, marathon dances were also staged here. Eventually, there was also a restaurant, and a pool was added later. The pavilion was a popular place for many social events. (Courtesy of Tim Auman.)

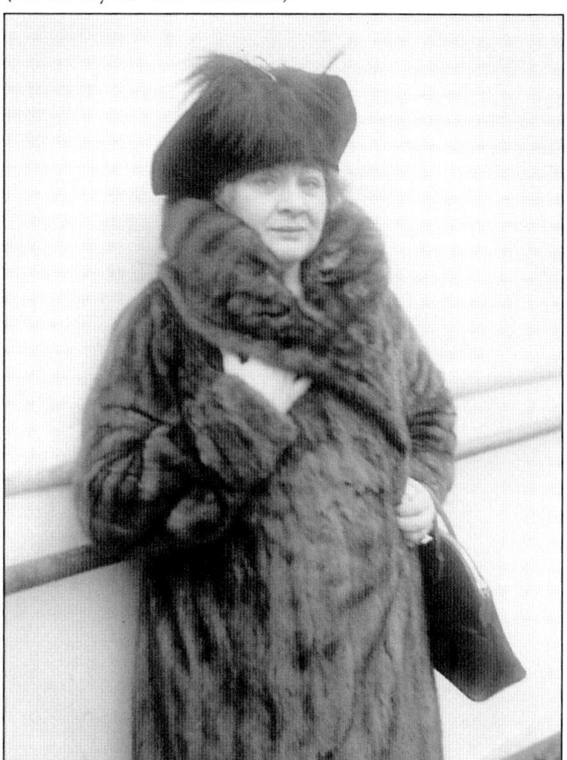

Sophie Tucker (1886–1966), who was born in Russia, became one of America's best-known entertains. She was a singer, comedienne, actress, and radio personality. She was often risqué, singing comical and ribald songs and was popular during the first half of the 20th century. Her nickname was "Last of the Red Hot Mamas." Tucker entertained the residents of Sunbury at the Chestnut Street Opera House. (Courtesy of the Library of Congress.)

Railroad tracks still run through the center of town today. This view is to the north up the tracks on West Third Street as seen from Market Street. In the old days, several churches in the area had to move as the train noise disturbed churchgoers. (Courtesy of Klaus Krippendorff.)

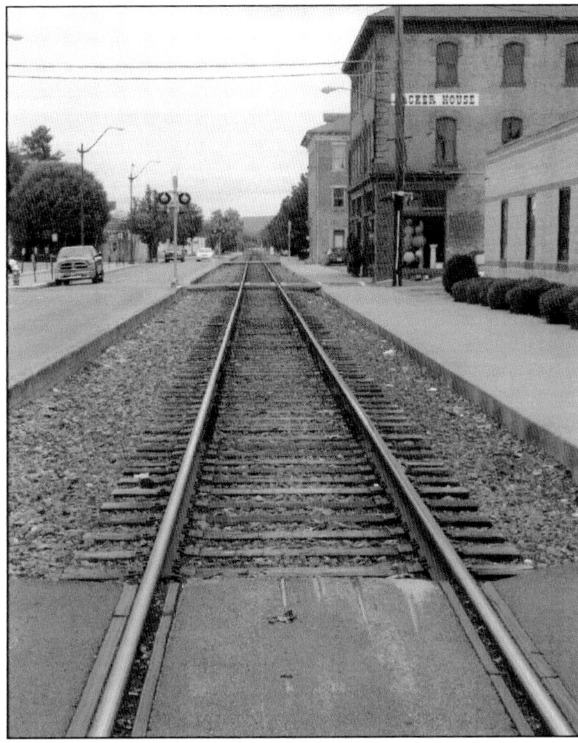

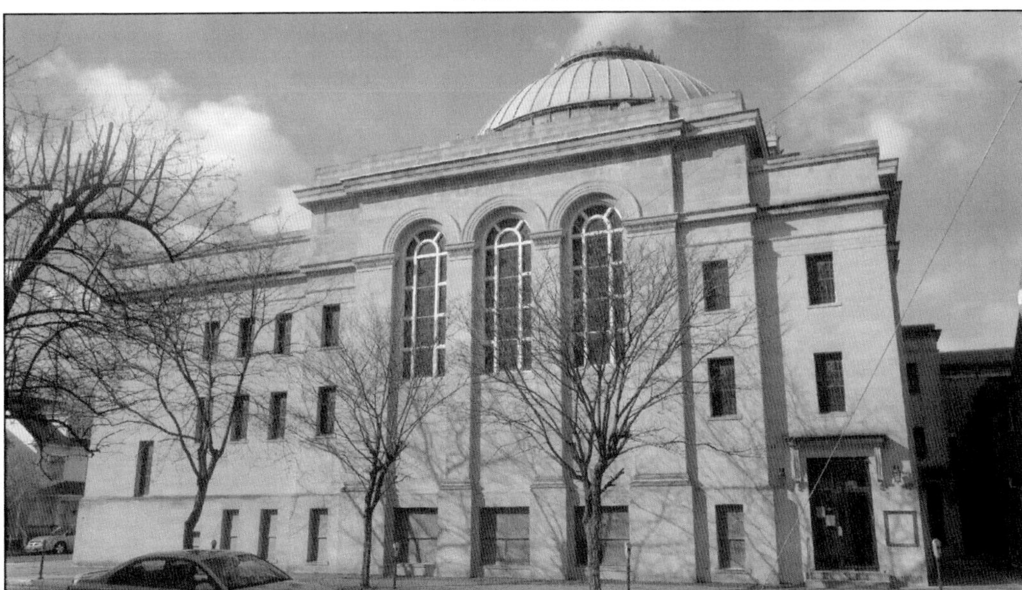

The beautiful Albright United Methodist Church, which closed in January 2011, is located at South Fifth and Chestnut Streets and is more than 80 years old. Its magnificent copper dome, with a green patina, and 32-inch thick granite walls add importance to downtown Sunbury. The cost to construct a building like this today would be around $10 million. The community is looking to use the structure as a performing arts center. (Photograph by Klaus Krippendorff, author's collection.)

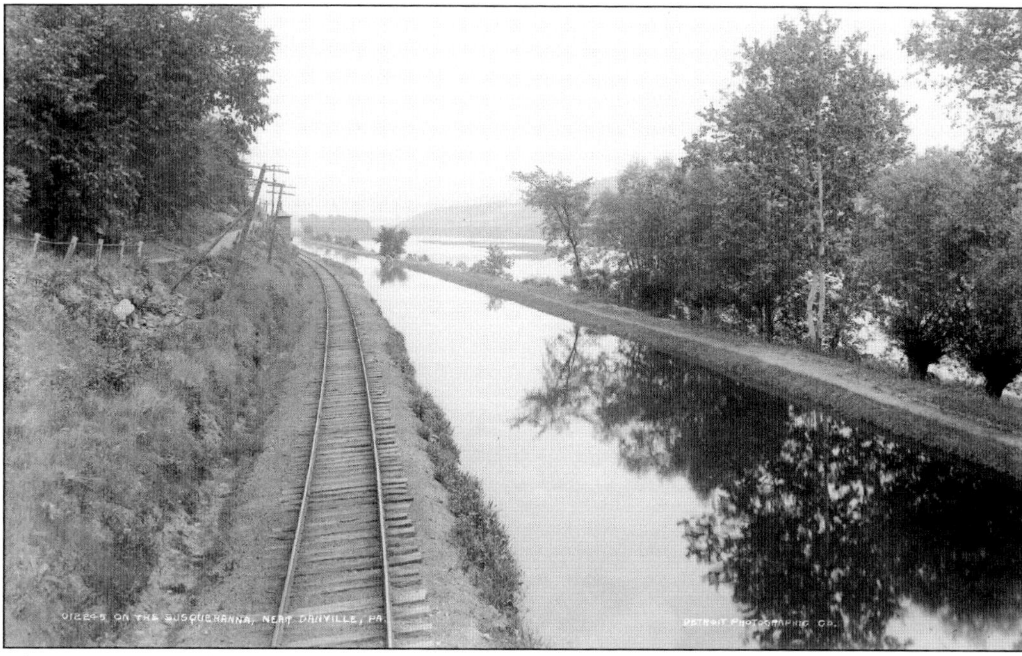

This is a view of the canal along the Susquehanna River and the railroad tracks. It helped transport material from Sunbury to other parts of the state and the Eastern Seaboard, which propelled Sunbury from a rural market town into a vibrant business community. (Courtesy of the Library of Congress.)

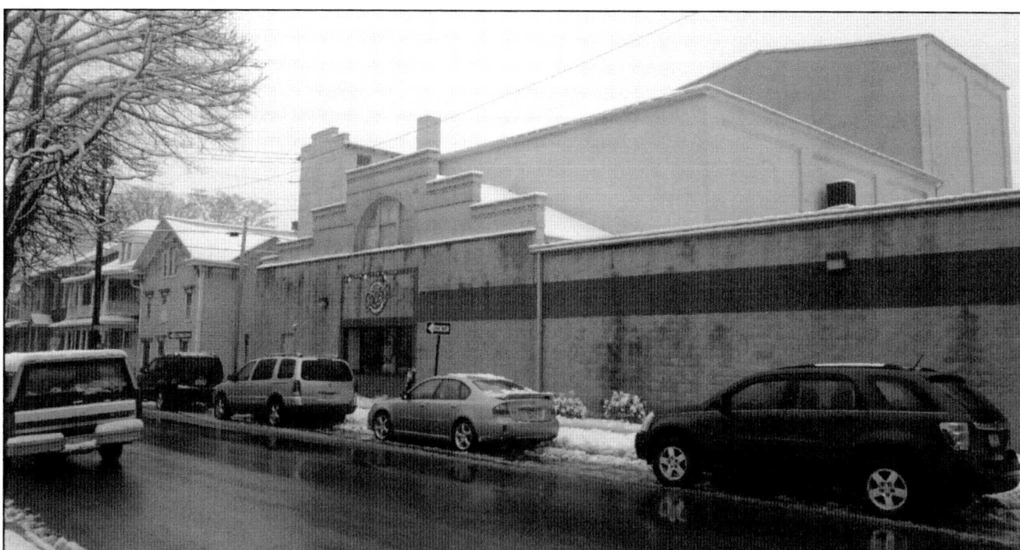

Present-day Cole's Hardware Store is located in the former Chestnut Street Opera House. The opera house opened on September 12, 1901, and could seat approximately 1,000 patrons. Many of the most popular vaudeville acts performed here, such as Sophie Tucker, Marie Dressler, Walter Huston, and Tyrone Power. Every city that considered itself civilized had an opera house that would book acts of all kinds—none of which were remotely connected with opera. Prior to this building's construction, "opera" was held at the Northumberland County Courthouse. (Courtesy of Klaus Krippendorff.)

Six

NCHS

Since 1925, the Northumberland County Historical Society has endeavored to preserve, promote, and publish the county's rich and diverse history. The society was chartered on October 26, 1925, with 138 members and incorporated on May 21, 1928. It now has more than 475 members from Pennsylvania, 21 from other states and the District of Columbia, and also from two Canadian provinces, each having a connection to Northumberland County or an interest in its history. Headquartered at the Hunter House, the site of Fort Augusta, at 1150 North Front Street, the society, a 501(c)(3) not-for-profit organization, operates a genealogical research library and a museum that includes a permanent exhibit about Fort Augusta and changing exhibits on other aspects of the county's history and material culture.

Over the years, the society has met in a number of different locations, including the Hunter House, the Northumberland County Courthouse, and the John R. Kauffman Jr. Public Library. In 1930, the Commonwealth of Pennsylvania acquired the strip of land where the two remaining fort features—the powder magazine and well—are situated. And in 1931, it also acquired the Hunter House tract. In 1987, Hunter House became the society's headquarters, and an extensive renovation restored the brick house to its original 1848 appearance and added meeting space at the rear of the structure. NCHS negotiated with the Pennsylvania Historical and Museum Commission to acquire the property in 2004. Volunteers continue to operate the library and museum. Fundraising efforts are underway to rebuild the Fort Augusta model on the front lawn of Hunter House, with construction slated to begin during the summer of 2013.

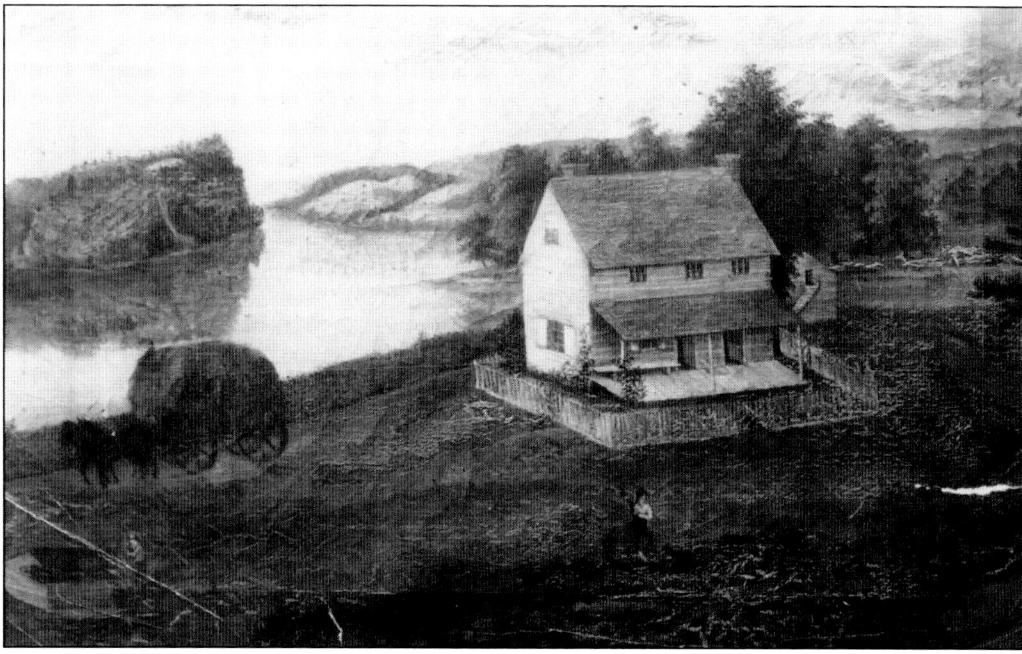

This is an unidentified artist's rendering of the early commandant's cabin on the site of Fort Augusta. It was the home of Col. Samuel Hunter, who continued to live there even after Fort Augusta deteriorated after the Revolutionary War. Colonel Hunter was responsible for the protection and support of smaller forts in the area. (Courtesy of NCHS.)

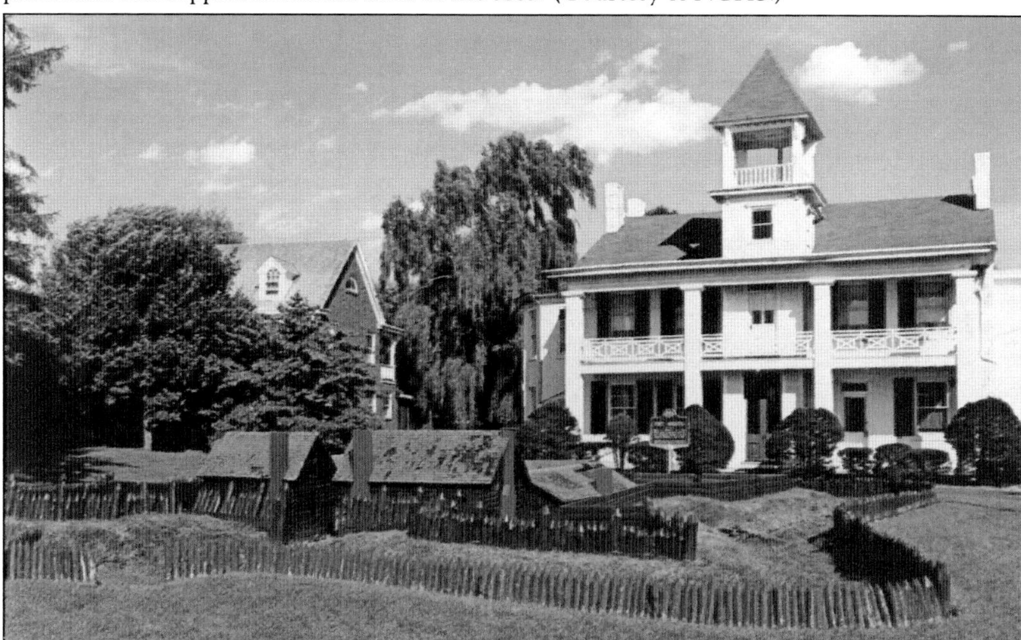

This is another view of Hunter House, with the elaborate changes that were made to the house. A scale model of Fort Augusta is shown in the foreground. Hunter's descendants lived there until 1848, when the log house burned down. The present Hunter House was built by a descendant of Col. Samuel Hunter. (Courtesy of NCHS.)

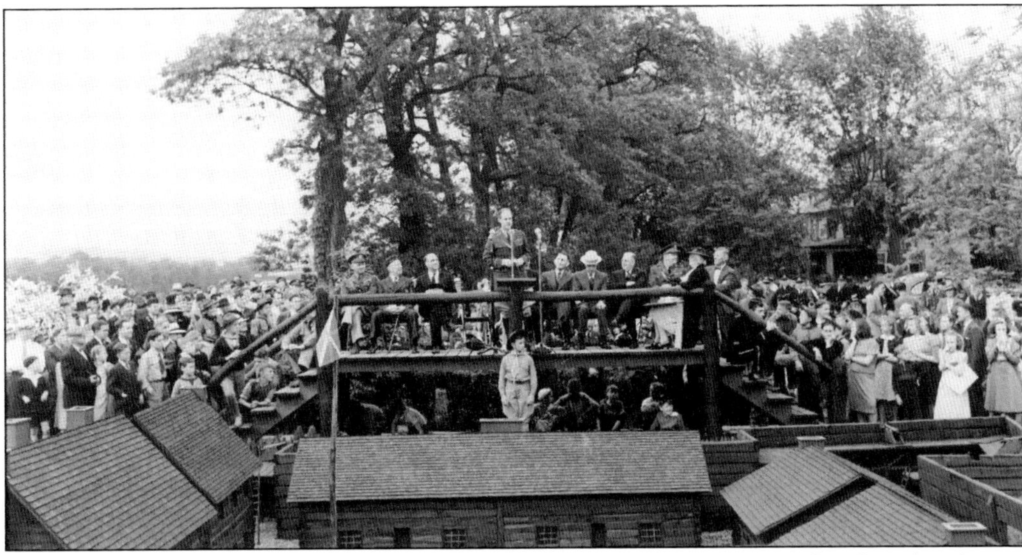

This photograph taken on the grounds of the Hunter House shows a crowd gathered in front of a large replica of Fort Augusta. Standing on the platform, an unidentified person addresses the people of the city of Sunbury. Also on the platform are members of the military and officials from NCHS. (Courtesy of NCHS.)

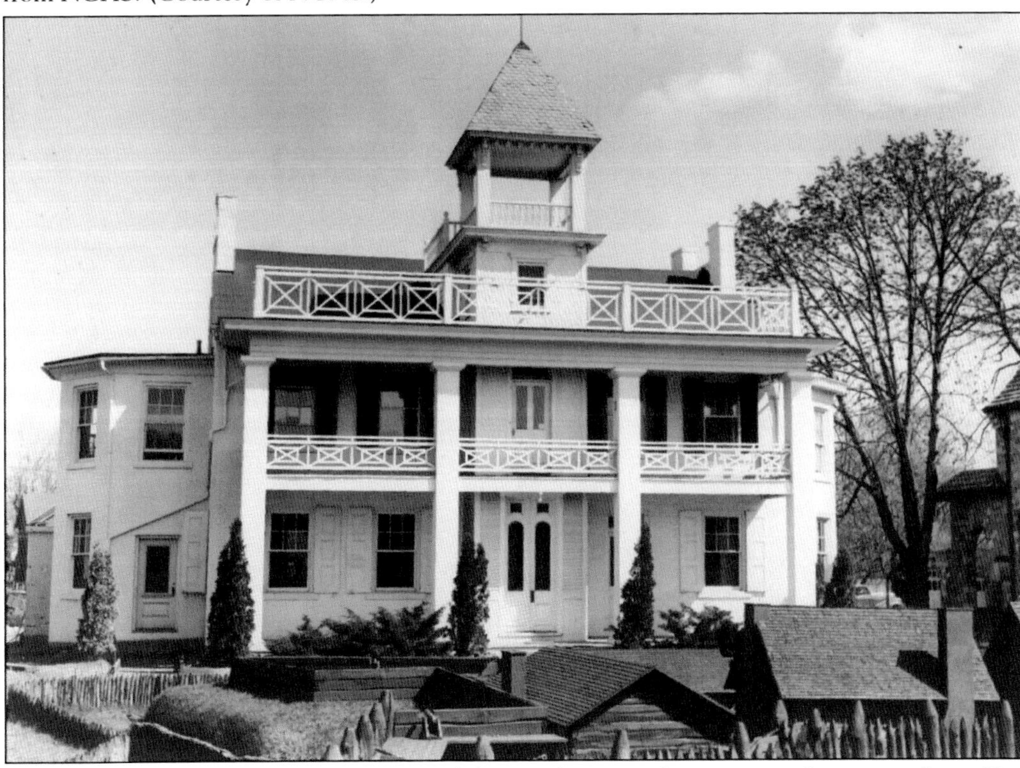

This photograph shows Hunter House, with large columns in front, a second-story porch, and bay windows on each side of the house. In addition to a porch to the top of the building, a cupola was also constructed. These elaborations were eventually removed to make the house more historically authentic. (Courtesy of NCHS.)

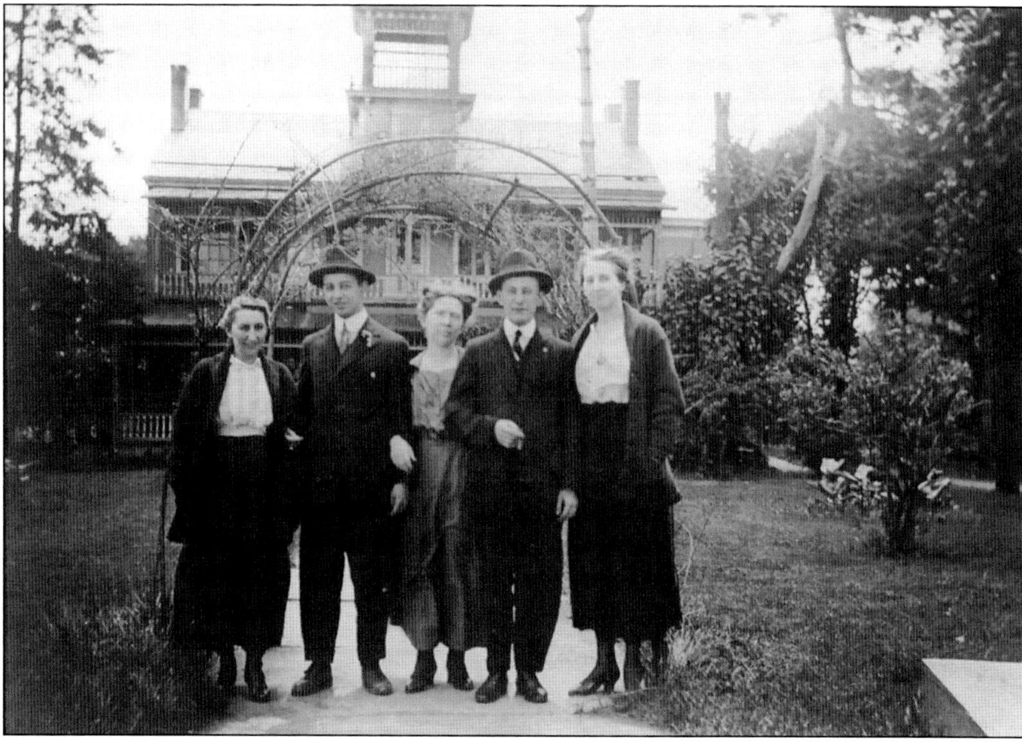

This very early and undated photograph shows five residents of Sunbury, one of whom is Edna Geisinger (center) of the family that started the Geisinger Clinic, now a huge medical complex 20 miles from Sunbury. They stand on the front lawn of Hunter House, before the columns and side additions were built. It is interesting to note the fashions of the day. (Courtesy of David Persing.)

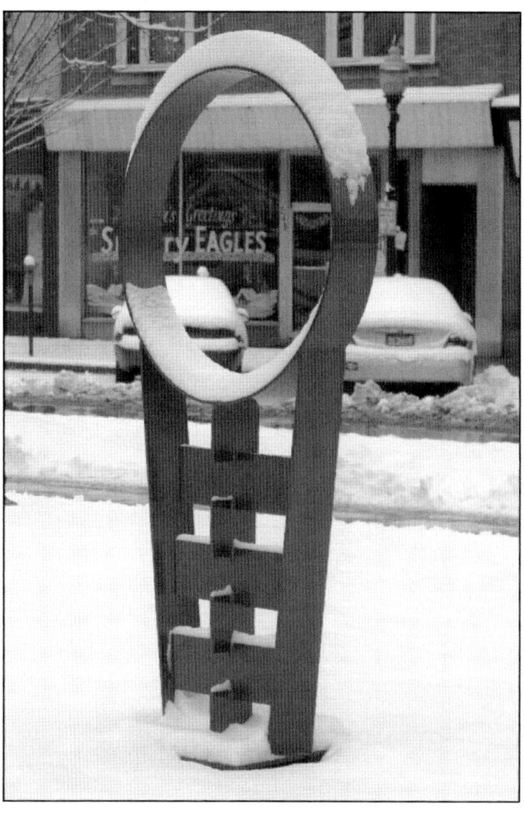

This unusual sculpture in Cameron Park in the center of Sunbury was fashioned and donated by attorney Jeff Apfelbaum. The freestanding piece, called *Optimism*, uses design elements from around Sunbury, like quoins from the courthouse and circles from the courthouse clock and the Presbyterian church. The geometric forms come from looking at the landscape in Sunbury. (Photograph by Klaus Krippendorff, author's collection.)

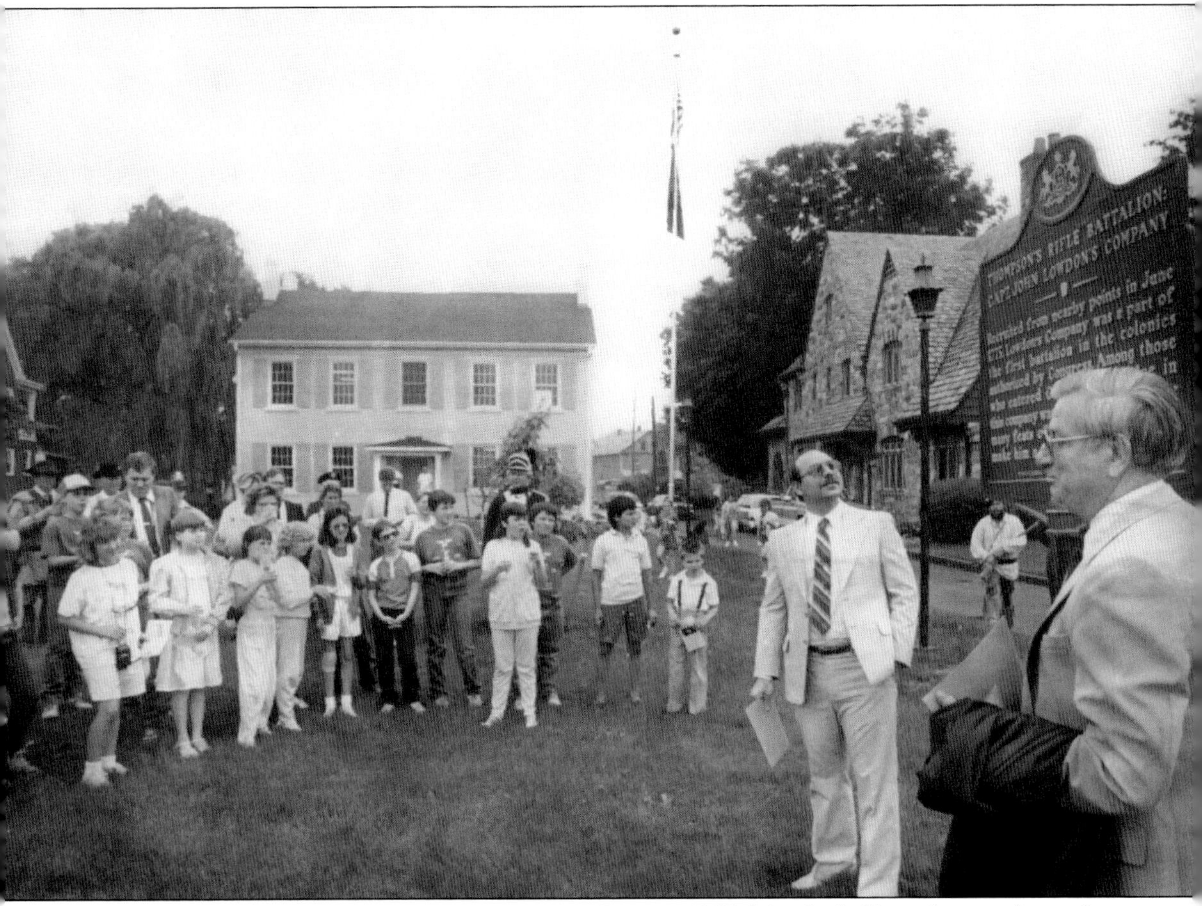

At the dedication ceremony at Hunter House on June 4, 1987, Maj. Jack Hetrick, president of the historical society (front), and teacher Mark O. Hagenbuch unveil a new historical marker in front of Hunter House as a fifth-grade class and others look on. Major Hetrick was president of the historical society from 1982 until 1989 and then president emeritus from 1989 until 1997. He wrote several books for the historical society, including *Some Afterthoughts on the Fort Augusta Dig* and *The Elliott-Davis House in Northumberland*. Major Hetrick was also in the Army and was an amateur archaeologist. (Courtesy of NCHS.)

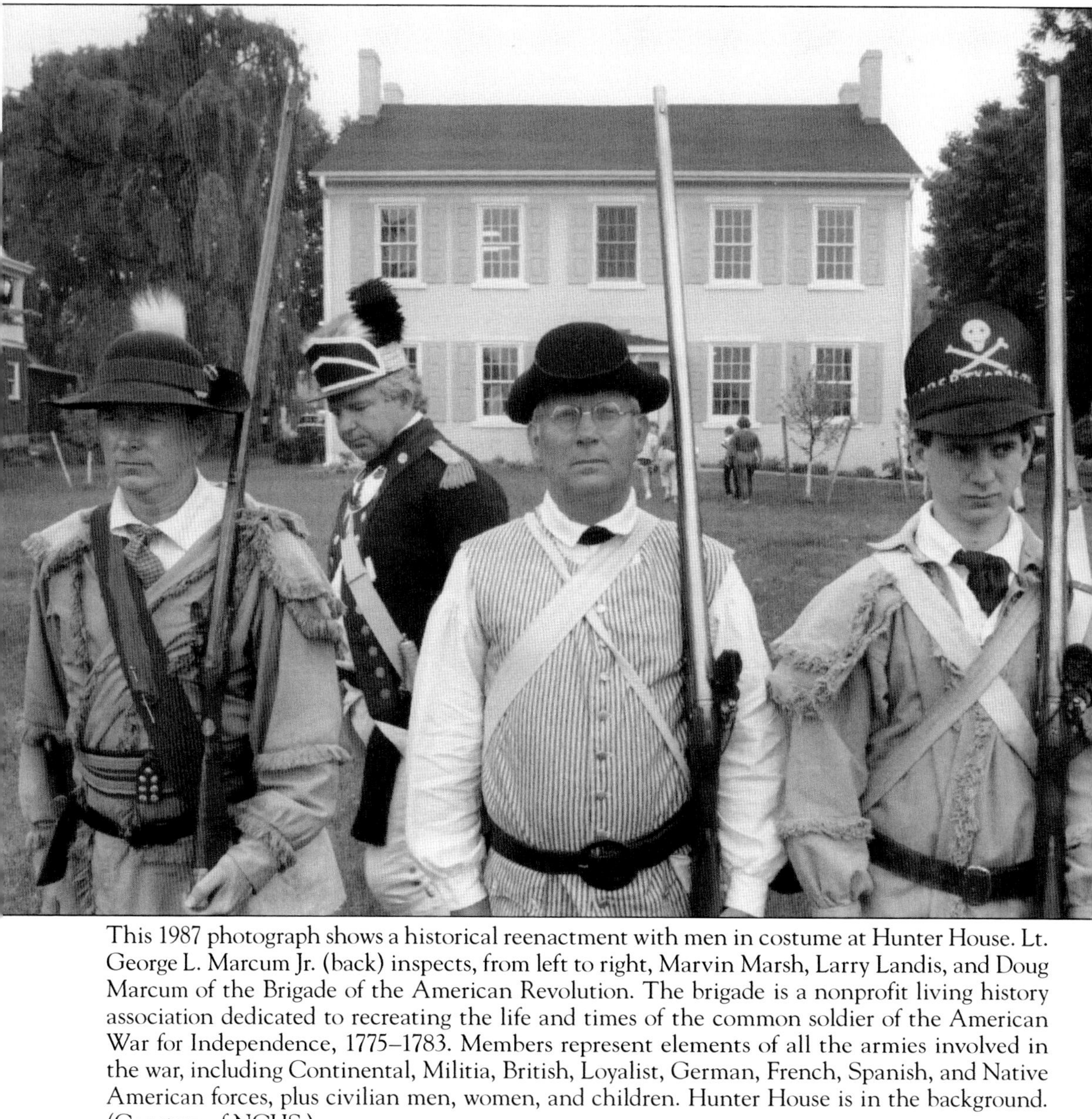

This 1987 photograph shows a historical reenactment with men in costume at Hunter House. Lt. George L. Marcum Jr. (back) inspects, from left to right, Marvin Marsh, Larry Landis, and Doug Marcum of the Brigade of the American Revolution. The brigade is a nonprofit living history association dedicated to recreating the life and times of the common soldier of the American War for Independence, 1775–1783. Members represent elements of all the armies involved in the war, including Continental, Militia, British, Loyalist, German, French, Spanish, and Native American forces, plus civilian men, women, and children. Hunter House is in the background. (Courtesy of NCHS.)

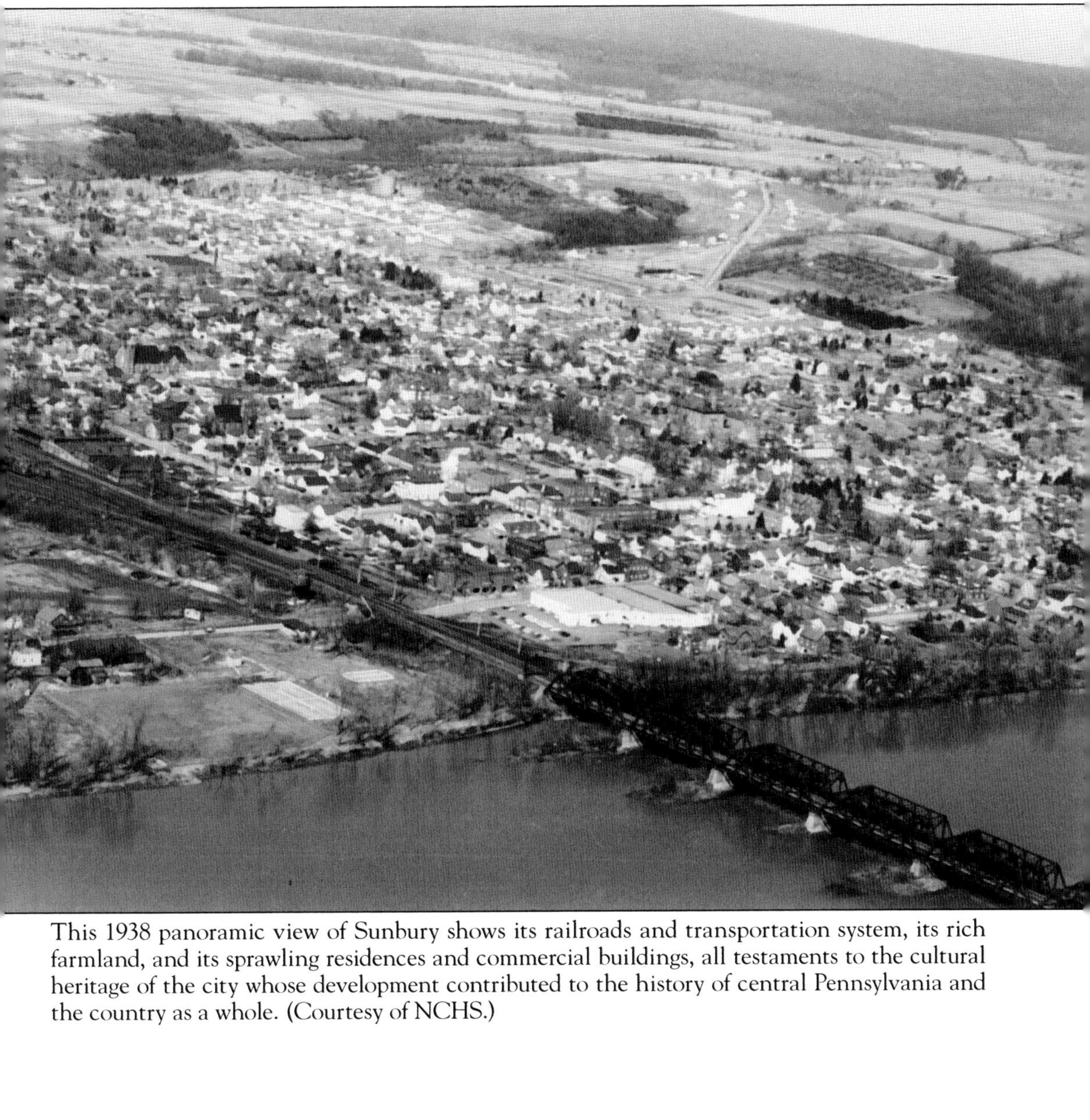

This 1938 panoramic view of Sunbury shows its railroads and transportation system, its rich farmland, and its sprawling residences and commercial buildings, all testaments to the cultural heritage of the city whose development contributed to the history of central Pennsylvania and the country as a whole. (Courtesy of NCHS.)

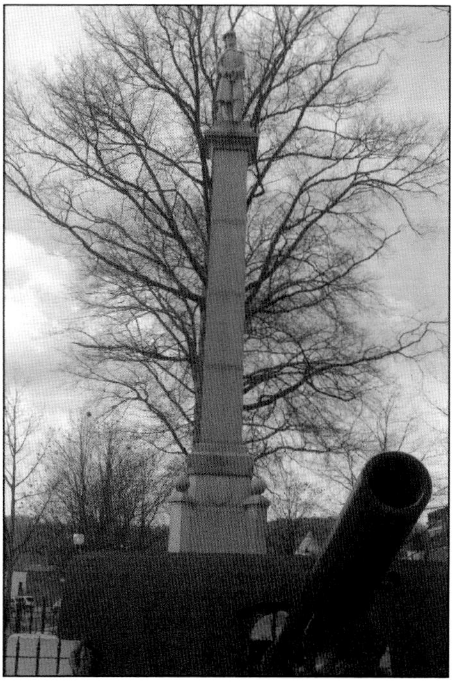

Today, this Civil War monument is the centerpiece of Cameron Park. The obelisk rises above the trees to commemorate the soldiers and sailors who served during that time. At the very top of the structure is a sculpture of Col. James Cameron, a native of Sunbury who fell during the Battle of Bull Run in 1861. Artillery and ship's cannons surround the memorial. A dedication to Colonel Cameron is inscribed on the base. Construction on this monument began in May 1874 and was completed on July 4, 1879. (Courtesy of Klaus Krippendorff.)

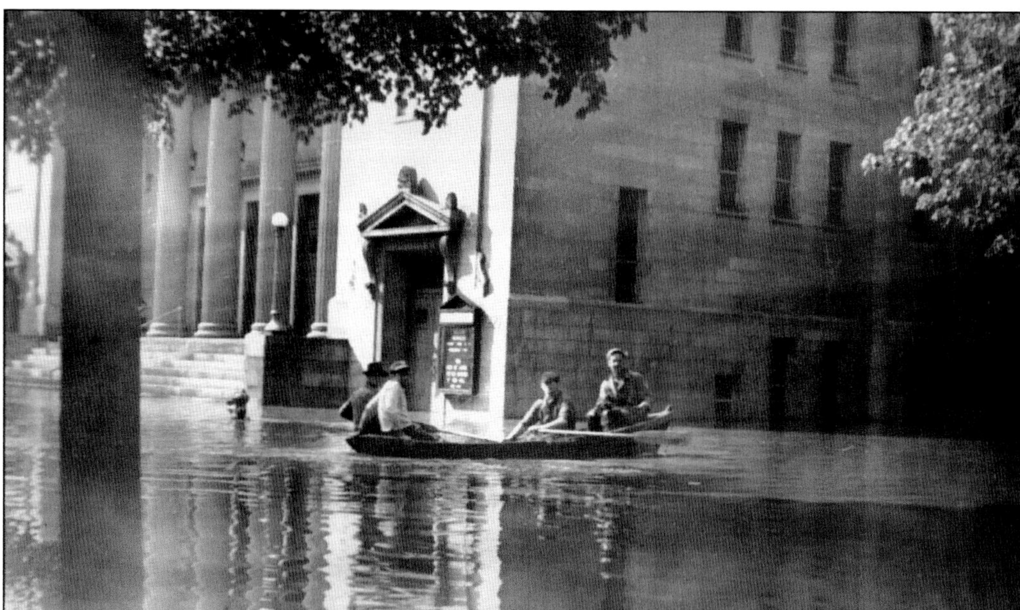

This picture is of one of the floods that submerged the city. Four people row down Market Street, surveying the damage to the town. This was not the first time residents rowed city streets. During some of the worst modern-day floods, power was interrupted, making it impossible for people to get information as water surged through streets and homes. During the 1936 flood, for more than 48 hours, many business, homes, and offices were underwater. Water was pumped from cellars, and rubbish and spoiled merchandise were hauled to a dump and burned. There was a $4,000,000 loss in property damage. Sunbury owes a debt of gratitude to Shamokin, Mount Carmel, and other communities for the food and supplies furnished. (Courtesy of NCHS.)

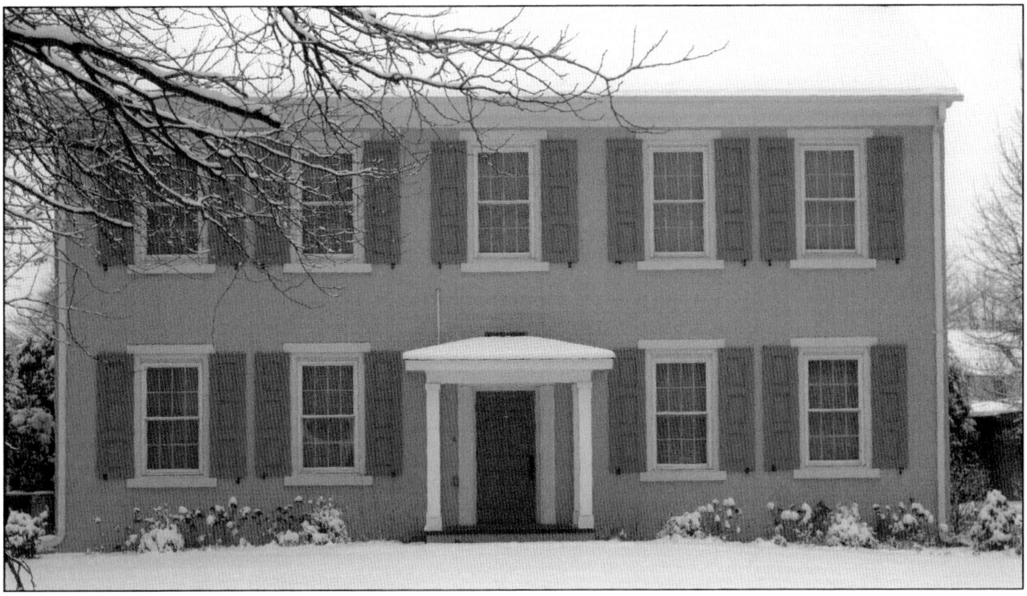

This wintertime picture is the Hunter House Museum today, the home of NCHS. Schoolchildren can attend camps here in the summer to learn about Fort Augusta and everyday life in Colonial Pennsylvania. Children engage in games, stories, crafts, and other events. (Courtesy of Klaus Krippendorff.)

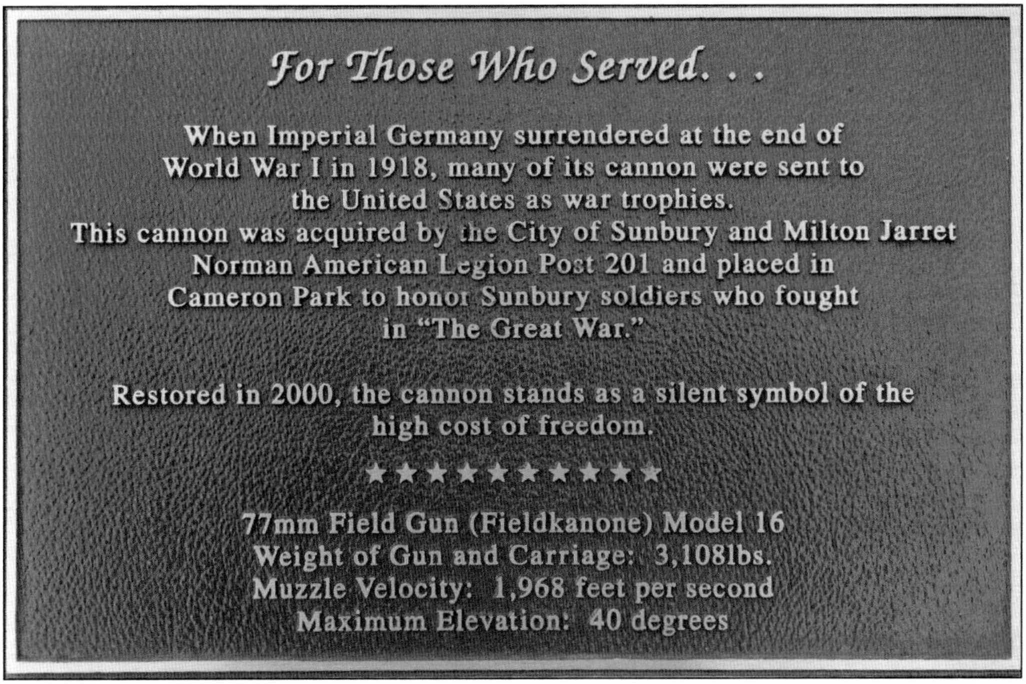

This plaque is dedicated to "those who served." The sign describes Germany surrendering at the conclusion of World War I, at which time many of the German cannons were sent to the United States as war trophies. The cannon was acquired by the City of Sunbury and the Milton Jarret Norman American Legion Post No. 201 and was placed in Cameron Park to honor Sunbury soldiers of the Great War. (Courtesy of Klaus Krippendorff.)

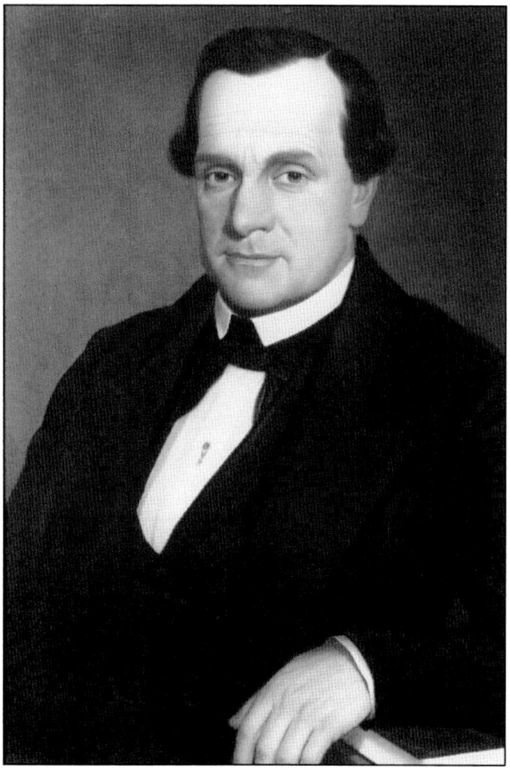

Amos E. Kapp was born in Harrisburg and came to the Sunbury area in 1832 by stagecoach. He quickly took charge of the stagecoach business there and was important in establishing the famous old line that carried passengers up and down along the river. He also organized the First National Bank of Northumberland, serving as its president, and was active in the lumber business. On February 16, 1841, he married Margaret Wighington, born on December 10, 1818, in Mifflinburg. She was the daughter of George and Catherine Wighington, who grew up in Sunbury. They had many children; several daughters lived for many years in the family farmhouse. (Both, courtesy of NCHS.)

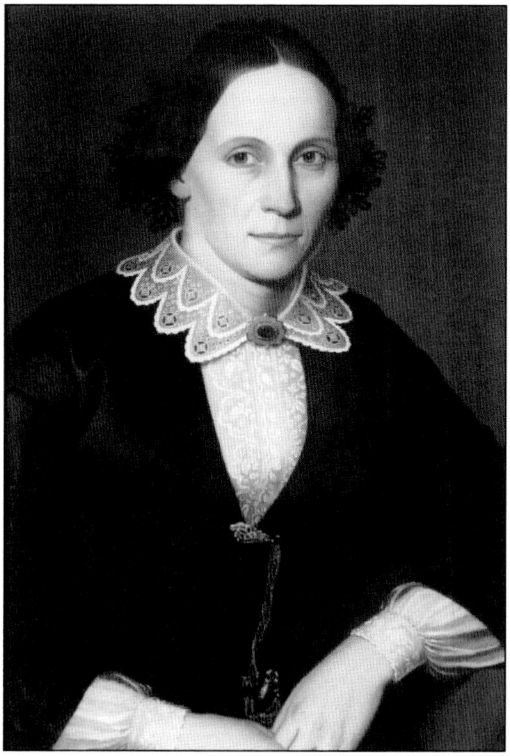

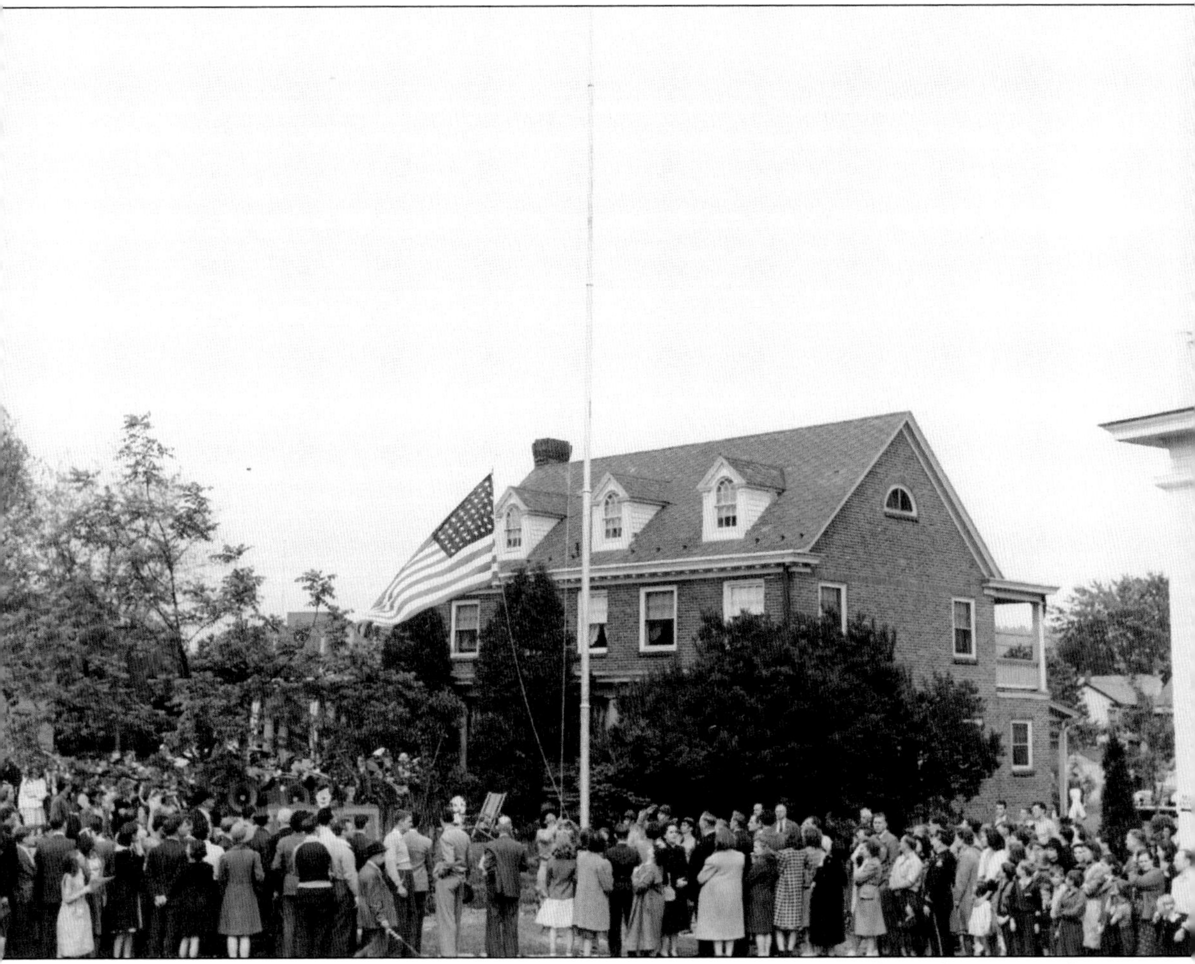

A crowd stands in front of the restored Hunter House as an American flag is being raised. The historical society, a repository of various artifacts, illustrates the history of Sunbury and Northumberland County. The museum offers historic and archaeological artifacts dealing with Fort Augusta, from the French and Indian War through the American Revolution. It also offers changing exhibits on topics of historic and archaeological interest. The Charlotte Darrah Walter Genealogical Library is housed at the museum. This library contains material on local history and thousands of records of families in Northumberland County. (Courtesy of NCHS.)

Bibliography

Bell, Herbert C. *History of Northumberland Country, Pennsylvania*. Chicago: Brown, Runk & Co., 1891.

The Diary of William Maclay and Other Notes on Senate Debates. Baltimore: Johns Hopkins University Press, 1988.

Genealogical and Biographical Annals of Northumberland County, Pennsylvania. Chicago: J.L. Floyd & Co., 1911.

Irwin, Jared C. *Reminiscences of Sunbury*. Sunbury, PA: T.J. Silvius, Printer, 1910.

Kidd, H.S. *Lutherans in Berks County*. Reading, PA: William S. Rhode Publishing Co., 1923.

Lossing, Benson John and Woodrow Wilson. *Harper's Encyclopedia of United States History*. New York: Harper & Brothers, 1905.

Wallace, Paul A.W. *Indian Paths of Pennsylvania*. Harrisburg: Pennsylvania Historical and Museum Commission, 1971.

www.visitcentralpa.org/pdf/sunburyWT.pdf

About the Organizations

The city of Sunbury is fortunate to have two organizations that support and contribute to the community of Sunbury and Northumberland County. For many years, the Northumberland County Historical Society has brought history to the community with archeological digs, special Revolutionary War and Civil War reenactments, and other important contributions to the culture of Sunbury. Sunbury's Revitalization Inc. is a nonprofit charitable organization dedicated to promoting economic development opportunities, spurring neighborhood reinvestment, and instilling pride and fostering a sense of community with the city of Sunbury. Both organizations have made significant contributions to the area—one by exploring the past and the other by focusing on the future of Sunbury.